ISLAND
— IN A —
STORM

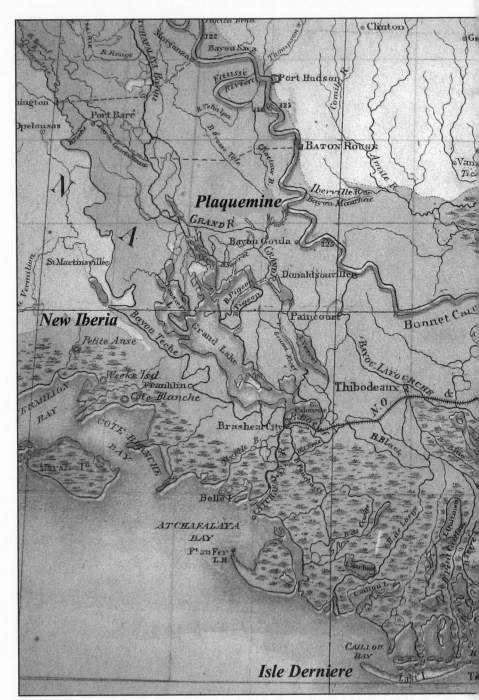

Central Louisiana surveyed in 1861 showing Isle Derniere relative to other major locales of *Island in a Storm*

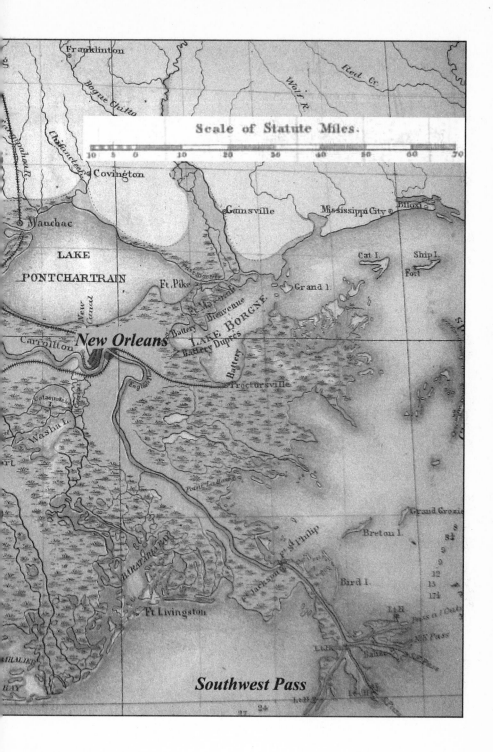

Scale of Statute Miles.

10 5 0 10 20 30 40 50 60 70

Franklinton

Bogue Chitto

Weir R.

Red Cr.

Covington

Manchac

LAKE

PONTCHARTRAIN

Gainsville

Mississippi City

Biloxi

Cat I.

Ship I.

Fort

Ft. Pike

Grand I.

Bienvenue

Battery

LAKE BORGNE

New Orleans

Battery Dupres

Carrollton

Battery

Proctorsville

English

Catacinche I.

Washa I.

Pont

Grand Groxie

Breton I.

Ft. St. Phillip

Jackson

BARATARIA BAY

Bird I.

Ft. Livingston

L. H.

Pass

Southwest Pass

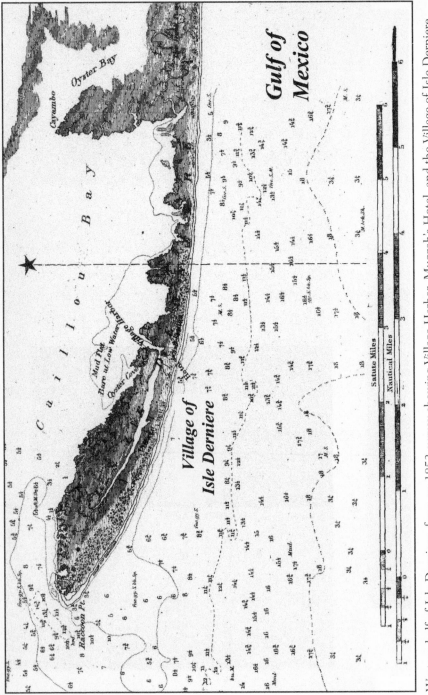

Western half of Isle Derniere, from an 1853 survey showing Village Harbor, Muggah's Hotel, and the Village of Isle Derniere

ISLAND
— IN A —
STORM

{ A RISING SEA, A VANISHING COAST,
AND A NINETEENTH-CENTURY DISASTER
THAT WARNS OF A WARMER WORLD }

ABBY SALLENGER

PUBLICAFFAIRS

NEW YORK

Designed by Pauline Brown
Text set in 11 point Fairfield Light

Library of Congress Cataloging-in-Publication Data

Sallenger, Abby.
  Island in a storm : a rising sea, a vanishing coast, & a nineteenth-century disaster that warns of a warmer world / Abby Sallenger.
      p. cm.
  Includes bibliographical references and index.
  ISBN 978-1-58648-515-3 (alk. paper)
  1. Hurricanes—Louisiana—Isles Dernieres. 2. Isles Dernieres (La.)—History—19th century. 3. Terrebonne Parish (La.)—History, Local—19th century. I. Title.
  F377.T5S25 2009
  976.3'4105—dc22
                                                                    2009000261
First Edition

10 9 8 7 6 5 4 3 2 1

Cover image: Bird's-eye view of central Louisiana drawn in 1861, showing the Isle Derniere as the last island to the west (left) and the passes leading from the Mississippi River to the Gulf of Mexico to the east (right)

Dedicated to Dee,
for giving me great joy and
standing with me through great tragedy,
&
to the late Dr. Shea Penland
of the University of New Orleans,
for first showing me the
Isle Dernieres

{ CONTENTS }

Windswept trees on a Louisiana barrier island, circa 1900

An Island Changed Forever

On the Gulf side of these islands you may observe that the trees—where there are any trees—all bend away from the sea; and, even of bright, hot days when the wind sleeps, there is something grotesquely pathetic in their look of agonized terror. A group of oaks . . . I remember as especially suggestive: five stooping silhouettes in line against the horizon, like fleeing women with streaming garments and wind-blown hair,—bowing grievously and thrusting out arms desperately northward as to save themselves from falling. And they are being pursued indeed;—for the sea is devouring the land.

—LAFCADIO HEARN, *CHITA: A MEMORY OF LAST ISLAND* (1889)

In the summer of 1856, Emma Mille traveled with several of her family members to Isle Derniere, or Last Island, the westernmost of the long, sandy barrier islands that line the Gulf of Mexico shore off central Louisiana. They crossed the inhospitable Mississippi River delta to reach Isle Derniere, where they planned to spend most of the summer. They would join a former governor of Louisiana and the state's speaker of the House of Representatives as well as hundreds of affluent planters, merchants, their wives and children on the narrow strip of sand that was emerging as a much-sought-after resort.

The Mille family departed from their sugar plantation near the Mississippi River town of Plaquemine (pronounced *plak-a-men*), located upriver from New Orleans and ten miles below Baton Rouge. Emma chatted with her family members in French. She was eighteen years old and excited about the trip. Her father had owned a house on Isle Derniere for several years, but the family had never used it until now. They likely rode in horse-drawn carriages several miles to the landing on Plaquemine's riverfront. There they boarded the steamboat *Blue Hammock,* which made the scheduled runs from Plaquemine to Isle Derniere, a straight-line distance of ninety miles. It was owned and often captained by Michael Schlatre Jr. (pronounced *Slaughter*), a relative and neighbor of the Milles.

The vessel's crew stoked the boiler fire, bringing a full head of steam. The two-story-high paddle wheel began to rotate, and the steamer slipped into the river's powerful current. The seventy-four-ton side-wheeler with twin smokestacks was one of hundreds of steamboats that plied antebellum Louisiana's waterways, the byways and highways of that time and place. During its journey to Isle Derniere, the steamboat would cross a remarkable sequence of diverse natural environments. It also would pass signs that foretold a coming disaster, though its passengers would not have recognized them.

Leaving the broad Mississippi River, the *Blue Hammock* threaded the delta's narrow bayous toward the Gulf of Mexico. These waterways cut into an easily eroded land composed of tiny bits of earth. Over thousands of years, the Mississippi had dumped these sediments into fan-shaped accumulations projecting tens of miles into the sea. "It is a place that seems often unable to make up its mind whether it will be earth or water, and so it compromises," wrote Harnett Kane in *Bayous of Louisiana*. "The result is that much of Louisiana belongs to neither element. The line of demarcation is vague and changing. The distinction between degrees of well soaked ground is academic except to one who steps upon what looks like soil but finds that it is something else." To Emma, this "something else" became increasingly apparent as she approached the Gulf of Mexico.

The steamer meandered through bayous shaded by two-hundred-year-old live oaks. They were squat trees with muscular, twisted limbs that dripped the silvery-gray hair of Spanish moss. In places their branches reached across the waterway in a canopy that brushed against the vessel. The steamer's dual stacks billowed black smoke through green foliage.

Soon the scene changed. The bayou swelled over its channel into the surrounding trees, submerging their roots in a swamp where oak gave way to cypress. Their flagpole-thin trunks rose from still water to heights of seventy to eighty feet. At the tops of these trees, branches and leaves were so close together, and the moss so thick, that they nearly blocked the light from reaching the ground. "The weird and funereal aspect of the place [was] perfect," observed *Harper's Weekly* of a Louisiana swamp in 1866, "presenting a forbidding appearance sufficient to appall a stranger."

The steamer followed the narrow channel through the forest. The air was stagnant, the confines ovenlike. Emma and the other women aboard sweltered in their floor-length hoop dresses and layers of petticoats. Their bodices had long sleeves to shield their arms from the sun. The only relief from the heat was found on the open deck. As the vessel cut through the muggy air, it created the semblance of a breeze against their faces.

From the deck, the passengers had a clear view of the environment around them. Stumplike roots, or cypress knees, rose out of the water to help the soaring trees breathe. Among them were alligators, only their eye sockets and snouts poking above the murk, and water moccasins, skimming wavy trails in green slime. Colorful birds darted under the mossy canopy; long-legged heron and crane stood in shallow water watching for prey.

Miles across the swamp, the forest began to diminish, trees began to die, as if the water engulfing their roots had been poisoned. The sun now blazed through thinning woods, and the passengers retreated to the shade under a cabin's overhang. Forest gave way to grass, willowy stems of Spartina, three to five feet high, massed into an endless prairie that was inundated by every high tide. The passengers rejoiced as they left the suffocating swamp and breathed in the fresh salt air that signaled the proximity of the sea.

The waterway splayed across the prairie, branching into an indecipherable maze of channels like veins on the back of an aged hand. The helmsman knew the correct route by pillars of grayed driftwood that had been driven vertically into the mud, marking the proper forks to follow to the sea. As the *Blue Hammock* navigated these turns, the wetlands of south Louisiana showed their richness. On nearby fishing boats, nets teemed with shrimp and fish. Oysters grew on channel-side bars, their exposed mass glistening in the afternoon sun.

Hours later, and miles closer to the sea, there were forks in the route that the driftwood no longer accurately marked, channel prongs that had broadened, merged, altered shape and direction, seemingly from one month to the next, one year to the next. Captain Schlatre had traveled this route many times over the years. He would have recognized lakes in the grassland that had once been ponds, and before that uninterrupted pasture. It was as if the grass had sickened and decayed, roots no longer binding mud together, pasture melting into water.

The vessel chugged from the marsh and into open water, a five-mile-wide bay. The hot, late-afternoon air rose over the delta and sucked a breeze in from the Gulf of Mexico, rippling the bay's surface. The passengers felt the change, the awkward roll of the flat-bottomed steamer as waves passed under its hull. The sea breeze dried and cooled their skin. They looked across the open water for the first signs of Isle Derniere.

From afar, the island would have been difficult to discern, merely a thread floating on the horizon, one line merging into the other. An 1853 chart of the region included a note to mariners: "Isle Derniere may be readily known by the numerous houses on the beach." As Emma's steamer drew closer, those buildings became clear, their roofs breaking above the horizon. Soon, the foundation on which the buildings were constructed emerged from the water, a narrow and low-lying accumulation of sand that extended along the coast for twenty-four miles. On the western end of this accumulation stood the Village of Isle Derniere with its majestic homes tucked amid oleanders and a bustling hotel packed with guests.

As the steamer neared the village, Emma and the other passengers could see across the strand to the Gulf of Mexico. The island was only a two-hundred-yard-wide strip of sand on its Gulf side, with a broader fringe of marsh on its bay side. Its total width was over one mile in places, much narrower in others.

There were no soaring sand dunes, like those found on some barrier islands that lined the eastern and Gulf coasts of the United States. The highest ground on Isle Derniere was at the crest of its beach, where the sand rose only five to six feet above the sea. The island's lack of physical presence was a symptom that it suffered from the same affliction that killed the cypress trees and the grass, the same affliction that made prairies develop ponds that broadened into lakes.

By the end of the summer of 1856, the Isle Derniere had changed forever. The homes and hotel were gone. The island was barren, as if swept clean, except for a strange forest standing in the surf. The trees were snapped off to stumps. Nothing but their scraggly tips rose above the waves. This forest in the sea was a sign of an island moving, diminishing. The Isle Derniere had been ravaged by a hurricane that killed many of the most prominent residents of antebellum New Orleans and the sugar plantations of south Louisiana. And it irreversibly changed the life of Emma Mille.

This is not the story of an isolated disaster that started with the first gust of wind and ended with the last survivor saved, the last body buried. It began centuries earlier, before Europeans arrived in America, and its implications will be felt on other coasts around the world through the twenty-first century and beyond.

This is a story of the sea rising relative to the land—and the land changing in ways that made Isle Derniere, and the people who lived there, vulnerable to a great storm. This is a portrait of a coast in motion, a delta whose surface rose and fell and whose shore systematically changed in position and form, evolving over centuries into a barrier island with degraded terrain that invited the sea to encroach and a storm to ravage.

This is the story of how the people on Isle Derniere came into harm's way, how they were driven to the island by unexpected consequences of human development of a dynamic land and by seemingly disparate, sometimes odd intersections of science, culture, disease, and agriculture.

In the end, this is the story of an island dying. Between the 1890s and 1988, the Isle Derniere retreated landward about two-thirds of a mile while losing three-quarters of its surface area. And it is a story that is not over. At its heart lies an image of a warmer world—and of what our children and grandchildren may endure from future hurricanes coming ashore on rapidly rising seas.

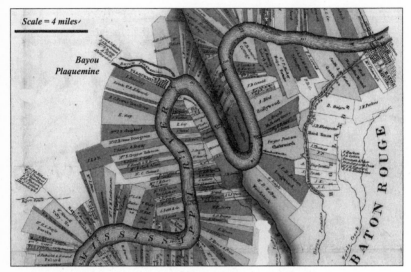

Boundaries of plantations—each labeled with the owner's name—along the
Mississippi River near Plaquemine and Baton Rouge, Louisiana, from 1858

{ PART I }

THE
ISLAND
AND THE
DELTA

The City
of the
Dead

They bury their dead in vaults, above the ground. These
vaults have a resemblance to houses—sometimes to temples;
are built of marble, generally; are architecturally graceful and
shapely; they face the walks and driveways of the cemetery; and
when one moves through the midst of a thousand or so of them
and sees their white roofs and gables stretching into the
distance on every hand, the phrase "the city of the dead"
has all at once a meaning to him.
—MARK TWAIN, *LIFE ON THE MISSISSIPPI* (1883)

New Orleans of the 1850s was alluring—a city of stunning architecture, a booming economy, unbridled opportunity—and
deadly, a black widow that enticed immigrants with its charm and promise, then devoured them. The stricken were disproportionately poor,
those without the means to evacuate when threatened, like the victims
of a flood that would engulf the city 150 years later during Hurricane
Katrina.

In an odd twist, however, when the rich people of the 1850s fled
from one peril in New Orleans, some unwittingly thrust themselves
into the jaws of another.

Many sugar planters traveled to New Orleans during the city's October to May business season to tend to their financial affairs, and some of them maintained homes there. Among the planters was Emma's father, Pierre Thomas Mille, who owned both a plantation in the country and a business as a merchant in the city. He was a Frenchman, born in 1800 in Cassis, a small fishing port in the south of France. Most of his life was spent in Louisiana, where he married twice. His first wife died in her twenties. He then married Pauline Dupuy, whose father was also French. They had five children together, two sons and three daughters, although one son died as a toddler.

Emma was the middle daughter, born on October 10, 1837, in Louisiana as French Creole. She was a devout Catholic, attending with her family St. John the Evangelist Church in Plaquemine, which was built in 1850. Beyond religion, she had little opportunity to acquire an education. When she was a child, there were no schools open to girls near her plantation. Her father either hired tutors or sent her away to school. Emma's younger sister was sent to the Sacred Heart Convent for girls established in 1825 by French nuns and located thirty miles downriver from Plaquemine in the small town of Convent, Louisiana. The curriculum available for young women at the time focused on arts and manners, which would prepare them to attract husbands. According to French historian Liliane Crete in *Daily Life in Louisiana*, the undertaking by a Creole woman of "formal study, whether . . . Latin, history, science, or philosophy, was actively discouraged as a betrayal of one's sex." Emma was expected to build and serve a family that would extend the Milles' French bloodline, not to follow ambitious dreams.

Her father's trips to New Orleans offered Emma and the rest of her family opportunities to escape the rural grind of plantation life and to experience the port's culture and excitement. Wealthy planters like Thomas Mille frequently brought their wives and children with them. The theater and opera offerings in New Orleans were among the most extensive in the South. Emma and her family could enjoy the latest productions from Paris at the Théâtre d'Orléans, which opened in 1815 on Rue d'Orléans.

On arrival in New Orleans, steamboats nosed into a landing on the Mississippi riverbank, joining a line of hundreds of diverse vessels. Stubby river steamers belched and whistled; sleek oceangoing steam and sailing ships flew colors from seaports around the world; rectangular flatboats rode low in the water with goods transported from interior ports like St. Louis and Memphis. Towering stacks of bales and boxes crowded the landing. Horse-drawn drays hauled merchandise from one stack to another, from one vessel to another. The area buzzed with loud, exotic voices, an indecipherable swirl of French and English, Spanish and German, Italian and Portuguese. Swarms of people pushed and shoved to board vessels bound for destinations as varied as Hannibal, Missouri, and Bordeaux, France.

This antebellum seaport rivaled New York's as the most prosperous in the nation. Corn, wheat, cotton, sugar, tobacco, whiskey, and furs and hides flowed down the Mississippi from America's midsection to New Orleans, where goods were transferred to ships for distribution around the world. International vessels arrived from far-flung locations brimming with salt, coffee, gold, silver, and a wide variety of manufactured products destined for the same middle American markets that exported downriver. New Orleans was the transfer terminal where cargo moved between shallow-draft steamboats designed for the river and deep-draft steam and sailing ships that moved through the sea.

Only a short walk from the river was the center of the Vieux Carré, or the "old square," the heart of New Orleans whose matrix of streets was laid out during the early 1700s in the crescent of a river meander. This district was home for many Creoles, and ultimately it became known as the French Quarter, or just "the Quarter."

The Vieux Carré's cobblestone streets were lined with ornate buildings, each several stories tall, with lacy wrought-iron galleries and central walled courtyards. "Their chief beauty," wrote Mark Twain in the 1880s, "is the deep, warm and varicolored stain with which time and the weather have enriched the plaster. It harmonizes with all the surroundings, and has as natural a look of belonging there as has the flush upon sunset clouds."

The Vieux Carré was sensibly positioned on high land, or on what passed for high land in Louisiana: a levee of the Mississippi River. When the river swelled over its banks, sediments fell from the water and built the ground vertically. Most of the sediment accumulated close to the channel, leaving the ground highest there. With each successive overflow, the accumulated sediments grew progressively higher, developing into rims that could contain small floods but were overwhelmed by large ones. Laborers bolstered this protection by heaping sediments on top of the natural levees to raise them even higher. The net result was an expanse of relatively safe land along the riverfront.

By Emma's time, New Orleans sprawled beyond the tight matrix of the Vieux Carré and the city's diverse population had segregated into distinct enclaves. The French-speaking Creoles who dominated the Quarter had neither room nor tolerance for the influx of Anglo-Americans seeking and finding their fortunes. The newly rich Anglos settled upriver from the Vieux Carré in the emerging Garden District, also perched on a levee. There they built an eclectic mix of mansions in styles ranging from Greek Revival to Queen Anne Victorian. These homes had wide verandas and decorative columns and stood on spacious and manicured grounds. "Something of Southern Europe lives in the Garden District," wrote the popular novelist Lafcadio Hearn in 1877, "with its singing fountains, its box-trees cut into distaffs, its statues and fantastically-trimmed shrubs, its palms and fig trees, and the yellow richness of its banana and orange orchards."

These relatively safe elevated neighborhoods were not available to everyone. Pouring into the city in the mid-nineteenth century were tens of thousands of impoverished European immigrants, many from Ireland and Germany, who had no means to take advantage of the economic boom. They escaped famine and tyranny in Europe for the promise of a better life in New Orleans, but the only jobs offered them were the most menial and arduous.

To accommodate these newcomers, the city expanded into the lowlands of surrounding swamps. Thomas Wharton, an architect who lived in New Orleans in the 1850s, wrote in his diary:

> The improvements are of the cheapest character, altogether for the poorer sorts of people. Plank roads at intervals are pushed far into the swamp. . . . The gutters filled with green stagnant ooze and the tenements jostle each other and are graced with innumerable stores of empty barrels, dilapidated wash tubs, remnant costumes, and old and new garments flaunting from clothes lines . . . and from within the yards, alleys, open doors and windows issued fragmentary specimens of every language spoken under the canopy of heaven.

This expansion of the city led to an odd class structure, where many of the poor lived on the lowest land in reclaimed swamps, and the rich lived closer to the river on the higher and safer levees. The rich shunned the highest land along the riverfront edges of the levees, however, because of the commercial bustle of wharves and warehouses. Here, some of the underprivileged settled in ramshackle homes and tenements, leaving the wealthy, in the words of author John Barry, "sandwiched between poor areas."

In addition to signaling one's social standing, elevation had far more serious implications, some but not all of which were known in the nineteenth century. Floods from river or sea were frequent threats and could submerge even the highest areas of the city. Visitors in New Orleans were startled to see steam and sailing ships on the Mississippi floating above them. "In high-river stage, in the New Orleans region," wrote Twain in 1883, "the water is up to the top of the enclosing levee rim, the flat country behind it lies low representing the bottom of a dish—and as the boat swims along, high on the flood, one looks down upon the houses and into the upper windows. There is nothing but that frail breastwork of earth between the people and destruction."

Another threat came from a bothersome yet seemingly harmless source: torrential summer downpours. Rain fell in the city and drained from high areas to low, filling the "empty barrels, dilapidated wash tubs," and other discarded containers strewn abundantly through the city's poor sections in reclaimed swamps.

On May 28, 1853, Dr. Erasmus Darwin Fenner, a prominent New Orleans physician and expert on southern diseases, plunged his scalpel deep into the flesh of James McGuigan, a twenty-six-year-old Irishman from Liverpool. McGuigan had died four hours earlier in one of Dr. Fenner's wards at Charity Hospital. His death was neither peaceful nor orderly—in his last hours, the man suffered delirium and the hospital's first case that summer of what was called black vomit. The throwing up of ingested blood that looked black and grainy was the most gruesome symptom of yellow fever. It "excited my apprehensions," Fenner wrote later.

James McGuigan had arrived in New Orleans on May 10 as a crewman aboard the oceangoing vessel *Northampton*. The ship had originated in Liverpool, bringing 314 immigrants from Europe, and made no stops on its passage to America. There had been no serious illnesses on the voyage, at least by the standards of the 1850s. The *Northampton*'s captain reported only "six deaths, four children and two adults; the former died by bowel complaints: one of the adults by hemorrhage of the nose." None of the deaths appeared to be related to the disease that attacked McGuigan.

Crowding around Dr. Fenner in Charity Hospital's "dead-house" were several New Orleans physicians, Drs. Stone, Choppin, and McGibbon, among others. Fenner had summoned them to observe the postmortem examination of McGuigan and to confirm the cause of death, knowing that he had to get it right because the diagnosis could cause panic in the city. Fenner also had to fight the press. "When informed of the first cases of yellow fever that appear in summer," Fenner wrote, the press "almost invariably denies the truth of the reports, and not [i]nfrequently, showers upon the heads of those whose duty it is to pronounce upon the character of the prevailing diseases, volumes of abuse and ridicule."

Antebellum New Orleans knew many deadly diseases—tuberculosis, smallpox, cholera, typhoid—but none of them generated terror like yellow fever. The disease attacked healthy persons, first provoking chills, muscle aches, and high fever, followed by liver failure and the jaundice that gave the disease its name. Finally, victims hemorrhaged from their gums, nose, and stomach. Typically, they were dead within one week. Mortality reached as high as 60 percent of those afflicted.

Yellow fever had ravaged New Orleans throughout the first half of the nineteenth century, killing thousands. However, the city had not experienced an epidemic since the summer of 1847 when 2,700 had died. In fact, by the early 1850s some thought the disease had finally been conquered. The editor of *Cohen's New Orleans Directory of 1853* wrote: "Five consecutive summers have now elapsed, since the scourge, which has made the name of our city a synonym for Lazaar house. . . . Yellow fever in New Orleans is now considered . . . an 'obsolete idea.'"

Dr. Fenner believed this not to be the case. He argued that the filth found in urban areas had to contribute to the disease, although he did not know exactly how. The medical community did not understand the cause of yellow fever or how it spread into epidemics. Some outbreaks could be traced to a single infected person, but others erupted from no known source. Even so, Fenner blamed the officials of New Orleans for doing nothing to clean up the decaying garbage or to drain the standing water. The city's streets were as disgusting as its architecture was stunning. "Worse and worse . . . ," an editor wrote in the *Delta*. ". . . Filth, dirt, decayed cabbage-stalks, dead dogs, and worse, are the fascinating ornaments of our thoroughfares. . . . Everybody suggests that 'something' must be done, and, day after day, that something ends in nothing."

Erasmus Fenner was one of the South's leading medical researchers, and the president of the Louisiana Medical Society, yet officials ignored his repeated warnings. "With deep regret," Fenner wrote in 1854, ". . . in vain have . . . important facts been laid before a heedless community . . . facts involving our own lives and the safety of those scarcely less dear to us than life itself."

Now, standing in the dead-house with the other doctors looking on, Dr. Fenner feared that the evidence of what could happen in New Orleans lay on the table before him. While the dead Irishman's neck and face were only somewhat yellow, his lower body was livid. Fenner carved complete organs from the cadaver and cataloged their size, color, and feel. He found the liver "partly the color of mustard," the brain "greatly engorged," and the stomach bloated with gas, containing "about four ounces of black vomit." The evidence was conclusive; no one observing the autopsy expressed any doubt about the cause of death.

On that day of May 28, the Irishman from Liverpool, James McGuigan, was duly recorded as the city's first death in 1853 from yellow fever.

Four days later the people of New Orleans were entranced by the breaking news in major newspapers, not of the death of James McGuigan, but of the verdict in a scandalous murder trial. The courtroom had been packed and crowds had congregated outside, waiting for any scrap of information about the fate of a young woman, Agnes Anderson, accused of her lover's murder. There was no dispute about what had transpired: she had willfully stabbed to death William Taylor. Her defense was simple. The man had seduced her with promises of marriage, then "refused to save her honor," wrote John Duffy in *Sword of Pestilence*. "Conscious of its obligation both to southern womanhood and American motherhood," the jury took five minutes to acquit.

In the clutter of trial news, there were no reports of the city's first death of the summer from yellow fever and what it might foretell. The masses of New Orleans were blissfully unaware of what had happened, although there were probably kernels of rumors germinating in the populace given that Dr. Fenner had certified a second yellow fever death in his ward at Charity Hospital on May 30.

It was unusually hot and strangely dry without south Louisiana's typical summer rains. The wealthier inhabitants of the city had begun their annual exodus, migrating to cooler climes of the Northeast or to the sea breezes of the Gulf beaches. Not only were these locations more comfortable from June through October, they were thought to be insulated from yellow fever. Many of the wealthy believed that summer's heat caused the fever by cooking the offal that soiled their streets, creating a deadly miasma that hung over the city until the first frost. Although the disease attacked mostly immigrants, who were typically poor and unacclimated to the environment, the rich and acclimated understood that they were not immune and evacuated the city as summer's temperatures rose.

On the same day that the trial's verdict was reported, and as many inhabitants contemplated leaving the city until fall, an advertisement appeared in the rural newspaper *Planter's Banner,* hailing a new summer destination to compete with more established waterfront resorts, such as those on the Mississippi coast in Pascagoula and Biloxi.

Last Island [Isle Derniere] Hotel
BATHING, FISHING, & c.

The undersigned has fitted up an extensive boarding establishment at Last Island, which is now open for the reception of visitors. The advantages of this delightful location, its unrivaled fishing and sea-bathing facilities renders it the most agreeable summer retreat on the whole summer coast.

Attached to the establishment is a well stocked Bar, Billiard and Bowling saloons, and a Livery Stable where horses and carriages can be procured to enable visitors to ride or drive on the extensive beach that bounds the island towards the Gulf. The Table will be supplied with the choicest delicacies of the season, and no pains spared to insure the comfort of the guests.

E. Pecot

Prior to the late 1840s, there were few structures on Isle Derniere. In 1819 an expedition to discover wood resources to build ships for the U.S. Navy visited the island. In their report, these explorers mentioned the presence of two huts and a shed for curing fish. By 1847 private homes had sprung up along the beach and the steamboat *Meteor* was used as a floating hotel; its owner advertised six-day sojourns to the island to fish and hunt and bathe. In July 1852, a letter to the editors of the *Daily Picayune* persuaded more people to vacation on the island. "Its southern shore looks out upon the wide, wide gulf from whose . . . waters roll . . . in ever fresh, ever beautiful surf. A southern breeze . . . [of] refreshing and invigorating character . . . almost constantly prevails." The letter also evaluated the accommodations then available on the island as "very good," including Pecot's establishment and a larger hotel owned by the four Muggah (pronounced *Mac-auch*) brothers.

Recognizing the enormous potential of Isle Derniere, Captain Dave Muggah and his siblings considered their hotel an initial step in developing a major resort. With their partners, the Muggahs planned to build a new, luxurious hotel that would lure summer visitors to the island from across the South.

On August 20, 1853, explosions rocked New Orleans.

Mayor A. D. Crossman had ordered the firing of cannon—fifty rounds at dawn, fifty rounds at dusk—from public squares throughout the city. Barrels of tar had been placed strategically at major intersections and set aflame. An acrid, choking smoke shrouded the city, burning eyes and throats, making the humid air intolerable.

The mayor was trying to rid New Orleans of a yellow fever epidemic that by August 20—eighty days after the first death in Dr. Fenner's ward—had claimed 4,805 lives, 1,302 of them in the past week alone. He was unsuccessful. The cannons were soon silenced for accomplishing nothing except frightening the sick and dying. In desperation, officials continued the burning of tar every night through the remainder of the summer, although its only benefit was to partially mask the odor of decaying human remains.

Dr. Fenner and his colleagues had worked tirelessly to understand the spread of the disease, how it skipped from one corner of the city to another, from one victim to another. Fenner discovered that the vessel of James McGuigan had been moored less than one hundred yards from another vessel that subsequently had confirmed cases of yellow fever. Still, there was no evidence of direct contact between the crews or passengers. Then, still early in the summer, Fenner learned of cases in a completely different part of the city, Gamby's Basin. This was a poor, unpaved area—"a filthy pond," Fenner later wrote, with "a canal leading from it to the swamp in the rear."

At first the disease moved slowly, taking 47 lives by the beginning of July. Nonetheless, rumors of an emerging "black vomit" epidemic swirled through New Orleans. The annual summer exodus turned into flight. "Our city has rarely been more completely deserted than at present . . . ," an editor wrote in the *New Orleans Bee*. "A regular and uninterrupted stampede has been in progress. Every steamer has carried away a living freight, and the process of temporary depopulation has continued so rapidly, . . . it is very questionable whether New Orleans contains one-half the number of those who reside amongst us during the winter."

Then the summer rains came, filling the low areas of the city and the accumulated barrels and jugs and containers of myriad types. Suddenly, the disease flashed into an inferno. Yellow fever snuffed 1,294 lives by the end of July, and nearly four times that number by the time the cannons thundered on Saturday morning, August 20.

Day and night, funeral processions clogged the city's streets. Most were simple, a cart drawn by a worn mule or horse, sometimes containing multiple bodies of the poor. The processions of the rich were more elaborate, with ornate carriages pulled by spirited horses. Sometimes grieving family members followed on foot, carrying in their arms vases of flowers to color grave sites. By the beginning of August, the city's cemeteries had been overwhelmed by the sheer numbers of corpses. Most bodies were no longer buried above the water-saturated ground in the crypts that Mark Twain called the city of the dead. Rather, they were thrown into hastily dug graves of a few feet or less.

By the end of the third week in August, family members held rags doused in camphor to their noses and mouths as they searched for the resting places of loved ones. They walked between crowded, muddy craters sprinkled with dirt and lime that failed to hide the coffins or to contain the smell.

The epidemic did not wane until early October. Dr. Fenner estimated the total cost of lives at 7,870, making the disaster one of the deadliest in U.S. history. And like so many other human and environmental disasters, it bred another in ways not understood.

New Orleans sat in the midst of the natural system of the Mississippi delta, where land and water and life interacted in complex, sometimes mysterious ways. Expansion of the city into surrounding swamps changed this system.

Swamps were cleared to make room for ramshackle tenements that became surrounded with refuse. Discarded containers filled with rainwater, providing an ideal habitat for the breeding of *Aedes aegypti*, a unique mosquito that carried the yellow fever virus, disliked natural swamps, and favored small containers of freshwater. Its population exploded. The insects flitted through the crowded tenements and fed on the immigrants who lived there. The mosquitoes extracted the yellow fever virus from immigrants who were already afflicted and injected it into those not yet sick. These people were new to the environment; their bodies had not yet built up resistance to the disease. *Aedes aegypti* feasted on the multitude of hosts, and yellow fever spread virulently.

In this complex system, even the most innocuous human activity could lead to unexpected consequences. In the city of the dead, family members tried to brighten the horrid scenes with vases filled with colorful flowers. The clean freshwater in the vases not only kept the blooms vibrant but also promoted the breeding of *Aedes aegypti*. The larvae matured into mosquitoes and spread the disease to grave diggers and visiting loved ones.

In the mid-nineteenth century, no one knew how human changes to the system of the delta exacerbated the scourge of yellow fever. And no one knew how other changes to the same natural system led to the dying cypress trees and drowning marsh grasses on the delta, and to the diminishing barrier islands along the Gulf shore.

{ 2 }

Chocolate
Gold

*No one has ever traveled upon one of those palatial steamers
bounding on the Mississippi, in the spring season of the year,
when the waters swell to the tops of the levees, lifting the
steamer above the level of the great fields of sugar-cane stretching away for miles to the forest on either bank of that mighty
river, who has not delighted with the lovely homes, surrounded
with grounds highly cultivated and most beautifully orna-
mented with trees, shrubs, and flowers, which come upon the
view in constant and quick succession, as he is borne onward
rapidly along the accumulated waters of the great river.*
—WILLIAM HENRY SPARKS, THE MEMORIES OF FIFTY YEARS (1872)

On return trips from New Orleans to their plantation home near
Plaquemine, the Mille family traveled upriver against the powerful current of the Mississippi River. The straight-line distance was
seventy miles, but the journeys were longer with the twists and turns
of the river. To ease the upstream fight, steamers stayed away from
the strong opposing current in the center of the channel and hugged
one of the riverbanks, where the flow was relatively weak. From here,
the passengers had a clear view of the remarkable scene ashore.

In the 1820s, Basil Hall described these riverbanks as "thickly peopled by sugar planters, whose showy houses, gay piazzas, trig gardens,

and numerous slave-villages, all clean and neat, gave an exceedingly thriving air to the river scenery." A half-century later, Mark Twain wrote about the same banks. "The great sugar plantations border both sides of the river all the way, and stretch their league-wide levels back to the dim forest walls of bearded cypress in the rear. . . . Plenty of dwellings . . . on both banks—standing so close together, for long distances, that the broad river lying between the two rows, becomes a sort of spacious street. A most home-like and happy-looking region." More elegant estates extended down the narrow bayous that fanned out from the lower Mississippi River toward the Gulf of Mexico. Even today, vestiges of the nineteenth-century grandeur can be found by driving along the famed River Roads that wind along both sides of the Mississippi from New Orleans beyond Plaquemine to Baton Rouge, passing restored plantations with oak-lined entranceways and columned manor houses.

On neighboring bayous near Plaquemine stood the plantations of Thomas Mille and Michael Schlatre, the owner and the captain of the steamer *Blue Hammock*. Born in 1819, Schlatre, a descendant of German immigrants, was nineteen years younger than the Frenchman Mille. Schlatre was a ruggedly handsome man and unusually tall for the time. At six feet, he towered over most people. Schlatre and Mille often found themselves thrown together; they were relatives by marriage, and their plantations were within a mile of each other. Michael Schlatre had long owned a Gulf-front house on Isle Derniere, where he spent summers with his wife and seven children. Thomas Mille bought the home next door, and his family's first visit was during the summer of 1856.

Planters like Mille and Schlatre were drawn to the banks of Louisiana's rivers and bayous by "gold the color of chocolate," as described by John Barry in *Rising Tide*—"gold that was not in the earth but was the earth." Every spring, ice and snow melt from 1.25 million square miles of middle America funneled into the Mississippi and wound its way to coastal Louisiana in a torrent colored brown by rich soil. This muddy brew of silt and clay had been washed from the slopes and plains of what today are thirty-one states from New York to Montana. Nineteenth-century engineers estimated that the Mississippi annually carried a volume of sediment that would fill a container one mile square and twenty-four stories high. Before humans heaped earth into embankments to contain floods, the river regularly spilled over its natural levees. There it deposited "the finest and most fertile . . . soil," according to a traveler during the 1800s, "collected from the most various quarters, and carried for great distances."

The first French settlers who came to the land their king claimed as Louisiana searched for a different kind of gold, the kind used to mint coins rather than to grow crops. These pioneers of the late 1600s and early 1700s envisioned a thriving community along the Gulf shore, where they hoped to discover precious metals and oysters bearing pearls. They planned to establish a trading post to barter furs and other goods. But they met with little success on the barren, sun-baked beaches of the northern Gulf of Mexico.

A young Frenchman, Jean-Baptiste le Moyne de Bienville, saved the fledgling colony through his vision of moving inland from the sandy coast and cultivating the muddy soils spread across the land by the Mississippi River. In 1718 he ordered an odd company of convicts and carpenters to cut a clearing on the river ninety miles above its mouth and construct an initial cluster of huts in the wilderness. Out of this settlement rose La Nouvelle-Orléans, or New Orleans. The planters followed.

Through the eighteenth century they came, enticed by offers of free fertile land. Large concessions were awarded to Frenchmen who were wealthy or noble or had fatefully served the crown. Louisiana's agricultural economy was initially established, however, through small grants to ordinary farmers. Some of them were German immigrants who, in the first half of the 1700s, were granted modest tracts on a riverbank thirty miles upstream of the burgeoning city.

"Every Saturday, they were seen floating down the river in small boats, to carry to the market of New Orleans the provisions which were the result of their industry," wrote the president of the Louisiana Historical Society in 1867. "From this humble but decent origin, issued some of our most respectable citizens, and of our most wealthy sugar planters. They have, long ago, forgotten the German language, and adopted the French, but the names of some of them clearly indicate the blood that flows in their veins. . . . The German Coast, so poor and beggarly at first, became in time the producer and the receptacle of . . . wealth."

During the second half of the 1700s, Acadians—immigrants of French descent from Nova Scotia—established small farms upriver from the Germans. The government provided them with the tools to cultivate the land and the authority to settle along both banks of the river from the German Coast to Baton Rouge. Part of this region became known as the Acadian Coast.

These coasts were subdivided into long, narrow tracts of land perpendicular to the river. Each had a slender width of valuable waterfront that was measured in French *arpents*, where one arpent is equal to about 192 feet. In 1770 the governor of colonial Louisiana provided a tract of land to each new family wanting to farm the rich soil next to the river. The grants were six or eight arpents along the waterway and forty arpents perpendicular. By Emma's time, many of these small garden-crop farms had been merged into plantations—a consolidation fueled by a Creole's gamble.

In the 1790s, on his plantation near New Orleans, fifty-four-year-old Etienne de Bore risked everything he owned, forgoing the delta's established but meager cash crop of indigo, to pioneer the cultivation of sugarcane. Although born in Louisiana, Bore grew up in France and served with the king's *mousquetaires*—the musketeers immortalized in the Alexandre Dumas novel—before returning to his homeland. He knew sugarcane was difficult to grow in Louisiana; the soil was rich, but unlike the warm, sugarcane-friendly Caribbean, planters faced the threat of frost wiping out their crops.

Even more difficult, Louisiana's sugar did not adequately dry into granules. It remained wet, and in an early attempt to export sugar to France, much of the cargo seeped from the containers while the ship was still at sea. Bore implemented a rigid discipline for planting and harvesting that avoided frost. He also developed the means to effectively granulate sugar so it could be shipped around the world. His initial crop sold for $12,000, a fortune in 1795—and triggered a stampede to sugar. "The people were electrified," wrote George W. Cable, a nineteenth-century writer known for his depictions of Creole culture, ". . . the agriculture of the Delta was revolutionized."

In the 1840s, Michael Schlatre joined the charge, buying a small tract of land on Bayou Jacob just above the town of Plaquemine. Though the tract had only 6 arpents (1,152 feet) of frontage along the natural levee, he built a sugar mill designed for a much larger plantation; the mill was 180 feet long and 40 feet wide and was equipped with a sugarcane grinder powered by a steam engine. The gamble paid off. Michael, then in his twenties, made sufficient money from his early crops to pay for his equipment and buy more land. Within ten to fifteen years, the initial small tract blossomed into a prominent sugar plantation, increasing in bayou frontage nearly fivefold.

By the 1850s, more than 1,300 sugar plantations lined Louisiana's rivers and bayous, many in the core of sugar production between New Orleans and Baton Rouge. An 1858 map showed on both sides of the Mississippi shoulder-to-shoulder plantations that were consolidations of the small farms of earlier times. They still were narrower along the river than they were deep, their boundaries protruding from the sinuous channel like ribs from the backbone of a snake.

Down a waterway called Bayou Plaquemine, several miles from where it spilled from the Mississippi River at the town of the same name, perched Milly Plantation. There Thomas Mille's family lived in a stately manor overlooking the bayou. Like Schlatre, Mille had seen his plantation grow, and during 1853 Milly became one of the highest producers of sugar in Iberville Parish. That year marked both a record crop and a tragedy for the owners.

Several months after Dr. Fenner plunged his scalpel into the chest of the first victim of yellow fever in New Orleans, Milly Plantation erupted into frenetic activity. It was the harvest season of 1853, and the fields around the big house were packed with flourishing stalks of sugarcane eight to nine feet high. "The green was so vivid," John Latrobe wrote of the delta's cane, "the foliage so dense, and the light wind waving it to and fro marked it with the varying shadows that rolled after one another like waves upon a sea."

Devouring this green sea were black men and women, slaves, dozens of them, wielding machete-like cane knives, felling every stalk near ground level. They moved in rows across the expanse of green, sweeping their blades in arcs, metal flashing in the sun. The older, weaker slaves and children followed, bowed to the ground, collecting stalks and dumping them into oxen-drawn carts. These carts rumbled over furrowed fields to the sugarhouse, where the cane was ground and boiled into a granulated residue.

Everywhere there was smoke. It billowed from the sugarhouse, where a steam engine turned grinders to pulverize cane and slaves stoked flames to fire cauldrons. It billowed from steamboats that puffed down the bayou and docked before the big house, where slaves muscled aboard thousand-pound hogsheads filled with sugar for market. And it billowed from bagasse, the damp remnants of ground stalks that slaves gathered, heaped into huge piles, and set aflame. They smoldered and smoked, Mark Twain wrote, "like Satan's own kitchen."

The plantation resonated with unique sounds. The crack of the overseer's whip and the pounding of his horse's hooves drove human combines to harvest the sugarcane before the first freeze. The clang from the bell tower signaled the start or end of tasks as precisely planned and sequenced as those of the Industrial Revolution's burgeoning factories in the North. And the songs of slaves rang from the fields.

"Verse . . . sweetens the toil of slaves," wrote William Cullen Bryant in 1850 about work in a Virginia tobacco factory. "We encourage their singing as much as we can," another observer of the facility explained, "for the boys work better while singing." Louisiana sugar planters agreed, one reporting that his slaves worked the fields late into the night while singing "some wild melody . . . that fairly made the old cane-shed shake."

Emma Mille had a passion for music, and the slave songs emanating from Milly Plantation's cane fields must have been forbidden fruit. Without an opportunity for formal education, Emma channeled her creativity into music. Since a child, she had studied to be a pianist, as did many of her female Creole contemporaries. Laura Locoul of Laura Plantation practiced daily for hours, as did most of the women in her family. But Emma explored beyond the acceptable minuets, waltzes, and polkas. She appreciated the music that grew out of slave songs, out of their sensual rhythms and chants, as well as their tales of joy and sorrow, hope and desperation. These were the first notes of what decades later would be called ragtime, music that the puritanical considered vulgar, even filthy. Regardless, Emma would come to compose and play her own rags, using the complexity of rhythm she first heard beat from the cane fields.

During the fall of 1853 on Milly Plantation, however, the sounds of harvest mixed with the cries of mourning. Emma's fifty-year-old uncle, Paulin Dupuy, who co-owned the plantation with Thomas Mille, had been stricken with yellow fever during the summer's record epidemic and suffered a grisly, painful death.

Dupuy's ancestry could be traced back to the poor French-Canadian immigrants of the 1700s who raised subsistence crops on small grants of land along the nearby Acadian Coast. With the stampede to sugar in the 1800s, Dupuy emerged as a successful and wealthy planter and prominent member of his community. In fact, Milly Plantation's productivity approached its zenith during the same harvest season as his passing. While Emma and her female family members mourned in sweeping black dresses, slaves cut and ground and boiled a near-record crop of cane yielding 452 hogsheads—or about a half-million pounds—of granulated sugar. As one of the deadliest disasters in U.S. history unfolded in New Orleans, Louisiana planters collectively produced the most sugar in their history, 40 percent more than the year before, shipping 25 percent of the world's sugar exports.

This was no coincidence. The concurrence of high sugar production and yellow fever epidemics was observed not only for the 1853 disaster but for other times as well. A planter wrote in 1834: "It was generally noted that yellow fever seasons were accompanied by a large sugar yield."

The connection was heavy rain. It both filled breeding containers for *Aedes aegypti* and nourished sugarcane in the fields, making the crops thrive.

As slaves on Milly Plantation harvested the bumper 1853 sugar crop, Bayou Plaquemine lay quiescent in front of the big house, the water nearly motionless, its surface smooth, reflecting the reds and yellows of the foliage along the banks like a mirror. The waterway seemed peaceful, even beautiful, yet deceptively so.

Two years earlier, in the spring, the Mississippi swelled with excessive runoff from across middle America. Water tumbled from the great river into Bayou Plaquemine, roiling it into a dangerous torrent that swept past Emma's house. A nineteenth-century boat crew encountered these conditions on the bayou. "Hardly had we started when our men saw and were frightened by the force of the current. The enormous flatboat [that drifted with the flow] . . . darted . . . like an arrow." Such violent water partially overflowed the channel and swirled through Milly Plantation's cane fields, reducing the sugar crop by one-third from the previous season. Widespread flooding in south Louisiana had a serious impact on the ability of planters to repay loans.

Sugar plantations required large outlays of capital. Planters had to consolidate small farms into commercially viable cane fields, purchase slaves at auction for $500 to $1,000 apiece, and acquire increasingly sophisticated equipment, like steam-powered machines that drained low-lying fields. Most had to borrow money to purchase and operate their plantations, and if their crops failed, they had to borrow more money to repay initial loans at rates of 25 percent or more.

During antebellum Louisiana's sugar craze, loans to purchase and operate plantations flowed like the river. "The money-lender gyrated around . . . with sweet smiles and open purse," wrote George Washington Cable. The planter "was mortgaged to the eyes, and still commanded a credit that courted and importuned him. . . . Borrower and lender vied with each other in recklessness." Sugar plantations had the potential to generate great wealth, but with the vagaries of nature they often brought ruin. They were high-stakes gambles, where winning required betting against nature and the recurrence of overflows.

By the time Emma was a teenager, human attempts to stack the deck in favor of the planters were well under way. By 1812, slaves and immigrant laborers had shoveled earth into artificial levees that lined the Mississippi on both banks from below New Orleans to more than 150 miles north of the city. By the late 1850s, artificial levees extended along the river for more than 1,000 miles.

Attempts to limit overflows continued through the remainder of the nineteenth century. After the Civil War, a congressman who had fought as a Union general in campaigns on the delta argued that nature had to be controlled for human benefit. "If we make the river what it ought to be we will make 40,000,000 acres of the best cotton and sugar lands on the face of the earth." In 1857 the state geologist of Mississippi made a prediction: "After the lapse of another century, whatever the delta of the Nile may once have been, will only be a shadow of what the alluvial plain of the Mississippi will then be. It will be the central point—the garden spot of the North American continent—where wealth and prosperity culminate."

Not everyone missed the irony of achieving "wealth and prosperity" by stopping the same natural process that brought riches to plantation owners through chocolate gold. W. W. Pugh, a Louisiana sugar planter who traveled with his family to Isle Derniere in the summer of 1856, found that annual overflows on lands without artificial levees brought more benefit from added soils than detriment from lost crops. "Time has shown beyond a doubt that the owners of these lands understood thoroughly what benefit would accrue to them after the lapse of a few years. The cypress swamps, which were but a few arpents from the bayou, have been filled by the deposits, and at this time, some of the most productive cane lands have taken the place of the deep cypress swamps."

On the delta, overflows and the sediments they deposited yielded a benefit in addition to the creation of fertile land. These soil accumulations built the delta vertically and countered a process of the system that deteriorated the land.

Evidence of this process was unearthed, literally, in New Orleans by an unlikely pair of men from starkly different backgrounds and cultures. One was considered an expendable laborer, nothing more than "food for fever," while the other was one of the nineteenth century's foremost scientists.

The Irishman stood in knee-high water and drove the blade of his shovel deep into the muck below. His shirt and hat dripped with sweat and filth. The air was thick with moisture, the water thick with mud and human waste. Hundreds of his countrymen stood around him in a swath of humanity sixty feet wide. From afar, they would have looked like an army of ants, laboring in concert toward a common goal to dig the six-mile-long New Basin Canal from New Orleans to Lake Pontchartrain, shovelful by shovelful.

In 1831 the New Orleans Canal and Banking Company began construction of this waterway that would compete with the Creoles' Carondelet Canal and open a new trade route to Mississippi, Alabama, and Florida for the growing number of Anglo-American merchants in New Orleans. Finding diggers, however, proved challenging. Slaves were too valuable. Slave owners would not permit their property to dig the canal because of the high risk of disease or injury. So company officials advertised in Ireland for workers, promising an impoverished people a better way of life.

Tens of thousands of Irish braved the crossing of the Atlantic and upon arrival in New Orleans were given a shovel or pick and a dollar a day to labor in the midst of snakes and alligators—and mosquitoes, swarms of them hovering in dark clouds. These immigrants had no choice but to live in the ramshackle tenements built in former swamps.

Here the Irish "lived in the utmost squalor," according to James Gill in *Lords of Misrule*, "died grisly deaths from yellow fever, cholera and malaria and, as elsewhere, were despised as a drunken, brawling and immoral subclass." A *New York Evening Post* advertisement on September 3, 1830, epitomized the social ordering of the time: "Wanted—a cook or chambermaid. They must be American, Scotch, Swiss, or African—no Irish."

After seven years of digging, the New Basin Canal opened in 1838 to vessels with drafts up to six feet. Over the next ten years, the channel was deepened to twelve feet and broadened from sixty to one hundred feet. The canal facilitated the flow of commerce to and from New Orleans through the nineteenth and early twentieth centuries, until the opening in 1923 of the Industrial Canal, whose floodwalls would fail during Hurricane Katrina in 2005.

The cost of the New Basin Canal was millions of dollars and un-counted Irish lives—tens of thousands of them according to some es-timates, their bodies buried in unmarked graves in the channel banks near where they fell. The digging of the canal likely created for the *Aedes aegypti* a lush habitat. Workers discarded innumerable contain-ers that filled with rainwater, and the mosquitoes fed on an endless supply of Irish. To make matters worse, runoff carried fecal matter into the canal, contaminating the water in which the Irish stood, trig-gering cholera, as chronicled in a ballad:

> *Ten thousand micks, they swung their picks,*
> *To dig the New Canal,*
> *But the choleray was stronger 'n they,*
> *An' twice it killed them awl.*

The excavation of the canal brought not only death but also a clue to a fundamental process of the delta. One day the anonymous Irish-man drove the blade of his shovel into the mud and met resistance. He had struck something hard. Further excavation showed that the blade had hit the trunk of a buried tree—a finding that would attract the in-terest of the world's most eminent geologist.

Sir Charles Lyell bumped down a shell road in a horse-drawn car-riage on March 5, 1846, his eyes studying the New Basin Canal that ran parallel to his path and was open to commerce. He was forty-eight years old, beardless, but with sideburns left broad and shaggy as if to compensate for his balding pate. "We found [the canal's] sur-face enlivened with the sails of vessels laden with merchandize," he wrote later. ". . . About a mile from the city we passed a building where there is steam machinery for pumping up water and draining low

lands." It was a pleasant scene of prosperity and progress, but the great
scientist's eyes probed the water of the canal as if trying to see through
it to the mud that lay below—to evidence of how the delta worked.

The Scotsman was in New Orleans on his second visit to America to study one of the major deltas in the world and to develop new
understanding for inclusion in his books, the best-known being *Principles of Geology.* It first appeared in the early 1830s and was followed
by thirteen updated versions through his life. Geology at the time was
a popular, lively topic among specialists and laypeople alike. Their
interest was fueled by Lyell's eloquent writings about the earth and
how it changed, as well as by the growing conflicts between science
and religion on issues such as Creation and the Flood. Unlike many
gentlemen-scientists of the nineteenth century, Sir Lyell did not have
independent wealth sufficient for his wants and needs; he worked
hard to make money from the sale of his books and attracted a broad
audience from scientists to artists.

Lyell's vision countered the prevalent geologic concept of catastrophism, whereby scientists conjured up some catastrophe to fill
gaps in knowledge, like the great flood invoked by geologist Lewis
Harper to explain the Mississippi's enormous breadth of deposits, or
alluvium. "The whole alluvial plain appears as a channel of an immensely large river . . . ," wrote Harper in the 1850s, "as if once an
immense quantity of water had rushed down in this gigantic bed and
formed it." Lyell, in contrast, explained the nature of the earth in terms
of known processes that were verified through observation, not assumed through speculation, and that operated over the vastness of
time. Hence, mountain ranges need not have been thrust up in an
afternoon by some imagined cataclysm, but could have gradually risen
over millions of years.

A devoted member of Lyell's audience was a young naturalist who
took one of Lyell's books with him aboard the HMS *Beagle* on an
1830s voyage of discovery. "The great merit of the *Principles*," wrote

Charles Darwin, "was that it altered the whole tone of one's mind, & therefore that, when seeing a thing never seen by Lyell, one yet saw it partially through his eyes." Darwin used Lyell's insights to develop *On the Origin of Species*, examining fauna and flora relative to geology and long-term processes. Without Lyell's guidance, Darwin would have been unable to understand what he saw.

While yellow fever raged in New Orleans in 1853, Sir Lyell published a new edition of *Principles* that continued his ongoing argument against catastrophism. "Many geologists, when they behold the spoils of land heaped into successive strata, and blended confusedly with the remains of fishes, or interspersed with broken shells and corals, . . . imagine that they are viewing the signs of a turbulent instead of a tranquil and settled state of the planet. They read in such phenomena the proof of chaotic disorder and reiterated catastrophes." To convincingly counter such proofs, Lyell needed to know what was below the surface of the land in the layers of the earth. Such information was not easy to find on the low-lying terrain of the Mississippi River delta, where there were few vertical cuts into the sediments exposing cross-sections of the layers.

Hence, Lyell was fascinated to learn why an Irishman could not drive his shovel blade into the mud of the excavation that would become the New Basin Canal. During Lyell's visit to the canal, it was filled with water and bustling with commerce; he could not see the channel walls and the layers of earth the Irishman had dug through. "But Mr. Bringier, the State surveyor, told me," wrote Lyell, "that when the great canal . . . was dug to the depth of nine feet from Lake Pontchartrain, they had to cut through a cypress swamp which had evidently filled up gradually, for there were three tiers of stumps of trees, some of them very old, ranged one above the other." The dead trees were still vertical, still in growing position, and though they had once lived in freshwater above the level of the sea, their remains were now well below the Gulf of Mexico.

Lyell deduced that this could have happened in only one way: "We must conclude that the land has sunk down vertically." The delta's subsidence did not occur in minutes or hours during some catastrophe, but slowly, persistently, over decades, centuries, millennia, as the land was being built. The sediments that flowed down the Mississippi River from middle America were dumped into a delta deposit that was both broad and thick. Under their own weight, the sediments gradually compressed and the surface of the delta sank. Trees slipped below sea level where they could not survive. This sinking of the land invited the Gulf to encroach on the delta, as if the level of the sea were rising. Saltwater crept across the land, inundating it, and poisoned the trees that Emma passed on her steamboat journey across the delta to Isle Derniere.

Continued unchecked, this subsidence would lead to the delta disappearing beneath the sea. But this natural system had resilience. When the river flooded and overflowed levees, sediments were spread across the delta, building the land higher and countering the subsidence. As Charles Lyell wrote in 1853, "the ground was slowly raised, year after year, by mud thrown down during inundations." Clay, silt, and organic material generated in the rich estuarine environment were deposited on the delta's surface, all building the land higher. If this vertical growth balanced or exceeded the sinking, the land survived. If sinking outpaced growth, however, the land vanished.

An imbalance leading to the land vanishing could be caused by human activity, such as the building of levees that limited overflows, but it could also be caused by nature. Hundreds of years before Europeans came to America, such a natural imbalance triggered an evolution in landform, where a muddy lobe of the delta was transformed into an elegant arc of sand.

{ 3 }

"The Summer Resort for the South"

*It . . . seems to be an advanced work of the principal shore,
thrown boldly out to sea, to receive the first shock of the
surging billows of the Gulf of Mexico. It is the last of the chain
of islands composed of Grand Tere, Grand Isle and Cheniere
Caminada, on the Louisiana coast, west of the Mississippi.
In the rear it has a fine bay ten miles in width, always calm
and clear as an inland lake; and in front the vast expanse of
the Gulf of Mexico, with its mountain waves, often . . .
wasting their fury upon its magnificent beach. On one side
is peace, on the other, the war elements.*
—NEW ORLEANS DAILY DELTA, AUGUST 20, 1854

In about AD 1300, approximately 550 years before Emma's time, Isle Derniere did not exist. In its place was soft mud from which grew waist-high grasses. The marsh extended in all directions in a vast, green prairie. Nearby, a channel of the Mississippi River carried a sediment-laden torrent through the marsh. There were no signs of the sand and surf of the Gulf shore.

Native Americans used the river as a highway, riding on it in canoes, as Europeans would later do in steamboats. Some of these neo-Indians were of the "Plaquemine culture"; they emerged about AD 1300 and survived until about 1700 on the alluvial and delta plains of the Mississippi River. One of their ceremonial centers, with two pyramidal temple mounds, was constructed near the present town of Plaquemine. They lived in small villages separate from their temples. Their huts had roofs of leaves and walls of poles, the cracks between them sealed with mud. The Plaquemine culture hunted bears and deer, gathered mussels and oysters, and cultivated corn and beans in the chocolate gold that would later bring riches to other people from other lands.

Like some of these other people, Native Americans would die by the tens of thousands as a result of a malady against which they had no defense. Before European immigration, smallpox did not exist in America. With no natural immunities, the Indian populations were ravaged by epidemics. Disease and slave raids combined to cause a collapse in the population of Native Americans of the lower Mississippi Valley in the late 1600s and early 1700s, just before Bienville sent a crew of convicts and carpenters to cut a clearing on the river from which New Orleans rose.

While the Plaquemine culture's end coincided with an abrupt change in the environment wrought by humans, its beginning coincided with an abrupt change in the environment wrought by nature—by a river that not only was shaped like a snake but moved like one. Every several hundred to several thousand years, the Mississippi River writhed sideways across the delta seeking a new and more efficient course to the sea. One of these natural course changes took place between AD 1200 and 1400, when the lower part of the river shifted eastward and cut a new channel near its present course. An abandoned channel was left behind. By the nineteenth century, it was no longer filled with a sediment-laden torrent. Its water had turned sluggish, quiescent, more like a long, narrow lake than a powerful river.

Before the river switched course, it had built an odd-shaped accumulation of sediment that projected into the Gulf a half-dozen miles farther than the shore during Emma's time. From above, it looked like a bird's foot whose skinny toes each carried a channel, or distributary, to the sea. After the river snaked away and no longer supplied new sediment, the Gulf's waves tore at the foot, consuming the land. The shore retreated at rates that would have been among the most rapid found anywhere in the world.

The erosion released mostly mud and some sand into the Gulf. The lighter mud swirled away in turbid water, while the heavier sand concentrated along the shore in small pockets. As more sediment was ripped from the land by waves, the pockets elongated into beaches, and then coalesced into an elegant arc of sand perched on the seaward edge of the vast marsh. It was a mainland beach, not a barrier island; a person could slog landward across marsh to the mainland without having to ford open water.

Over the five and a half centuries between the Mississippi River altering its course and Emma's arrival on Isle Derniere, this arc of sand grew miles longer, its curvature smoother, more streamlined into the waves, as if it were trying to protect itself from further ravages. Nevertheless, the abuse of waves and storms continued, and the strand retreated landward for miles.

Behind the sandy arc, the mainland marsh starved; the river had taken its flow elsewhere, leaving few sediments available to be deposited during floods. Unable to build vertically and to compensate for the sinking of the land, the marsh slipped beneath the sea and the grasses died. Without roots to bind the mud, the sediments sloughed away. Lakes and ponds broadened, and then coalesced, one joining another, then another, opening five-mile-wide Caillou Bay between the arc of sand and the mainland. The sand was now surrounded by a moat of water, transforming it into a barrier island that would be known as Isle Derniere.

Through a centuries-long evolution that made it particularly narrow and low, the sandy strip had become perfect for unobstructed views and daily promenades that attracted the rich and prominent to its shores.

White water boiled under the two-story-high paddle wheel, black smoke belched from dual stacks, and the steamer began to decelerate. It was June or July 1856, and Emma was nearing the end of her trip across the delta to Isle Derniere. Behind her stretched the open water of Caillou Bay, the low-lying mainland barely visible on the horizon. In front of her was an expanse of marsh that formed the landward side of the narrow island. The vessel nosed into a natural channel carved into the marsh and glided toward the island's Gulf side. There, rising from a sandy beach, was the Village of Isle Derniere.

Three years prior to Emma's voyage, maps of the island were published by the Coast Survey, a federal agency established in 1807 by President Thomas Jefferson. In the early nineteenth century, the shipwrecks that were common on America's uncharted shoals and coasts had drowned seamen and disrupted commerce. The Coast Survey's mandate was to produce accurate navigation charts of the coastal waters of the United States—a mammoth undertaking given that U.S. shorelines were longer than those of any other nation at the time.

In its first several decades, the Coast Survey struggled under limited funding and bureaucratic meddling and made little progress, mapping only parts of the mid-Atlantic while the rest of the coasts remained uncharted. It was not until the 1840s that agency director Alexander Dallas Bache organized separate parties to survey the different parts of the nation's coasts simultaneously. The resulting charts were remarkable considering the limitations of mid-nineteenth-century technology. Surveyors at sea sounded hundreds of thousands of depths by lowering lead weights on marked lines to the sea bottom, while surveyors on land plotted thousands of miles of shoreline by ranging on rods held by assistants walking along the water's edge.

One of those maps was 1853's "General Reconnaissance of the Gulf Coast of Louisiana," which showed Isle Derniere as a narrow, continuous, twenty-four-mile-long island. Such maps were becoming more widely available to mariners because of another innovation during Bache's tenure at the Coast Survey: mass copying and distribution.

A more detailed map called "Preliminary Chart of Ship Island Shoal, Louisiana," also published in 1853, displayed the ragged shoreline of marsh on the island's bay side where Emma's steamer slipped between two muddy promontories into Village Harbor. Its channel cut halfway across Isle Derniere before turning right, to the west, and paralleling the smooth shoreline of sand on the island's Gulf side for more than two miles. Here, sailing vessels of various sizes and types were moored behind the homes and businesses of an elongated village that was a few buildings wide and several miles long.

The steamer docked at the landing near the eastern end of the village at the elbow where the harbor channel bent parallel to the Gulf shore. Between the landing and the beach was Muggah's Hotel, a center of entertainment for visitors to the island that offered bowling lanes, billiard tables, a fine restaurant, and a ballroom. Also in the village were Pecot's boardinghouse, a stable where horses and carriages were available for rent, a beach pavilion, and a gaming establishment.

With only a small seaward slope, the beach was smooth and firm enough for carriages to whir along as if the sand were a paved road. This thoroughfare was bordered on one side by gentle surf and on the other by Gulf-front residences. These homes were large and comfortable, most with two stories and wraparound galleries. Many were propped above the sand on stubby piles. Behind them were clusters of smaller buildings, including slave quarters, kitchens, and stables. Since the late 1840s, the village had developed many of the attractions and homes needed to make itself into what a newspaper called "the summer resort for the South."

A half-mile to the west down the beach from Muggah's Hotel was a line of three residences. At one end stood the home of Paul Octave Hebert, a French Acadian who had graduated first in his class at the U.S. Military Academy and served as governor of Louisiana from 1853 to 1856. Michael Schlatre owned the center home. Next to Schlatre was the home of Thomas Mille.

Two Mille family members had not traveled to the island. Emma's older sister remained on the mainland with her husband, while her younger sister was in a convent school. Settling into their beach house for the first time were Emma, her parents, her brother Homer, his wife Althee and their infant, plus a visitor from New Orleans, Mrs. Rommage.

From their home on clear nights, the Mille family could see the beacon of a lightship moored eighteen miles offshore, where the sea floor rose sharply into Ship Shoal. The primary shipping lane between Galveston and New Orleans ran past the Isle Derniere, and many vessels would dip landward of the dangerously shallow water and pass within several miles of shore. The ships came close enough that in 1854 a slave was ordered to hail a vessel to take on a passenger who did not want to wait for the next scheduled river steamer.

The people on Isle Derniere were well aware of the presence of Ship Shoal. They may have been unaware, however, of the similarities between the shoal and the island. Both were relatively narrow and a few tens of miles long. Both of their long dimensions were oriented parallel to shore. Both had surfaces of sand.

None of the people realized that both shoal and island began the first stage of their lives as an accumulation of sediment projecting into the sea in the shape of a bird's foot. And none realized that both entered the *last* stage of their lives by slipping beneath the sea, transforming an island into a submerged shoal.

Emma Mille was a few months shy of her nineteenth birthday and unmarried at a time when Creole girls commonly wed at sixteen. She wore her long, dark hair pulled back in a chignon knotted at the back of her head or wrapped on top of her crown. (It was considered unseemly for a woman to wear her hair down in public.) Her complexion was stylishly pale; when outside, a bonnet or parasol sheltered her visage from the sun to prevent the development of unsightly blemishes, like a tan or freckles. She had a broad, rounded face, less classically beautiful than strong, with large, dark, penetrating eyes.

Emma and the other women on the island looked forward to the late-in-the-day promenades along the strand to seek cooling breezes, as well as to see and be seen. "This famous beach teems every evening with people," the *Daily Delta* reported in 1854, "composed of sober-sided old gentlemen as pedestrians, alert young men and beautiful ladies on horseback, and in carriages innumerable whirling along at a pace that would astonish frequenters of Shell Road [in New Orleans]."

The ladies picked their outfits for promenade with care, having brought to the island extensive summer wardrobes. "If ever there were clothing to die for, the ladies of Isle Derniere possessed it," wrote Bethany Bultman in her account of the storm. "These bite-your-tongue Victorian-era damsels were judged on their ability to defy gravity and nature with the body-modifying fashion confectionery wonders of the Industrial Age."

They wore corsets stiffened with whalebones. Female house slaves strained to cinch the corsets' stays as taut as a fiddle's strings. Any exertion made faces glisten in sweat. The summer heat and humidity were oppressive. With no screens, they could not throw the windows open to capture a breeze without inviting bloodsucking flies and mosquitoes into their bedrooms. To kill these menaces, blown-glass fly-catchers were distributed about the rooms, each partially filled with sugar water to attract insects through a narrow opening that would trap them inside. The only effective escape from the insects came at night when the women lay in bed under fine-mesh netting.

Night or day, there was no escape from the heat. The soaring ceilings mitigated the discomfort slightly. They were designed in many antebellum homes to allow the hottest air to rise above heads. Standing in their rooms, most of the women on the island would have appeared short, not only relative to the ten- to twelve-foot-high ceilings, but also because of the small stature of the people of the time. From 1840 to 1865, the average height of women measured in a community in the U.S. Northeast was five feet, while today the average height of U.S. women with high incomes has grown to about five feet, four inches. Evidence for this difference can be seen today in some of Louisiana's surviving big houses, where doorknobs of the eighteenth and nineteenth centuries were installed nearly half a foot below the standard elevation for the twenty-first.

In spite of the hot weather, the ultimate choice of an outfit was not dictated by temperature. Rather, as Catherine Clinton wrote in *The Plantation Mistress*, "purity ruled appearance." The women left little skin exposed, blanketing it in the stylish yet suffocating multilayered clothing of the time, like the hoop dress over petticoats, the fashion rage of the mid-nineteenth century. Toward the end of the 1850s, some of these dresses had hoops with diameters of twelve to fifteen feet.

On her way to join her family in the promenade, Emma would squeeze her hoops through the door leading from her bedroom to the second-floor gallery of the Mille home. Some antebellum house designs had no internal hallways; rooms opened into adjacent rooms. The external galleries and their external stairways were used to navigate the house. Downstairs, off the first-floor gallery, was the parlor where the family would greet visitors. A central stairway led from the first-floor gallery down to the sand.

It was far shorter than the entrance stairway Emma was accustomed to at the big house on Milly Plantation that rose to the family's living areas—the parlor, dining area, and family bedrooms—on the second floor. The first floor of the big house was reserved for storage and quarters for the family's most trusted house slaves. Emma had seen the reason for this design: the high water that swirled over the banks of Bayou Plaquemine and through not only the cane fields but the first floor of the big house.

In her beach home, however, her family's living areas were lower, propped above the sand on piles whose height was spanned by a mere four steps.

Emma and her family joined some of the most prominent people of Louisiana in the promenade, including sugar-planter-turned-politician Colonel William Whitmell (W. W.) Pugh, who was the speaker of Louisiana's House of Representatives, Paul Octave Hebert, who had recently completed his term as governor, and their families. As they walked along the beach, the men would cluster together and usually talk of agriculture and business. This summer, however, the planters and merchants on Isle Derniere shared a deep concern for national politics. Many people in Louisiana were not initially for secession from the Union. But many sugar planters were incensed at the insults hurled at a fellow slave master on the floor of the U.S. Senate in Washington on May 19–20, 1856.

"The senator from South Carolina has read many books on chivalry, and believes himself a chivalrous knight, with sentiments of honor and courage," intoned Massachusetts senator Charles Sumner, referring to Andrew P. Butler. "Of course he has chosen a mistress to whom he has made his vows, and who, though ugly to others, is always lovely to him; though polluted in the sight of the world, is chaste in his sight;—I mean the harlot Slavery."

The fury of slave owners on Isle Derniere was soon assuaged. Several days after Sumner's speech, Congressman Preston Brooks of South Carolina, a nephew of the elderly senator who had been disparaged, slipped into the Senate chamber to seek satisfaction.

According to the *Tribune* of New York, "Mr. Sumner was struck un-awares over the head by a loaded cane and stunned, and then the ruffianly attack was continued with many blows. . . . No meaner exhibition of southern cowardice—generally miscalled southern chivalry—was ever witnessed."

Most editorialists in the South and many of the planters on Isle Derniere saw it differently. "For Mr. Sumner we have not the least sympathy," wrote a Georgia newspaper. "When he delivered that com-pound of vulgarity, abuse and falsehood called a speech, he knew that he violated all the laws of decency, and deserved a severe corporeal castigation, but he relied upon his position as a Senator to protect him. We believe there are some kinds of slander and abuse, for the perpetration of which, no office or station should protect a man from deserved punishment."

Debates swept the country and sometimes turned violent. The confrontations were most intense in the territories where the slavery question had not been settled, like Kansas. On May 21, 1856, pro-slavery forces sacked the antislavery stronghold of Lawrence, attack-ing a hotel with cannon and fire and destroying newspaper businesses. Soon, antislavery forces retaliated. The abolitionist John Brown and his men were hurrying to defend Lawrence when they heard that it had been sacked. In fits of rage, they murdered five slave owners.

The deaths sent a chill through the sugar masters on Isle Derniere. They worried about such news reaching their slaves, en-couraging them to resist, inflaming them against their owners. On a typical Louisiana sugar plantation in the early 1850s, about eighty-five slaves worked the fields and sugar mill and big house, outnumbering the master, the overseer, and their families by as much as eight to one. In spite of their firearms and whips, the planters were well aware that slave revolts on their plantations would overwhelm them. On Isle Derniere, however, the masters needed only relatively small numbers of cooks and body servants and hostlers, and the threat of conflict was reduced. The slave owners had a sense of security that allowed them to enjoy the peace and tranquillity of the island.

Standing on the crest of the beach and looking landward, they had unobstructed views across the broad expanse of Caillou Bay, its ruffled surface in gentle, almost imperceptible motion. Turning around, they faced the open Gulf of Mexico, where "the water is clear and salt," wrote a visitor to the island in 1848, "and not over five feet deep, for a distance of two-hundred yards from the shore, and when the tide is coming in, the waves roll upon the beach one after another in so beautiful succession, that any one who looks upon them must be gratified at the sight."

The people of Isle Derniere appreciated the island's hard-packed sands that invited walking and carriage riding unobstructed by prominent dunes. "[It is] certainly one of the finest places for promenading I have ever seen," continued the visitor. "Its surface is smooth and firm, it is always cool on account of its being contiguous to the salt water which so uniformly washes its surface, a gentle sea breeze is always floating across it, and health and vigor seemed to be inhaled at every breath by those who visit it."

The dangers of the time must have seemed distant to those on Isle Derniere. The island was a refuge from yellow fever, from the growing fervor against slavery, and from the constant fear of slave revolt. The planters felt safe in the isolation of the strand, as if the surrounding water shielded them from harm.

{ 4 }

The Law
of Storms

*It is generally believed that within the tropics hurricanes are
more frequent during the months of July, August, and
September. . . . Learned astronomers have, from time to time,
attempted to account for these periodical visitations. . . .
We have not yet been favored with any satisfactory solution
of their causes and severity, and can only submit to the laws
of nature regarding them.*
—NEW ORLEANS DAILY CRESCENT, AUGUST 16, 1856

M any afternoons during the summer of 1856, thunderstorms
boomed over or near Isle Derniere. No one thought much
about the storms. They were a routine part of summer in coastal
Louisiana. Sometimes they came with fierce winds, often with driving
rain, but they were short-lived, seldom destructive, and life continued
when skies cleared.

In late July or early August, such a routine thunderstorm developed somewhere over the sea. No one knows the exact location, but
it was at least six hundred miles southeast of Isle Derniere near Cuba,
or farther east in the tropical Atlantic. The seawater where the storm
fired up was uncomfortably warm, 80 degrees Fahrenheit or more, and
this warmth extended beyond the sea surface to depths of at least 160
feet. The hot and humid air just above the sea was relatively light, so

it rose, cooling as it gained altitude, condensing water vapor into rain, and releasing energy as heat that made the air continue to rise. Cumulonimbus clouds, or thunderheads, billowed high into the atmosphere.

There were no large changes in wind speed with altitude to shear the columns of rising air and clouds apart. The fledgling meteorological system persisted and grew. Other thunderstorms developed nearby and joined the first, forming a ragged cluster of soaring clouds. Then more storms fired up around the periphery of the initial cluster and coalesced with it, broadening it into a huge but still amorphous mass of clouds that started to move to the west or northwest—and to spin.

Scientists of the time hypothesized that storms were governed by what they called a "law." This law incorporated some of the fundamental characteristics of storms that needed to be understood in order to develop forecasts. Through much of the first half of the nineteenth century, what constituted the "law of storms" was under considerable dispute.

On Wednesday, August 6, 1856, Michael Schlatre packed his valise, preparing to leave the island aboard the *Blue Hammock*, which was docked at the landing in Village Harbor behind Muggah's Hotel. Around him in his oceanfront home, children played and servants worked. Staying in the main structure and in the slave quarters behind it were "17 souls of us," Michael wrote later, "consisting of wife and seven children also four grown servants and three small ones, with a servant of Mrs. Robertson with us, old Hannah."

Michael Schlatre had lived in Louisiana most of his life. His grandmother had come down the Mississippi as a young girl aboard a flatboat, powered only by the river's current through a gauntlet of what Schlatre described as "hostile Indians lining both banks." She and her family had been drawn to Louisiana by stories of a land so productive that "feathers grew on trees." Michael's grandfather, Jacob Schlatre, endured the treacherous voyage across the Atlantic aboard the ship

Hope as one of America's German immigrants. They were a hardworking people who first showed how Louisiana's rich soils could be
cultivated into rich harvests. Schlatre inherited this drive to succeed
that made the German Coast downriver from Plaquemine into Côte
d'Or, or the Gold Coast. Schlatre was also an educated man; he had
attended St. Louis University for two years, until deciding that Missouri's climate did not suit him. He returned south and entered
Louisiana's Centenary College, where he completed studies in navigation, surveying, and engineering. Schlatre put his drive and education to good use, becoming both a steamboat captain and a sugar
planter, highly respected occupations of the time.

On this Wednesday in early August, the thirty-seven-year-old
Schlatre looked forward to assuming command of his vessel. He was
going to deliver a load of hoops to sugar plantations along the western
margin of the delta. The hoops held together large sugar containers,
called hogsheads. He then planned to steam to Plaquemine and load
more passengers for a return run to Isle Derniere. But in the evening
his plans changed. J. A. Dardenne, who had piloted the steamer on its
last trip to the island, came to Schlatre's house and said that he had
business on the mainland in Plaquemine and wanted to return there
in the morning. "Such being the case I told him that [I] would remain
on the Island, if he would command the boat home and back, to which
he agreed."

On schedule, at 2:00 AM, Thursday, Dardenne took the *Blue
Hammock* from Village Harbor and into the darkness of Caillou Bay.
Michael Schlatre was left behind in his island home, where, he wrote
later, "it fell to my lot to witness what followed."

Pierre Thomas Mille stood before a mirror in his bedroom and inspected his appearance. Other hands appeared in the reflected
image before him, black hands straightening the cravat around his
neck, snugging it tight against his white skin. On a nearby table or

dresser, those black hands had neatly stacked the gloves, hat, and coat that Mille would don before venturing outside into the heat and humidity. To many wealthy French and Creole men of the time, appearing in public when not properly attired, even at the beach, was unthinkable. The hands of his body servant were ever present to assure that the unthinkable never occurred.

Although born in France, Mille had lived most of his fifty-six years in Louisiana with Creoles, who "retained a deep nostalgia for mother country," according to Liliane Crete, "and continued to cultivate French manners, customs, and tastes." Unlike the coarse Anglo-Americans crowding south Louisiana, he would not have chewed tobacco and spat the brown juice onto the ground or into a spittoon. He also would not have imbibed shots of whiskey. Rather, Thomas Mille would have greeted ladies with a kiss on the back of their hand, savored fine cigars, and sipped black coffee during the day and sherry in the evening. And he lived in a Creole culture whose males, according to Crete, had "haughty bearing, . . . pride, and . . . indifference to those outside [their] class." They considered themselves part of a "superior race."

Creoles had different backgrounds from French Acadians, whose ancestors were expelled from Canada with few belongings and little money and forced to build new lives elsewhere. In contrast, the first Frenchmen who came to Louisiana were "the first blood and rank in France," according to William Henry Sparks in 1872; they included "the Ibervilles, the Bienvilles, [the] St. Denises." Their Creole descendants grew up in wealth and kept it, passing their money from generation to generation. Some of the Mille family's wealth came from the inheritance received by Emma's mother, Pauline, after the death of her rich French father.

French Creoles were not known for industriousness. Many were satisfied with their personal wealth and chose not to engage in the constant, unending pursuit of more and more riches. Instead, they indulged in enjoying life, appreciating their families and socializing with their friends. George Washington Cable maintained in his 1884 book *Creoles of Louisiana* that they "expended the best of their energies in trivial pleasures, especially the masque and the dance."

Compared to the German descendant Schlatre, the Frenchman Thomas Mille would have been focused more on his next pleasure than his next challenge.

As a steamboat captain, Michael Schlatre was wary of his surroundings, wary of the changes in the water or the atmosphere that could bring sudden danger. He navigated his steamer in river and bayous with numerous hazards. "Alluvial banks cave and change constantly," wrote Mark Twain, ". . . snags [from submerged trees] are always hunting up new quarters, . . . sand-bars are never at rest, . . . channels are for ever dodging and shirking."

Sometimes a shroud fell over the banks and snags and bars. Hot humid air over cold northern water created a fog that followed the course of the river. During grinding season, this fog mixed with the smoke from the burning of bagasse on the sugar plantations. This shroud hid the hazards, leaving a steamer captain like Michael Schlatre essentially blind.

He would have tried to sense changes in conditions before they occurred, like the sudden gusts of wind that whisked fog and smoke from the river but slammed against a side of his top-heavy steamboat. While the vessel's hull dipped into the water only several feet so it could negotiate the hidden shoals of river and bayous, its cabins towered three stories above the water. This exposed superstructure acted like a sail. Even a moderately strong wind could push it, driving the vessel into a bank or snag or bar.

The captain knew that missing a single sign of danger could lead to loss of property and life. Mark Twain described what was at stake: "[the loss of] a quarter of million dollars worth of steam boat and cargo in five minutes, and maybe a hundred and fifty human lives in the bargain." Yet on Isle Derniere, Schlatre may not have anticipated the potential dangers as thoroughly as he would have on the river. He and his family were there to escape disease, to relax after a long planting season, to enjoy the bathing, the fishing, the promenade. Schlatre undoubtedly remained conscious of the weather and its vagaries, conscious of the potential for storms. Yet heavy winds had come and gone and the Village of Isle Derniere still stood.

Just a year earlier, on September 16, 1855, a major hurricane had swept ashore close to the mouth of the Mississippi River. It was the most destructive gale in over three decades. According to the *New Orleans Crescent*, the losses along the coast were "truly deplorable." Though the lightship moored eighteen miles offshore over Ship Shoal was ripped from its mooring, the island emerged unscathed. About this time Schlatre's wife wrote her brother in New York, telling him of the confidence the storm had given her. Their house was so well constructed that it was hardly even damaged. She felt that her family was safe on the island. When the Schlatres traveled again to Isle Derniere for the summer of 1856, everything had returned to normal. They could even see the evening glow of the repaired and reanchored lightship.

The Schlatres and many others on the island were lulled into complacency, a sense that nothing had happened to them and hence nothing was going to happen—a sense still common today along barrier islands lining the U.S. Atlantic and Gulf coasts. "Having been at the Island for so many seasons," Michael Schlatre wrote, "and in all kinds of weather I felt no apprehension." Schlatre felt like he had come to know the island and the sea from observing them, just as he had come to know the bars and snags of the river, and one observation would soon stand out among the others. During the 1855 hurricane, the wind was probably strong enough that people on the island would have had difficulty standing erect, but these gusts came persistently from the land, not the sea. Because the Village of Isle Derniere endured the event with few lasting impacts, strong winds from the land did not seem to pose a serious threat.

Michael's practical experience as a captain was aboard steamboats navigating inland rivers and bayous and bays. He had little experience plotting a course that would take his vessel away from, rather than toward, a great storm at sea. This was the concern of captains of seagoing steam and sailing ships. On the other hand, he had studied ocean navigation in college in the late 1830s or early 1840s and may have been exposed to some of the techniques then being developed to identify and avoid powerful storms. He may also have been exposed to a nasty debate that raged among some of the nation's most prominent meteorologists in regard to establishing the law of storms.

During the nineteenth century, like today, scientists clashed about the veracity of research findings out of the public view at technical conferences and in scholarly journals, where criticisms and point-by-point rebuttals were published. In the early to mid-1800s, some of the more contentious debates gained a wider audience through an explosion of information. Before this time, what people knew of their world came mostly from what they heard from the pulpit. Yet with progressive improvements in printing technology, sermons became increasingly supplemented by the written word as the number of newspapers and periodicals published in the United States increased from less than 200 in 1800 to more than 2,500 by midcentury.

In addition, a grand experiment in adult education known as the lyceum movement created lecture halls around the country. Its mission was to cure "gossip, intemperance, ignorance, and sectional strife," and by 1835 more than 3,000 lecture halls had been established. Some of the most noted people of the nineteenth century spoke in them, including Ralph Waldo Emerson, Henry Ward Beecher, and Horace Greeley, as well as renowned scientists such as Sir Charles Lyell and Louis Agassiz. Flocking to their lectures were artisans, salespersons, factory workers, and clerks.

With the opening of a Lyceum in New Orleans in 1844, Michael Schlatre would have had the opportunity to hear about the most recent research of the time. The public was fascinated and alarmed by the sudden appearance of great storms that would take lives and destroy property with no warning. During the War of 1812, the Great Louisiana Hurricane unexpectedly struck New Orleans. The parishes south of the city were submerged under fifteen feet of water. In 1831 the Great Barbados Hurricane left 2,500 people dead from multiple landfalls from Barbados to Louisiana.

In presenting their findings in lectures and writings, however, some meteorologists chose to criticize competing scientists personally. "We regret that the discussions which unavoidably arise among different investigators," the first director of the *Smithsonian Institution* wrote, "have not always been carried on with the calmness and moderation with which the pursuit of truth should always be conducted. Indeed, meteorology has ever been a source of contention, as if the violent commotions of the atmosphere induced a sympathetic effect in the minds of those who have attempted to study them."

During the 1830s and 1840s, James Pollard Espy stood at podiums across the country, gazing over his audiences with confidence and command. Photographs show that he had a clean-shaven face with elegant, almost handsome features and a slight smile tinged with arrogance. He was a social, enthusiastic person who engaged his audiences with his personality and ideas. They paid rapt attention to his words, and Espy gloried in their interest. He was a star, touring across the country from Lyceum to Lyceum, where people flocked to hear the man introduced as "the Storm King" reveal the secrets of hurricanes. Considering the popularity of the movement, his audiences were probably large. A British agricultural scientist at the Smithsonian Institution drew 1,200 to 1,500 for his lectures.

Espy had the rare skill of being able to express complex scientific principles in interesting and understandable terms. His training enhanced this talent. Like Sir Charles Lyell, he began his career as a lawyer, developing his oratory skills, before devoting himself to science. Espy studied languages and science at Transylvania University, and in 1817 he became a professor at the Franklin Institute of Philadelphia, where he first delved into detailed investigations of meteorology.

Professor Espy developed a theory of storms that he elucidated in a series of papers in the *Journal of the Franklin Institute* and summarized in his 1841 book *The Philosophy of Storms*. He argued that great storms are driven by warm, humid air rising in a column. The air cools as it rises, and since cool air cannot contain as much moisture as warm, the water vapor condenses as clouds and rain, releasing its latent heat and warming the surrounding air. The warmer air becomes lighter, more buoyant, and continues to rise, reinforcing the updraft. In addition, Espy argued, the rising air is replaced by air rushing from all directions toward the center of the column, feeding the upward flow. "Thus the law will become general . . . ," Espy wrote, "the wind will blow toward the centre of the storm."

Alexander Dallas Bache, who led the Coast Survey in the first effective mapping of the nation's coasts, wrote of Espy's work: "Founded on the established laws of physics, and upon ingenious and well-directed experiments, this theory drew general attention to itself, especially in the United States." By the early 1840s, the theory had gained acceptance in Europe. In fact, a prominent French scientist remarked, "France has its Cuvier, England its Newton, America its Espy." In 1843 Espy was offered a job in the U.S. War Department to pursue his studies. Professor Joseph Henry of the Smithsonian Institution said that Espy's research on storms made the first weather forecasts possible.

Support for Espy and his theory was not, however, universal. He came under sharp criticism from other meteorologists for taking his arguments to the public in his lecture tours. "It had been sneeringly said . . . by a distinguished Professor," Espy lamented in the preface to his 1841 book, "that I had failed to convince men of science of the truth of my theory, and that I had appealed to the people, who were incapable of judging." The most devastating challenge to Espy's research, however, came from an amateur scientist.

William C. Redfield had no university education and was taught the most basic subjects in the most common schools. He was born in 1789 in Middletown, Connecticut. In the early 1800s, before steamboat and railroad travel became routine, Redfield had inadequate finances to purchase a horse or passage aboard a stagecoach. So he walked. On one journey he covered seven hundred miles to visit his mother, making thirty-two miles of headway per day. Much of the land he encountered in the northeast United States was still covered by dense forests with few paths or roads cut through them.

During his walks, Redfield examined the environment around him, developing and honing his skills of observation. Every evening he updated a log with notes and sketches of what he had observed about the forests and towns and people he passed during the day. Walking through a Connecticut forest in the fall of 1821, Redfield documented the unique signature left in the devastation of a great storm.

He noted that a violent wind from the southeast had snapped off trees and laid them down pointing toward the northwest. As he kept walking across Connecticut and into Massachusetts, he was surprised to see trees laid down with their heads in the opposite direction. From talking to people in villages along his route, Redfield discovered that during the storm the wind was blowing in different directions at different locations at the same time. Mystified, Redfield continued walking and noting the directions of fallen trees and questioning people who had experienced the storm. He concluded that the storm was a whirlwind that moved forward. In this progressive whirlwind, the air rotated around the center of the swirl. In contrast, Espy argued that air rushed directly toward the storm's center.

Redfield's observations might never have been widely known if not for a chance encounter aboard a steamboat nearly a decade later. "A stranger accosted me," wrote a professor of natural history and astronomy at Yale College, "and modestly asked leave to make a few inquiries respecting some observations I had recently published." That stranger was Redfield, and during the ensuing conversation he related his interpretations of progressive whirlwinds. "This doctrine was quite new to me," the professor wrote, "but it impressed me so favorably, that I urged him to communicate it to the world." Redfield felt uncomfortable doing so, telling the professor that he was merely "a practical man little versed in scientific discussions." Yet the professor persisted and helped guide him through the publishing process. Redfield's milestone paper, "Remarks on the Prevailing Storms of the Atlantic Coast," appeared in the *American Journal of Science* in 1831.

Espy and some other scientists of the time found Redfield's "Remarks" and his subsequent studies more nonsense than breakthrough. Espy argued that Redfield's research suffered from the "practical evils arising from unfounded rules." Professor Robert Hare of the University of Pennsylvania, who had published numerous scholarly papers in the *American Journal of Science*, wrote, "I cannot give to this alleged theory the smallest importance while the unequal and opposing forces, on which it is built, exist only in the imagination of the author." Redfield might have understandably shrunk from such attacks, and from further scientific discussions, given the stature of his attackers.

Instead, Redfield overcame his reticence and engaged the scientific giants of his time with a verbal slap in the face. "The grand error into which the whole school of meteorologists appear to have fallen, consists in ascribing to heat and rarefaction the origin and support of the great atmospheric currents." Espy did not hesitate to slap back, accusing Redfield of misrepresenting his data. "I did not anticipate so complete an evasion of all the distinguishing points at issue, and so barren an effort at confusing and mystifying." Redfield kept swinging, charging that "Espy misquoted [me], confused facts well established by observations, and—most damning of all—stole [my] ideas."

During the decades-long slugfest, Redfield's interpretation of a "progressive whirlwind" was gradually accepted by other scientists—notably by Lieutenant Colonel William Reid of the Royal Engineers, who incorporated it into his 1838 book *An Attempt to Develop the Law of Storms by Means of Facts.* Espy's argument that air rushes straight toward the center of a storm was wrong. Rather, the rotation of the earth gives the air "some spin," and it spirals progressively inward, turning counterclockwise in the Northern Hemisphere. As the air winds toward the eye, the spirals become tighter and speeds become higher in the whirlwind deduced by Redfield.

Some of Espy's other findings, however, were correct and important. The key role of convection, the vertical movements of air due to heating and cooling, has become fundamental in understanding the development and maintenance of storms.

The criticisms that Espy received did not stop him from promoting his ideas or continuing his popular lectures. Had Professor Espy stood before an audience at the Lyceum of New Orleans, he would have presented himself to the public as the legitimate "Storm King." He would not have provided Redfield's side of the argument—at least not without a sneer. "Mr. Redfield insists . . . ," Espy wrote in his 1841 book, "that all of the West Indian hurricanes . . . whirl contrary to the hands of a watch!"

At such a lecture, the audience would have heard nothing but contempt about progressive whirlwinds.

As dawn broke over Isle Derniere on Thursday, August 7, 1856, it was already fully light in Washington, D.C., where workers were preparing to open the Smithsonian building to the public for the day. In this city known for its white marble, passersby gawked at the recently completed edifice's ruby sandstone walls and soaring, castle-

like towers that still stand today. In 1856 in the great hall of this building, Joseph Henry, the first director of the Institution, hung a unique
map that showed weather conditions over much of the United States,
using observations transmitted via the telegraph. Despite their antag-
onism on the law of storms, William Redfield and James Pollard Espy
agreed on the importance of this revolutionary communication device
in understanding and forecasting changes in the weather.

In the 1830s, before becoming the Smithsonian's director, Henry
had shown that messages could be sent over long distances with the
telegraph, setting the stage for Samuel Morse in the 1840s to demon-
strate the device's commercial viability. By 1847 one major telegraph
line had wound its wires over 1,200 miles from Washington, D.C.,
through Raleigh, Columbia, Macon, Montgomery, and Mobile before
terminating eighty miles from Isle Derniere in New Orleans.

Joseph Henry and his fledgling Smithsonian Institution implemented weather telegraphy in the United States by first cobbling together in the late 1840s a small group of telegraph operators who signed
on each day with a brief description of the local weather. Over the years
the network grew; by 1858, thirty-two operators participated in it. At
about ten o'clock every morning, the stations reported and Henry's map
in the Smithsonian building was updated with current conditions.

A card of a specific color was hung at each station: the different
colors distinguished different weather conditions—rain, snow, cloudy,
clear. Visitors to the Smithsonian crowded around the map to check
the weather at their hometowns. Henry would sometimes join visitors
and regale them on the map's use. By this time, meteorologists knew
that winter storms, or cold fronts, generally moved from west to east
across the country. By updating the weather map with periodic observations from telegraph stations, the approach of such storms to ports
and cities on the Atlantic coast could be monitored and forecast.

On August 7, 1856, weather conditions in New Orleans—"Hot
sunshine[,] West wind"—indicated nothing ominous. There were no

telegraph stations farther west than New Orleans to detect a system approaching from that direction. Further, weather telegraphy could not detect tropical storms feeding on the warm water of the lower latitudes and threatening Louisiana from the south, from the Gulf of Mexico.

With no aircraft or satellites, the only way to monitor the approach of a tropical storm to Isle Derniere would have been from observations by crews aboard ships. But in 1856 wireless telegraphy was several decades away. Hence, ships at sea could not warn the mainland of an approaching storm in the same way that Henry's land network could warn ports on the Atlantic coast of an approaching cold front from the west.

It would be seven days hence, after the steamships *Texas* and *Daniel Webster* had docked safely in New Orleans, that the *Daily Picayune* would report what their crews had seen and experienced.

On Thursday, August 7, the people on Isle Derniere were blind to what had happened to a cluster of thunderstorms far at sea. Over the next few days, however, signs of its evolution would appear on the island—signs dictated by the law of storms.

{ 5 }

Secrets
of the
Deep

*We did not know then as we did afterwards that the voice of
those many waters was solemnly saying to us, Escape for thy
life. Scientists may smile, but the wisest of them will own that
the deep has not yet given up all its secrets to the philosopher.*
—Reverend R. S. McAllister,
Southwestern Presbyterian, April 9, 1891

Michael Schlatre awoke on Friday morning, August 8, to an
odd buffeting of his house. He felt a sense of unease; a strong
wind must have sprung up during the night. Coming from the Gulf,
it would bring rough seas and disrupt steamer traffic between Isle
Derniere and Brashear City (called Morgan City today) on the mainland. The previous morning his steamboat, the *Blue Hammock*, had
made that run, following a course to the west of Isle Derniere across
fifteen miles of open Gulf of Mexico before ducking northward
through marsh channels and bays to the Atchafalaya River. The *Blue
Hammock* and the other packet boats that served the island were designed with flat bottoms to skim shallow bayous, rather than rounded
hulls to cut large waves. As a consequence, when a strong onshore

wind ruffled the Gulf's surface, the steamers could not safely venture offshore.

From the second-floor gallery at the rear of his house, Schlatre would have felt the wind against his face and seen the bay's surface speckled white. The wind pushed up steep, choppy waves and sheared off their caps into froth. Yet any concerns that crossed Schlatre's mind about the wind, and what it could do, diminished after he determined that the wind was not blowing from the sea. Rather, it came from the land, whipping across the delta and five-mile-wide Caillou Bay toward the marshy side of Isle Derniere. Later he wrote that it was "nothing extraordinary."

The conditions were similar to those of the "northers" that recurred every few weeks during winter with the passage of cold fronts, except the air this day was hot, not cold. As with northers, the wind swept off the land and pushed the water of shallow Caillou Bay against the bay side of the island, submerging its marsh fringe and filling Village Harbor behind Schlatre's house almost to its brim. The moored sailing vessels, which the day before drifted lazily at anchor, had now snapped to attention, turning in concert to face the wind, each of their anchor lines pulled taut. Having spent considerable time on the island over a number of years, Schlatre would have seen such minor bay-side flooding before and would have found it, like the wind that rattled his home, to be "nothing extraordinary."

What was extraordinary was unfolding on the Gulf side of his house. Schlatre heard the breakers before seeing them. They sounded like thunder. Normal waves coming ashore on Isle Derniere from the Gulf of Mexico were gentle. A typical wave breaking against the shore was no taller than a few feet. The shallow and muddy seafloor offshore of the island usually sucked the energy from the waves before they reached the shore.

On this day, however, in spite of the muddy shallows offshore, in spite of the opposing wind from the land, "the billows [from the sea] . . . grew . . . larger and higher," wrote an observer on the island, "ran more and more swiftly, and assumed, continually, a greater variety of form. Retaining an erect posture, and riding forward impetuously upon the surface of the apparently solid main." The wind blew against the waves as they started to break, holding their erect faces vertical for an instant longer than gravity would have allowed alone. Then the crests tumbled landward and exploded into white water, the wind shearing their spray seaward, in the opposite direction of their fall, in feathery, sallow plumes. The scene was exciting, even beautiful, yet perplexing.

A strong wind blowing over water pushed up waves that ran with the wind, not against it. The stronger the wind and the longer the distance over which it blew, the taller the waves would grow. A strong onshore wind from the Gulf could generate waves as tall as houses. But the wind was blowing offshore, sweeping from the north over Caillou Bay and generating waves there that broke against the marsh fringe on the island's bay side. These waves were substantially smaller than those on the Gulf side; their heights were limited by the bay's narrow width and shallow depth.

Meanwhile, the waves on the Gulf side of the island grew taller even though the local wind continued to blow against them. These waves came from a distant source, the winds in the growing expanse of clouds that had swirled into the Gulf of Mexico through the Florida Straits in between the Keys and Cuba. That storm was spinning "contrary to the hands of a watch" and propelling waves outward in all directions.

Unaware of the distant storm, Schlatre found the large waves in the Gulf peculiar but nonthreatening. His attitude was shared by most of the people on Isle Derniere that day, even though there were other signs of danger. These signs had become part of the background and were easy to walk or ride past with no notice. The sands of Isle Derniere were strewn with driftwood—thick trunks of large trees that were appreciated by the people of the island for offering a ready source of fuel for cooking fires. Few of them considered the implication of having such easily accessible wood. Past storms had inundated the island and left the logs behind. "Though there were some trees lying about and [they] had evidently found a resting place after some storm, an inundation of the island in the past . . ." wrote Speaker of the House W. W. Pugh, "the idea did not occur to any one of the gay throng, that what had taken place in the past might be repeated."

In spite of the breakers, the people on the island continued to try to enjoy themselves. "Toward night" on August 8, according to Pugh, "the water assumed an angry appearance, and the waves on the Gulf were quite high, though it [was not] deemed dangerous to those who ventured to take a bath among the breakers."

From the gallery on the bay side of his house, Michael Schlatre would have seen the bright sails of pleasure boats running hard among the whitecaps that crowded the surface of Caillou Bay. There were several excellent sailing vessels kept on the island for pleasure trips in surrounding waters, including the *Atlantic*, a ten-ton bark that the year before had been sailed to Isle Derniere from New York.

As evening approached, Schlatre might have noticed the *Atlantic* with its distinctive three masts, slipping into Village Harbor after an exhilarating day of sailing. The vessel anchored near the landing where the steamer *Star* was moored. The *Star,* a packet steamboat, was owned by the Muggah brothers and, like the *Blue Hammock*, regularly brought visitors to the island. Schlatre's eyes would have been drawn to the steamer's dual stacks, which rose above the roofline of the two-story hotel. He would have seen no smoke coming from those stacks, indicating that the steamer's boilers were cold. The captain was not preparing to make a run for the mainland and, hence, must have also been unconcerned about the weather.

"So little was thought of a storm, and its consequences," recalled Pugh, "that on Friday [August 8] one of the gentlemen expressed a great desire to witness a gale, so that . . . he might learn whether the descriptions he had read were true[;] he lived to witness it but not long enough to relate his conclusions on the subject."

Captain Thomas H. Ellis of the steamer *Star* had been aboard the *Atlantic* for a day of enjoyable sailing, along with a large group of men and women from the island. Upon the *Atlantic*'s anchoring in Village Harbor, they rowed ashore in skiffs and made their way across the sand to their homes or to their rooms at Muggah's Hotel. Ellis had just arrived at his hotel room when the cabin boy from the *Atlantic* interrupted him and said the vessel's captain, Old Jimmy, wanted to see Ellis back on board right away.

Ellis was tired and wet from sailing through bumpy seas, and he wondered what could be the problem. When he made his way back to the landing, he saw Captain Jimmy with several other seamen on the deck of the *Atlantic* waiting for him. Ellis jumped into a skiff and after several strokes with the oars joined them aboard.

Unlike the planters and merchants vacationing on the island, these seamen were alarmed by what they saw going on around them. They pointed to the harbor's flooded shores, to the marsh fringe now being submerged, to the water lapping against the sand of the island and the planks of the pier. None of them had ever seen the water level higher. This was an unusual blow, the men told Ellis, not a norther, like those that brought the cold air of winter. They feared a bad storm and severe damage to the island.

Captain Jimmy and the others motioned to the steamboat *Star* and advised Captain Ellis to fire his boilers and leave the island as soon as he made steam. All of them knew it would be a rough run, a flat-bottomed boat trying to power through steep, white-capping waves for miles across shallow Caillou Bay before reaching the protected waters of one of the mainland bayous. But if he got under way soon, he'd probably make it across the bay safely. The storm was as much as one and a half days away, but the old seamen said that it was surely coming to the island.

Ellis respected the seamen and valued their opinions, yet he had to refuse to do what they suggested. He had promised passage to a number of islanders, and he could not leave them behind. Before the men left the *Atlantic*, Ellis treated them to a drink, then sat down with the bottle and Captain Jimmy, who had four decades' experience as a sailor. Together they decided that Ellis might have a little more time and that he should try to persuade his passengers—a Major Nelson and several women—to depart Isle Derniere in the morning. Ellis knew this would be difficult; a ball was planned at Muggah's Hotel for the next night. The women looked forward to attending the ball and would not want to leave the island.

Later in the evening, using what he called "fright and persuasion," Ellis convinced his reluctant passengers to join him aboard the *Star* for a morning departure.

At 5:30 PM on August 8 in Galveston Harbor, Texas—240 miles west of Isle Derniere—the oceangoing steamship *Nautilus* prepared to get under way. This was a much larger vessel than the river steamboats *Blue Hammock* and *Star*. It was designed with a rounded hull and a sharp bow to slice through ocean waves and a single smokestack and paddle wheel set amidships. By the 1840s, coastal steamship lines had developed in the United States such that all of the key U.S. Atlantic ports had regular steamer service, with some northeastern lines servicing major southern ports like Savannah and New Orleans. By August 1856, the *New Orleans Daily Picayune* was filled with announcements of steamships arriving from and departing to ports around the world.

On August 8, Captain John S. Thompson—dressed in trademark blue clothes, his face covered with scraggly black whiskers—stood on the deck of the *Nautilus* and railed against the crew. Most of his wrath was probably leveled against one person, the vessel's steward, Jim Frisbee. A day earlier, the *Nautilus* had been at sea a few hours when Frisbee had the unfortunate duty to inform the captain that they had not taken on enough ice to keep their provisions fresh during the voyage. Since they had more passengers than usual, Captain Thompson had no choice but to return to Galveston and load more ice, an operation that had delayed their departure for New Orleans by twenty-four hours.

Finally the *Nautilus* slipped away from a wharf on the bay side of a barrier island that was similar in some respects to Isle Derniere. "The appearance of Galveston from the Harbour is singularly dreary," wrote Francis Sheridan in the late 1830s. "It is low flat sandy Island about 30 miles in length & ranging in breadth from 1 to 2. There is hardly a shrub visible, & in short it looks like a piece of prairie . . . that had quarreled with the main land & dissolved partnership."

This "quarrel" formed one of the finest natural harbors on the Gulf coast, the barrier island protecting a body of relatively deep water that spurred economic opportunity. About the time of Sheridan's visit in the late 1830s, the first wharf for ocean steamers was built and the city of Galveston consisted of nearly one hundred buildings and sixty families. By the late 1840s, the population of the port had boomed to nearly five thousand.

On August 8, 1856, as the *Nautilus* steamed from Galveston Bay through a narrow inlet leading into the Gulf of Mexico, there were as many as ten wharves lining the island's bay side, an infrastructure that fueled a race between Galveston and nearby Houston for commercial dominance. In the decades to follow, Galveston would surge ahead, becoming by the dawn of the twentieth century the largest cotton port in the United States and the third most prosperous port overall. The race was brought to an abrupt conclusion, however, by the death and devastation in Galveston during a 1900 hurricane, from which the city's commercial center never recovered.

Captain Thompson ordered his helmsman to steam northeast along the coast toward the Mississippi River, following a course that on a clear day would have taken them within sight of the houses lining the beach of Isle Derniere. As Thompson steamed toward Louisiana, he might have felt something unusual in the motion of his ship. On the coastal waters of the Gulf of Mexico, waves tended to be choppy and crowded together, with short lengths between adjacent crests, making round-bottomed vessels roll back and forth, sometimes jerkily, in about a half-dozen seconds. This was not the case on August 8. The Gulf's waves were sleek and long, rolling the vessel slowly, smoothly, over cycles lasting fourteen or sixteen seconds or more.

If he noticed this motion, Captain Thompson might have found it curious, but not ominous. He was behind schedule, and his primary concern was making up lost time. The *Nautilus* had to deliver the U.S. mail, dozens of passengers, and a living cargo of horses and cattle that filled much of two decks. He felt compelled to press on to New Orleans.

In front of a secluded oceanfront boardinghouse on Isle Derniere, a half-mile farther down the island from the westernmost cluster of homes in the village, Reverend R. S. McAllister and many of the other boarders stood on the beach staring in awe at the huge breakers. They "looked like things of life," the reverend wrote later, wearing "upon their heads ornaments of snowy foam. . . . [A] countless number were at the same moment visible, those in the rear eagerly chasing yet never catching those in the van."

These waves were taller in height, and more crowded together, with less time between successive crests, than the long, gentle waves that rolled under the *Nautilus* 240 miles to the west. While the ship's crew and passengers barely detected the long rollers, McAllister wrote later that the boarders on the island had a "bewitching spell" cast over them by powerful breakers "madly intent upon exhibiting to the universe all that was grand and beautiful."

Twelve people were spending the summer in that boardinghouse, including the host couple, their three children, a cook, the cook's child, the reverend, Roland Delaney, and "three ladies, young, single, cultured and beautiful." Delaney had fallen in love with one of these women, but after the stirring of a relationship she had rebuffed him. The young man then fell into what the reverend called "pale melancholy" and kept to himself. Nearly everyone else stayed on the beach for hours, recalled McAllister, watching the waves, "as to enjoy to the utmost an exhibition so marvelous that we might not hope to see it again."

Emma and her sister-in-law Althee were anxious, not because of the waves breaking in front of the Milles' Gulf-front home, but because of the ill health of Althee's three-month-old baby. Like Emma, Althee was eighteen years old and French Creole. She had long dark hair pulled up off her shoulders, revealing delicate, striking features. Emma and Althee knew that their lives of privilege could not completely shelter the baby from the ever present specter of death. Cholera, typhoid, and smallpox attacked with little warning and killed quickly, particularly the very old and the very young. The women did not know what afflicted the baby, Althee's only child. Anytime an infant developed a cough or a fever, however, it was reason for concern, and if symptoms persisted or grew in number or severity, concern turned to fear, then panic.

Emma knew of the vulnerability of the very young from her visits to St. John's Cemetery in Plaquemine. There she encountered monuments marking the graves of many local children, including those of two of her stepsiblings from her father's first marriage, one a toddler under two years old, the other an infant of only three months.

Emma and Althee hoped and prayed that the therapeutic sea air of Isle Derniere would soon make Althee's baby well.

The slaves on the island were also nervous. One was a body servant named Richard, the owner of the black hands that had appeared in the mirror and straightened Thomas Mille's cravat. He had been preparing his master's appearance for the daily promenade. Richard groomed Mille's nails and hair and made sure his clothes were clean and packed for trips. He would have been the slave who accompanied Thomas Mille in stagecoaches and steamers to New Orleans, to Milly Plantation, to Isle Derniere—who hovered in the background, present but unseen. During an interview with the *Times Picayune* decades later, Emma could not remember Richard's last name. Perhaps she could not recall because, like many slaves, he did not have one. Plantation documents and Bibles commonly recorded lists of slaves using only first names.

Today little is known about Richard—what he looked like, whether he was young or old, whether he had a wife or children. He was probably purchased by Thomas Mille at the New Orleans slave market, which became the largest in the United States during antebellum times by feeding the appetite for labor of the Mississippi delta's sugar plantations. Slaves were auctioned under the grand rotunda of the St. Charles Hotel and sold by trading firms along Chartres Street in the French Quarter.

On Isle Derniere, Richard lived with the other Mille slaves behind the main house in quarters that were small, single-story structures of ramshackle construction. On plantations, these boxy quarters were arranged in the neat rows of a planned community, but here on the island there were far fewer quarters to accommodate far fewer slaves. The buildings were not elevated, but erected at ground level; some, if not all, had floors of sand. The walls of many were left with gaping cavities between rough-cut timbers that were not sealed, like those of the main houses, with bousillage, a mixture of mud and moss and animal hair. On still summer nights, biting insects swarmed through the openings, seeking fresh blood.

This evening, however, as Richard settled into his home, he would have felt the air ripping through the walls. The cavities helped the wind grip the structure and shake it. Richard knew the quarters were vulnerable to being blown apart. It was about this time that he began to consider what he would do if the wind continued to increase.

As dusk edged toward darkness over Isle Derniere, Michael Schlatre would have noticed that the waves on the Gulf side of the island had grown even taller. He might not have noticed another change in the waves, a subtle one that was particularly ominous. Through the course of August 8, the time between successive waves breaking in the surf gradually decreased, from a high of perhaps fifteen or sixteen seconds down to maybe ten seconds. By evening, this more frequent breaking made the surf appear increasingly furious.

This change would have been easier for Captain Thompson and his crew and passengers to detect at sea aboard the *Nautilus* as they steamed from Galveston toward the mouth of the Mississippi, every mile bringing them closer to Isle Derniere.

Over the hours they would have felt it, the roll of their ship becoming faster, the back-and-forth cycles decreasing in time, the cargo of cattle and horses shifting nervously with the quickening roll as the vessel drew closer to the source of the waves—and as the source drew closer to Isle Derniere.

The flooding of Isle Derniere by waves and surge on August 10, 1856
(*upper illustration*: early flooding; *lower illustration*: complete inundation)

{ PART II }

THE
ISLAND
AND THE
STORM

{ 6 }

Force 12

Lord of the winds! I feel thee nigh,
I know thy breath in the burning sky!
And I wait, with a thrill in every vein,
For the coming of the hurricane!
—William Cullen Bryant, "The Hurricane" (1840)

It had no name, just a number, 12, or at least that was how a mariner in the nineteenth century would have described the wind that still lay far out at sea at 6:00 AM, Saturday morning, August 9. Fifty years earlier, Captain Francis Beaufort of the British Navy had jotted into his journal a numerical scale to describe the force of the wind, cobbling together the practices of earlier seafarers with his own experiences to make a system of abbreviations that is still used today, with some variations, as the Beaufort Scale. "Hereafter I shall estimate the force of the wind," he wrote in January 1806, "according to the following scale, as nothing can convey a more uncertain idea of wind and weather than the old expressions of moderate and cloudy, etc. etc."

In subsequent journal entries, Beaufort tinkered with the scale by expressing the wind force in terms of the performance of a ship's sails. This was something that all seamen could understand and apply, and it removed at least some of the subjectivity from estimates of the wind at sea. He was trying to develop a system for categorizing and documenting the wind that would be easy to use and reasonably accurate and reproducible. For example, Force 1 referred to "light air" that would be "just sufficient to give steerage way"; Force 2 was a "light breeze" that would propel "a well conditioned man-of-war, with all sail set . . . 1 or 2 knots"; Force 10 was a "whole gale . . . with which she could scarcely bear close-reefed main-topsail and reefed foresail"; and the highest level, Force 12, was described as a "sail-splitter," or a condition "which no canvas could withstand."

This numerical scale was first officially used to note wind forces in the early 1830s aboard the HMS *Beagle* during Charles Darwin's five-year voyage of discovery and was soon thereafter adopted by the British Admiralty for use aboard all its warships. The scale was chosen as an international standard for characterizing wind forces in 1853, and newspapers, such as the *New Orleans Daily Crescent,* published daily weather reports that included Beaufort force levels. In fact, at 7:00 AM that Saturday, August 9, as Force 12 winds were splitting any sails present in the central Gulf of Mexico, observers in New Orleans reported winds from the northeast at Force 3, "a gentle breeze" that would propel a man-of-war under full sail "3 to 4 knots." As author Scott Huler wrote in *Defining the Wind*, "Beaufort turned the sailing ship into an anemometer."

Such an "anemometer" lying hundreds of miles southeast of Isle Derniere that early Saturday morning would have faced serious difficulties. The ship would have been unable to make headway and forced to bring in all its sails. Winds of Force 12 are those of a hurricane. The storm at this time had a sustained wind speed later estimated at one hundred miles per hour. Under such conditions, the air and sea would have had a distinctive appearance, as described by German sea captain P. Peterson in the 1920s: "The air is filled with foam and spray; sea completely white with driving spray; visibility very seriously affected."

The air whipped across the sea, swirling in a counterclockwise direction around the hurricane's eye. The strongest winds were concentrated in an eyewall, described by Kerry Emanuel in *Divine Wind* as a "stadium of thick, white cloud[s] surrounding the eye." Today the look of these clouds from inside the calm and clear air of a hurricane's eye has been revealed in photographs taken from aircraft. "Imagine a Roman coliseum 20 miles wide and 10 miles high," wrote Emanuel, "with a cascade of ice crystals falling along the coliseum's blinding white walls." In the 1850s, from the deck of a ship caught in a hurricane's most intense winds, a seaman would have discerned the eyewall as where the sea surface was the whitest, where the air was most filled with foam and spray, where visibility was most obstructed, and where his vessel was most in peril.

The eyewall is also where the air is the most humid, the moisture coming from the evaporation of warm seawater as the wind spirals inward across the sea surface. This evaporation is one of the most important sources of heat to drive the hurricane. Initially, this heat lies dormant as humidity; it is not unleashed until the air reaches the eyewall and turns vertical in violent updrafts through the "stadium . . . of clouds." As Espy argued, the air cools as it rises and its moisture condenses, releasing heat. This heat warms the air, makes it more buoyant, and reinforces the updrafts in the eyewall. This natural system operates like a heat engine with enormous power. "The amount of power dissipated by a typical mature Atlantic hurricane . . . is on the order of 3 trillion Watts," wrote Kerry Emanuel, which is "nearly equal to the worldwide electrical generation capacity as of January 1996. This is enough to light 30 billion 100-Watt light bulbs."

In the Gulf of Mexico on August 9, 1856, the storm was feeding on ample warm seawater and growing stronger, more powerful. In twelve hours, from 6:00 PM Friday to 6:00 AM Saturday, the hurricane's winds had increased in speed from eighty miles per hour to one hundred miles per hour. (Hurricanes have winds greater than seventy-four miles per hour.)

The winds ruffled the sea surface into waves of a broad spectrum of heights and lengths. It was a confused sea, the ugly kind, quite different from the tall, majestic waves that bewitched Reverend McAllister and the others on Isle Derniere or the long, smooth waves that rolled under the *Nautilus* after it left Galveston. The storm's confused sea was a mixture of waves of different lengths. The longest of these waves traveled the fastest and ran before the storm. Some reached as far as the *Nautilus*, rolling subtly, almost imperceptibly, under the vessel's keel. Closer to the storm on Isle Derniere, the long, smooth waves were also arriving, but with waves of shorter lengths and taller heights, creating awe-inspiring breakers.

As the storm continued to move toward the northern Gulf coast, more of the mixture of waves reached the island. The breakers became taller and less uniform, and they broke more frequently. The surf turned ugly—and majestic waves evolved into monsters.

Michael Schlatre awoke that Saturday morning to the rumble of a waterfall—and to the trembling of his house. Throwing the doors open to the second-floor gallery, he could see the source of the sound—"the sea that was white with foam"—and feel the source of the shudder—the wind that had grown into a gale. It "blew hard but steady," still opposing the waves on the Gulf side of the island while swelling the water on the bay side, piling it up in a storm surge that now completely covered the marsh fringe and encroached on the sand.

Schlatre spied a schooner in the Gulf, with its trademark fore and aft sails, beating its way eastward in the white foam along the coast toward the mouth of the Mississippi River. With rough seas and dark clouds, the captain must have had second thoughts about proceeding; indeed, as Schlatre watched, the vessel anchored eight miles offshore of his house, apparently waiting for conditions to calm. Soon, however, the captain changed plans again. The schooner "brought home her anchor and ran before the northeast wind in the direction of Galveston, and was soon out of sight."

Michael Schlatre did not share the captain's concern about the weather. He walked in the wind, striding a half-mile down the beach to the parlor of the hotel where islanders gathered to discuss business or play at gaming and pool tables. Most of the others on the island were also calm about the conditions, although some faced an unwelcome reception when they tried to take their morning bath in the Gulf. Those "who ventured in the water," wrote W. W. Pugh, "were disgusted with the roughness of Neptune's greeting, and beat a hasty retreat." The strong wind from the land persisted through the day, and many bathers on Isle Derniere decided to watch the surf from the beach.

Michael Schlatre probably had everyday issues on his mind, but he would have seen and heard something unusual on his walk when he passed the island's corrals. The cows were pacing back and forth and "lowing in a plaintive way." They seemed to know something the planters and merchants on Isle Derniere did not.

The paddle wheel of the steamer *Star* groaned as it dipped into the water and eased the vessel away from the landing behind Muggah's Hotel. Deckhands scurried to stow mooring lines, and Captain Thomas Ellis ordered more power to counter the wind that pushed broadside against the vessel's expansive superstructure. The *Star* was stacked like a layer cake, with two enclosed lower decks for passengers and cargo extending nearly the entire length of the vessel. A smaller pilothouse was on the third level, or hurricane deck, containing the steering wheel, compass, and chart table that the captain and helmsman used to guide the vessel. As the *Star* slid away from the dock, it turned into the wind, minimizing its exposure and gaining speed and control. It puffed dual columns of smoke that the wind laid horizontal and sent streaming toward the Gulf in the opposite direction of the vessel's movement.

Aboard were Major Nelson and the ladies whom Ellis had convinced to leave the island. They had grudgingly agreed to depart after

Ellis promised to see them safely to Brashear City, near the terminus of the new railroad line that ran through the swamps and marshes between New Orleans and the coast. On boarding the *Star*, Ellis had probably warned his passengers of the coming wet and wild ride across Caillou Bay. They would have sought protection from the wind and waves in cabins on the first or second deck.

Captain Ellis had difficulty detecting the location of the channel to follow to the bay, since the scene around the steamer had changed—Village Harbor had vanished. The water had poured in from the bay, spilling over the banks and obscuring the main channel as if it did not exist. The marsh around the harbor was now discernible only by random tips of three- to four-foot-high grasses broaching the water's surface.

Looking along the shore from the hurricane deck, Ellis could see that the island had significantly narrowed. The broad expanse of marsh on the bay side had disappeared, leaving only the narrow strip of sand on which the houses of the Village of Isle Derniere were built. So the captain set a course following what he thought was the channel, guided by his remembrance of its bends and turns and by the wooden stakes emerging from the water ahead that marked where the bayou spilled into Caillou Bay. Beyond those markers, as far as Ellis could see toward the mainland, was white water from steep waves pitching forward and breaking.

As the steamer passed the marker stakes and entered Caillou Bay, the passengers felt the distinct change, the flat-bottomed vessel lurching through the white water. The waves in Caillou Bay were smaller than those in the Gulf, their heights limited by the bay's narrow width and its shallow depth. The waves the *Star* faced that day would have been no larger than the water was deep, averaging about six feet. Although not huge, these waves were hazardous: the vessel had no sharp hull to cut through their steep faces, and the pilot had only a half-dozen seconds or less to maneuver between successive crests. Pitch-

ing fore and aft, the steamer plowed through these waves, making passengers nervous and their stomachs queasy.

On deck, the waves were breaking over the river steamer's blunt
bow, sending streams of white water running along passageways to
either side of the cabins before spilling off the stern.

By Saturday morning, the oceangoing steamer *Nautilus,* on its voyage from Galveston to New Orleans, had left Texas waters and
was churning eastward through the Gulf of Mexico along the muddy
mainland shore of western Louisiana. With a spyglass (a small hand-
held telescope), Captain John Thompson could determine his vessel's
position by the coastal terrain. It was a mainland shore that was mostly
low and flat, except for ridges of sand and shells rising from mud and
marsh. The coast of western Louisiana was marked with five such
ridges, or *cheniers*, paralleling the shoreline. Each was tens of miles
long. They were made prominent by the oak trees that flourished along
their crests. (Their name was derived from *chene*, which means oak in
French.) "To see a chenier from afar," wrote Gay Maria Gomez in *Wetland Biography*, "is the equivalent of seeing a mountain range from
across a broad plain."

Captain Thompson was not pleased. The vessel's position alongside these ridges confirmed how far behind schedule he was. By now,
the *Nautilus* should have been steaming, not off western Louisiana,
but 180 miles ahead on the quiescent waters of the Mississippi River
close to their destination of New Orleans. His frustration was still directed toward his ship's steward, James Frisbee, who had loaded insufficient ice in Galveston and cost them an entire day of sailing.

Anxious to make headway, the captain looked forward to reaching
central Louisiana's well-traveled "islands route," where ocean steamers and sailing vessels hugged the sandy barrier islands—the first of
which would be Isle Derniere—on their passage to the mouth of the
Mississippi. His son, Powell, was with him aboard the *Nautilus* on

this voyage. It was an opportunity for Thompson to show his son how a captain commanded his vessel, how he ensured the safety of lives and cargo, how he dealt with adversity.

The cargo on this voyage could not only be seen but heard and smelled. Aboard were 176 horses and cows and mules. They filled the ship between decks and also on the forward part of the main deck that was exposed to the elements. It was a living cargo worth $30,000, a fortune at the time. Also aboard were approximately seventy passengers, about two-thirds of whom were wealthy enough to afford individual cabins—what would be called first-class accommodations today. The remaining one-third were booked into steerage, the third-class or economy space, where people were packed uncomfortably close together, like the livestock on the ship's decks.

The first part of the voyage had been easy on both two- and four-legged cargo. The weather was fine and the water smooth—except for the slow undulations of long symmetrical waves created by the Force 12 winds of a faraway storm. At first, these barely perceptible undulations were noticeable aboard the *Nautilus* only as gentle cycles of motion. Through most of the voyage thus far they had grown in height and decreased in length, but the *Nautilus* rode them easily without bumping or jerking.

Now, though, the ride had turned rough. The change began at 3:00 AM, Saturday, when a "fresh breeze sprung up," recalled James Frisbee. It blew from the northeast and generated steep, choppy waves like those the *Star* plowed through on Caillou Bay. These waves rode atop the long ones. They grew taller and combined with the long waves to make an increasingly ugly mix of different heights and lengths and directions of movement.

Captain Thompson may have considered the wind an opportunity to save fuel. He could stop stoking the boiler fires and unfurl his sails to continue the vessel's forward progress toward New Orleans. Many early steamships were outfitted with three masts and auxiliary sails—

as if the designers had not yet decided whether sail or steam was preferable and compromised by providing both. The sails were used in the event of mechanical trouble as well as to save fuel. This was a time of change in transportation on the high seas, although it came about slowly. Screw propulsion systems had been introduced but not yet perfected. At the same time, marine architects were designing sleek clipper ships that optimized the use of sails. In the 1850s, these vessels set speed records hurrying passengers from New York to San Francisco and California's gold fields.

The *Nautilus* pitched back and forth, and rolled side to side. The passengers did not welcome the erratic motions. One of them, Reverend Twichell, had felt ill since they departed Galveston and planned to spend the entire voyage in Captain Thompson's stateroom. All of his meals were sent down to him. The captain's son stayed with the reverend, perhaps to tend to his illness. The stateroom became a haven where they could retreat from the other passengers, the livestock, and the elements.

On this morning of August 9, 1856, the *Nautilus* was one of many steam and sailing vessels from around the world converging on New Orleans, the second-largest port in the antebellum United States. The approaches to the river were crowded, and the river below New Orleans to its mouth was congested with ships coming and going, the steamships under their own power, the sailing ships tied behind steam-powered towboats. All of them entered the river or left it through one of the passes cutting through the bird's-foot delta; the deepest and most commonly used was Southwest Pass, to which the *Nautilus* had set its course.

These entranceways to the river were about to be slammed shut.

While the *Nautilus* steamed along the western Louisiana coast, the sailing ship *Manilla* lay far to the east in the Gulf of Mexico, within sight of Southwest Pass. Standing on deck, Captain Rogers of Bath, Maine, would have heard the northeast wind whistling through his rigging and felt the giant swells from the south rolling under his keel. After a long and risky transatlantic voyage from Bordeaux, he was anxious to make safe harbor. In addition to the crew, the *Manilla* carried seventeen passengers: three who had booked passage in the cabins and fourteen others who had endured the long voyage on deck. The wealthy sugar planters and merchants of south Louisiana looked forward to the delivery of what the *Manilla* had packed in its hold: hundreds of casks of fine French wine.

Rogers was undoubtedly pleased when he spied two steam-powered towboats chugging toward his vessel. One came alongside so that a pilot with local knowledge of the changing shoals off the mouth of the river could clamber aboard. Crewmen scrambled to attach hawsers from the towboats to the bow of the *Manilla*. With dense streams of smoke puffing from their stacks, the two small but powerful tugs pulled the lines rigid and hauled the much larger sailing vessel toward the shallows of Southwest Pass.

From the first clearing of land along the Mississippi River in the early 1700s to establish New Orleans, the inhabitants of the port had recognized that a key to their success would be maintaining navigation in the river—and nowhere was this more important, or more difficult, than at the river mouth passes. "The commerce of [the Mississippi River Valley] will, in time, certainly exceed that of any other in Christendom," wrote Elmer Corthell in 1880, "and the mouth of the great river constitutes the only natural gateway through which the immense products of that region will henceforth find their way to the various nations of the earth."

As the Mississippi River draws near to the Gulf of Mexico it broadens and shoals, separating into outlets or passes. Basil Hall compared the terminus of the delta "to an arm, of which the hand at the end, with the fingers opened as widely as possible, might represent the different outlets. These are called the South-west, the South, the South-east Passes, and the most eastern of all is called in the books the 'Passe à l'outre.'"

Water laden with sediment from across middle America poured through these "fingers" and swirled into the emerald-blue Gulf, where the current slowed and the sediments settled. The smallest particles—silts and clays—fell in deep water where they were lost from the delta, never again available to nourish the land. The largest particles—sands—fell just seaward of the passes into accumulations that were shaped by waves and river currents into formidable sandbars across the river mouth.

These bars were in near constant motion. During river floods, the strong currents pushed them seaward into deeper water, farther away from the passes. But when the flow from the river was weak, waves shoaling from deep water transported the grains of sand back landward, returning the sandbars close to the passes, where the water became so shallow over the bars that ships ran aground. "All the inland wealth of agriculture and minerals," wrote Elmer Corthell in his history of the passes, "was land-locked by an obstruction that had baffled every effort for its removal."

Many attempts were made to deepen the channel at the mouth of the river, the earliest being a 1726 effort to "[drag] iron harrows over the bars," yet none of these alterations had more than modest and temporary benefit. For example, in 1852, with a $75,000 appropriation from the federal government, the bar blocking Southwest Pass was successfully deepened by stirring up the bar sediments with machinery so that natural currents would then sweep them away. By 1853 the channel was eighteen feet deep, but the improvement was temporary. Three years later it had once again filled in with sediment, leaving no sign of the deepening. The channel was closed again to shipping.

For more than one hundred years, keeping this gateway open for navigation proved challenging. The shifting shoals frequently clogged the passes, making them too shallow to accommodate ever larger ships with ever deeper drafts. It became common for vessels to wait for weeks at dock in New Orleans, or at sea off Southwest Pass, until natural currents swept away clogging sediments and deepened the channel. In March 1859, thirty-five ships would be trapped inside the pass, unable to slip over the sandbars and leave. Three ships remained aground on the bars from failed attempts to negotiate the pass, and seventeen others waited offshore at anchor for an opportunity to enter.

On this morning of August 9, 1856, as the two towboats hauled the *Manilla* closer to the river mouth, Captain Rogers looked ahead to wild and heavy waves breaking on the bar across Southwest Pass. After a voyage of thousands of miles across unpredictable seas, safe waters seemed tantalizingly close. The captain knew that just beyond the gauntlet of dangerous surf, calm river waters would lead them to New Orleans.

Adding to Captain Rogers's difficulties that Saturday morning was the narrowness of the continental shelf off the passes. Here the delta had pushed far into the Gulf of Mexico, the river building its accumulations of sediment into progressively deeper water. Nineteenth-century charts of the U.S. Coast Survey showed that only nine miles seaward of Southwest Pass, the Gulf was six hundred feet deep. Twenty-five miles off the pass, depths reached three thousand feet. Compared to the broad shelves elsewhere off Louisiana, the narrow shelf off the river mouth would have sucked less energy from waves and allowed larger waves to range closer to shore.

Also adding to the difficulties for the *Manilla* were the offshore winds. They pushed water away from the mainland coast, lowering the sea level there. As a consequence, water over the bar decreased and the large waves broke harder, more completely, churning the sea white.

As the *Manilla* approached the surf, the waves pitched and rolled the vessel crazily. Captain Rogers knew that he could not run the gauntlet without risking the loss of his ship. Frustrated, he ordered it towed back into deep water, where he set "both anchors ahead, and sent down royal and top gallant yards, fore and aft," to wait for the waves to calm and for the water over the bar to deepen. He must have felt trapped there, with wind howling from the land and huge waves rolling from the sea, but Rogers had no safe recourse. He could have ordered an immediate departure for a distant port like Mobile to the east or Galveston to the west, or he could have tried to slip through the other treacherous shoals guarding one of the many shallow bays tucked behind Louisiana's barrier islands. Rogers dismissed all these options, knowing that any of them could prove hazardous to his ship and crew and passengers.

Off the cheniers of western Louisiana, Captain Thompson of the *Nautilus* continued to press onward with all available speed toward Southwest Pass without realizing that he was steaming into the same trap that had snared the *Manilla*.

Through the eighteenth and nineteenth centuries, the closing of the entrance to the Mississippi River was usually viewed in terms of its economic consequences. For example, a few years after the *Manilla* could not cross the bar, the New Orleans Chamber of Commerce reviewed the impact of river-mouth closings and reported financial losses of more than $7 million, a huge amount for the mid-nineteenth century.

The slamming shut of the Mississippi's gateway on Saturday morning, August 9, 1856, however, would have consequences far more dire.

M ost of the young women on Isle Derniere awoke Saturday morning looking forward to the dance planned for that evening at Muggah's Hotel. Emma Mille, however, was an exception. Whereas many Creole women loved attending balls, she told the *Times*

Picayune years later, "I was never fond of dancing." She planned to spend the day, not preparing her finest outfit, not twisting her hair into a waterfall of curls, but sitting at her piano composing a melody and perhaps helping care for her sister-in-law's sick infant. Like the others on the island, she felt and heard the wind and the surf, but since this was her first visit to Isle Derniere, Emma did not know what to expect and was not overly concerned. The day did not seem exceptional, until she noticed the look on her father's face.

Thomas Mille seldom dirtied his hands. He hired an overseer to face the unpleasantness of plantation life, to crack a whip and drive slaves into hoeing and planting, cutting and hauling. On Isle Derniere, however, he had no one to face the unpleasantness that now surrounded him, to buffer him from the eerie creaking and swaying of his home or the deepening roar of the surf.

And etched into his visage, Emma saw the first signs of fear.

{ 7 }

The
Opening Roar

*. . . No sleep till morn, when youth and pleasure meet,
To chase the glowing hours with flying feet.
But hark!—that heavy sound breaks in once more,
As if the clouds its echo would repeat;
And nearer, clearer, deadlier than before;
Arm! arm! It is—it is—the cannon's opening roar! . . .*
—LORD BYRON, "THE EVE OF WATERLOO"

As slaves lit the way with torches, or lanterns, Michael Schlatre and his wife of ten years, Lodoiska, emerged from their ocean-front home and descended the four steps to the beach on their way to the ball at Muggah's Hotel. It was about 7:00 PM, Saturday, August 9. Through the day Michael had walked the half-mile "backwards and forwards, to and from the hotel," but now, with the wind and showers, and he and his wife dressed in their finest, he would have ordered his slaves to bring an enclosed horse-drawn carriage to the front of the house. Gathering the hoops of her dress and lifting their edges above the sand, Lodoiska scurried toward the shelter of the brougham's cab.

Like many of the other planters' wives and daughters on Isle Derniere that night, Lodoiska undoubtedly found the weather conditions maddening after she and her lady's maid had spent hours preparing her clothes and hair and makeup for the ball. She did not, however, find the conditions threatening to herself, her husband, or their six sons and one daughter. Lodoiska's confidence in the safety of the island was still bolstered by her beach home successfully weathering a powerful storm the year before.

Michael had dressed in his formal attire, as though he were preparing to attend Mass at St. John the Evangelist Church in Plaquemine near the cane fields of his plantation. A formal photograph taken several years later showed him wearing a white shirt with a tall stiff collar that contrasted sharply with a thin black cravat and black jacket. He combed his hair flat on top and left it bushy at the sides. When he and Lodoiska dashed across the sand and climbed into the brougham, his coiffure and his wife's cascade of curls would have been mussed by a wind that he later wrote "blew with much the same force, strong and regular."

As the carriage's four wheels whirred across the sand toward the hotel, Michael and Lodoiska could have looked outside the passenger compartment to see white flashes emanating from the dark surf. They could not have seen well enough to confirm that the waves had grown taller, but they could have heard their roar. With the wind from the land persisting, the steamboat owner and captain would have been worried about the river steamer *Star*, which had departed that morning for the mainland. Nothing had been heard from the vessel since it left, and Schlatre was anxious about its scheduled return at 10:00 PM.

On a clear evening, Schlatre would have been able to see offshore beyond the breakers to the glow of the beacon at the top of the lightship marking the shallow waters of Ship Shoal, eighteen miles seaward of the island. This night, however, he could not see any lights at sea; the clouds and showers and distance obscured his view, not only of the lightship but of two other vessels enduring wild wind and seas.

The *Nautilus* rolled heavily as it tried to make headway along the central Louisiana coast, following an eastward course that hugged the shore. The vessel ran more parallel to the waves than it had earlier, creating a side-to-side motion that was not smooth and periodic, as it had been on departure from Galveston. Waves now attacked the *Nautilus* from both sides. The tall and long ones rolled under the ship from the south, or starboard, side, while the steep and short ones exploded against the north, or port, side. These waves were out of sync. One would heel the vessel over and then, in midroll, a rush of white water on the opposite side would jerk the ship back in an erratic motion that would have sickened both experienced seamen and novice passengers alike.

Captain Thompson stood near the helm, his hands wrapped around a railing to remain erect, his black whiskers and blue clothing dripping from wind-whipped spray and rain. He had not left the exposed main deck "from the time the gale sprung up." In the darkness, he had difficulty seeing the livestock before him, but he would have known that they were shifting and stumbling side to side with the exaggerated motions of his vessel. Though their sounds were muted by the wind, they would have been crying out in fear and confusion. Thompson's concerns were mounting. He could only hope that he had seen the worst of the storm.

At 7:00 or 8:00 PM Saturday evening, Thompson peered off his ship's port side but could not detect the lights of the Village of Isle Derniere. The ship must have been close to the barrier island. He had just spotted the flash of the lightship moored over Ship Shoal, where five years earlier the steamer *Galveston* had run aground and been lost. "It shoals suddenly to five feet on the inshore, or northern side," wrote a hydrographic surveyor in 1853, "the three-fathom [eighteen-foot] curve extending east and west eighteen miles, with a mean breadth of three miles."

For the *Nautilus* this night, however, the normally dangerous shoal was more help than hazard. Captain Thompson directed his helmsman to duck inside Ship Shoal and pass between it and Isle Derniere on their rush to Southwest Pass. The shoal would serve as a protective breakwater that incoming waves from the Gulf of Mexico would break heavily over, dissipating their energy. Calmer waters would prevail in the shoal's lee. Soon the captain felt the rolling of his vessel reduced. The *Nautilus* was now pounded mostly on its port side by the short choppy waves driven by the wind from the land.

Captain Thompson knew that below the main deck, in his cabin, his son Powell and the ill reverend would be relieved by the smoother ride. Only moments before, a kaleidoscope of shadows and light would have been sweeping about the cabin from lanterns swinging wildly on hooks. The reverend and the young man would have kept their bodies from being thrown against the ship's bulkheads by gripping the railings or strapping themselves to their bunks.

Thompson also knew that the calmer waters would persist for only a few hours until they emerged off the east end of the shoal and entered the open Gulf of Mexico again. Then they would have another seventy miles of exposed waters to cross before they could finally slip across the bar at Southwest Pass and into the river.

He did not know that the gateway was closed, that ships trying to gain entrance had anchored off the mouth in a growing fleet with no place to go, no place to hide. And he did not know of the entry written in the log of one of those trapped vessels that foretold what was to come.

"At 6:00 P.M. [Saturday, August 9], it was blowing a strong gale still from the Northeast, took in all sail, except a close reefed maintopsail, put double on all sails, and made all possible preparations for a hurricane."

About the time Captain Thompson scoured the darkness for the glow of the Village of Isle Derniere, the captain of another vessel stood in the elements outside his pilothouse trying to detect those same lights. Abraham Smith had taken command of the river steamboat *Star* for its return voyage to Isle Derniere and did not understand why he could not see the window lights of the miles-long row of two-story buildings. By his calculations, the *Star* was in Caillou Bay and should have drawn near to the bay side of the island hours earlier. Even with the intermittent poor visibility, he should have been able to see at least a glimmer to guide him into Village Harbor, but the sky was black.

Earlier in the day, under the command of Thomas Ellis, the *Star* had steamed from the island through the white caps of Caillou Bay to the mainland shore. There the vessel turned westward to cross fifteen miles of exposed Gulf of Mexico waters before slipping into a mainland marsh channel and steaming inland to the new railroad terminal. There it offloaded passengers and took on board cargo and travelers for a return trip to the island. The conditions had not deteriorated further. "The weather [was] threatening," wrote Ellis, "but [there was] no indication of danger." The vessel immediately departed on its voyage with Captain Smith in command. Thomas Ellis came along as a passenger. The *Star* retraced its course down the Atchafalaya River and across Fourleague Bay, leaving the mainland marsh and entering the Gulf of Mexico shortly after nightfall.

As Thomas Ellis sat at a gaming table in a second-deck parlor, playing cards with other passengers, a man threw the door open and rushed inside, "his hat gone, and looking frightened." Rising from his seat to question the man, Ellis felt the vessel heave and knew that something was amiss. He clambered down the ladder, or stairs, to the main deck and emerged outside into a gale. "It took but a moment to realize that the boat was not where she ought to be and in great danger of being blown to sea."

Ellis grabbed a lengthy rod from the *Star*'s mate, plunged it into the water, and probed for the bottom. His fear was confirmed. The water was far too deep for Caillou Bay, and far too deep for where the vessel should be on its return voyage to the island. They were still in the midst of the most treacherous leg of the voyage: somewhere in the fifteen miles of open Gulf of Mexico that they had to cross before ducking into Caillou Bay. Ellis knew that the wind was overpowering the thrust of the vessel's paddle wheel, pushing the three-story super-structure away from the mainland. Further, he knew there was no bar-rier island between them and the Gulf of Mexico to stop the *Star* from being swept offshore onto deep water.

Ellis bounded up two flights of ladders to the hurricane deck to warn Captain Smith. He was "as good and gallant [a] man as ever trod the deck of a steamboat," Ellis wrote later, "but with little or no expe-rience with outside navigation." Ellis found the captain peering in-tently into the darkness off the vessel's starboard side, looking for the lights of Isle Derniere. "I told him he was looking in the wrong direc-tion." They had been blown dangerously off course. Ellis said the is-land should now be off the port side.

At first Smith did not believe him. Together they scrambled down to the main deck to recheck the depth. This time Smith drove the sounding pole vertically into the water, but the steamboat had now been blown so far seaward, and into such depths, that the rod did not reach the seabed, and the captain "was compelled to let the pole go to prevent being dragged overboard."

With every passing minute, the *Star* was being blown into deeper water and into huge waves that the flat-bottomed, top-heavy river steamer had no chance of surviving.

The hotel ballroom was filled with motion and sound, the dancers swirling, the watchers clapping, the fiddler fiddling. The men wore formal coats with tails, and the women long dresses with hoops.

Nearly everyone visiting the island—"the best people of the country"—
were believed to be attending the ball that night. These included
planters and their wives, such as Michael and Lodoiska Schlatre and
W. W. and Josephine Pugh. Prominent single men were there as well,
such as Seymour Alexander Stewart, the youngest son of one of the
richest families in New Orleans, and Dr. Alfred Duperier, a physician
and widower from western Louisiana. The hosts of the event were the
brothers Muggah, sugar planters and entrepreneurs who had constructed and owned the resort hotel. These "best people" represented
remarkably diverse ancestries, from the German blood of Schlatre to
the Anglo of Pugh, the Irish of Stewart, the French of Duperier, and
the Scottish of the Muggahs. This night, however, they had "set aside
their cultural disapproval of one another," wrote Muggah descendant
Bethany Bultman, "to rock away the hours."

Unlike many of the other men present, Dr. Alfred Duperier felt
uncomfortable at balls; he did not enjoy fashionable society and would
have preferred a quiet night at home with his young daughter. She
had not accompanied him to the island, however, and he was staying
alone in the hotel. He would have been unable to escape the loud
music and voices, whether he had come to the ball or not. An appearance there allowed him to pay respects to his patients among the
dancers. He had tended to a new patient just that afternoon. Emma's
brother, Homer Mille, had come to the hotel and asked Dr. Duperier
to prescribe medicine for his and Althee's sick baby. Alfred did so and
promised to visit the Mille house and thoroughly examine the child
the next day.

The thirty-year-old physician worked toward his medical degree at
Charity Hospital in New Orleans in the 1840s. He studied under the
Dr. Stone who would later witness Erasmus Darwin Fenner plunging
a scalpel into the chest of a dead Irishman and confirming that yellow
fever had claimed the first of thousands of victims in the 1853 epidemic. Alfred Duperier built a prominent practice in his birthplace,

La Nouvelle-Ibérie, or New Iberia, in southwest Louisiana. He was Creole, his French grandfather having served as "Chevalier Royale et Capitaine" in St. Domingue before being killed with his wife during a slave revolt.

For a moment the hotel dance floor was motionless, with pairs of women facing pairs of men, all of them frozen in place four or five steps apart; then, at the head of the ballroom, a fiddler slowly raised his bow to his strings. Although orchestras usually played at balls in and around New Orleans, a single fiddler often provided music in the country. In fact, a good dance fiddler was heavily sought after and could demand as much as three dollars for an evening's work. In mid-nineteenth-century Louisiana, many musicians were slaves, but the fiddler playing that night at Muggah's Hotel was an immigrant from Germany. One of the guests would later write, "I recall with sadness the skill and taste of the old German whose violin furnished the exquisite music, which charmed so many."

When the fiddler began his tune and hit a predetermined note, the pairs of men and women suddenly came to life, stepping toward each other to switch places, each of their movements timed with the rhythm, offering their right hand to their partner as they passed. These were the initial movements of the *quadrille de contredanses* that had become a favorite dance in the royal palaces of Europe as well as in the haunts of sugar planters in Louisiana.

The women on the floor looked remarkably similar. They all wore hoops, they all had their hair piled high on their heads, and they all had stylishly sallow complexions, although today we would consider the hue ghostly. Many antebellum women puffed a white powder onto their cheeks and chins and foreheads to pale the skin and mask unwanted blemishes. By the mid-1800s, they used harmless zinc oxide for makeup powder, a huge advance over the earlier practice of covering their faces with lead oxide, which achieved a corpselike pallor sometimes more effectively than desired, since lead poisoning could lead to death. The quest for beauty at this time, however, was still far from safe. Some women had eyes that were impossibly bright and impossibly wide, a sought-after look induced by putting drops in the eyes of an extract of the toxic plant called deadly nightshade—or *belladonna*, which in Italian means "attractive lady."

Despite similarities among the women, Alfred Duperier would have been able to distinguish many of the French Creoles present. They had characteristically dark hair, and their dresses were typically more colorful than those worn by women of other cultures, more "flowing, diaphanous," according to Liliane Crete in *Daily Life in Louisiana*. And the Creole women danced, as Perin du Lac observed at a Louisiana ball, "to the point of madness." Alfred longed, however, to find a different kind of Creole woman. He sought a mate for himself, and a mother for his daughter, who was comfortable away from the dance floor and who would be less driven toward such madness.

Seymour Alexander Stewart had come to Isle Derniere less interested in a wife than in a good time. He was celebrating his twenty-first birthday. His father was a builder in New Orleans and one of the few Irishmen who rose to great wealth and success there. His mother was Creole, born in a home at the corner of Rue d'Orleans and Royal in the French Quarter. Hence, Seymour had been exposed to the Creole philosophy that young men should learn the ways of the world by sowing some wild oats. In contrast, mothers and chaperones shielded young Creole women from those oats. That night at the dance on Isle Derniere, Seymour would have had chaperones' eyes following his every move.

As he ventured through the ballroom, Seymour carried with him a unique present from his mother in commemoration of his birthday: twenty-one shiny gold coins. He was concerned about having them stolen, so he carried the coins in his pocket at all times.

After about 10:00 PM, the *Nautilus* began to roll heavily again. The huge waves had returned and approached the vessel on its Gulf side, while short steep waves continued to come from the landward side. Captain Thompson remained on deck in the elements, still clinging to a railing to keep his balance as the ship gyrated under his feet.

He could no longer see the beacon of the Ship Shoal lightship, and he never saw the lights from the buildings of Isle Derniere, although his ship had passed within a dozen miles of them. With the poor visibility, and the land to his port side and a shoal to his starboard, the captain would have ordered a crewman to repeatedly lower a weighted line to the seafloor to ensure that they were not slipping into dangerously shallow water.

With the renewed rolling of his ship, though, Thompson knew that he had cleared the east end of Ship Shoal. They had been steaming in the lee of its elongated crest since about 8:00 PM. Now they were once again exposed to the open Gulf of Mexico and its growing waves. Captain Thompson braced himself for a wild run to the mouth of the Mississippi River.

For hours after discovering that they were being blown off course toward the open Gulf of Mexico, the *Star* had fought its way northward into the wind. Captains Smith and Ellis believed this course would take them back to a mainland location near Caillou Bay. They were shrouded in darkness and saw no lights or markers confirming their position.

Regardless, they had no choice but to continue ordering the crew to stoke the boiler fires and generate as much steam as possible. The vessel plowed into the steep short waves that were breaking over the bow every few seconds. The vessel struggled to make headway against the wind and waves of what had become a full gale.

Before midnight in the hotel ballroom, many of those watching the dancers would suddenly appear startled. They had become accustomed to the flex of the wooden floor under their feet as the dancers stepped in unison to the fiddler's rhythms, but occasionally they also sensed something else, something random, sharp—sudden tremors coursing through the building. With each shock, eyes would leave the dancers and search for something amiss around the ballroom, but would detect nothing except the sway of the chandeliers, their flames casting moving patterns of light and shadow.

Many of those watching began to worry about the storm that had blown for days but would not go away. W. W. Pugh wrote: "Before the dance ended the wind arose, and blew in gusts, causing some of the ladies present to express their fears as to the effect of the storm." Each of those gusts shook the building to its core.

To calm the fears of those gathered in the ballroom, Dave Muggah announced that they were now being hit with the most severe part of the storm. He said, "If the storm doesn't blow over by the morning, no fear, the steamer *Star* will soon arrive to take you all back to the mainland." Dave and his brothers not only owned the hotel but also had an interest in the 1840s vintage *Star*, which they had outfitted for passenger service to deliver guests to their island properties. The vessel had not tied up to the dock behind the hotel by its scheduled arrival time of 10:00 PM, and many of the people at the ball expressed concern. Not among them was Michael Schlatre, who had concluded "that the . . . Star . . . would not venture out of [O]yster [B]ayou [on the mainland] in such a gale."

With still no signs of the steamer, the dance ended around midnight. Some of the people attending, like Stewart, Duperier, and Pugh, departed the ballroom for their rooms at the hotel.

Others, like Michael and Lodoiska Schlatre, ventured into the wind and rain to meet their carriages or to walk to their homes on the beach. They would have sensed from the shocks of the gusts that the storm was getting stronger.

In New Orleans, Thomas Wharton tried to sleep. English-born, he was an architect and the superintendent of the huge new Customs Building that still stands today on Canal Street between the antebellum French and American Quarters. Wharton lived with his wife and child in a neat one-story home on Camp Street on the American side, and he railed against customs practiced on the French side. "A very serious accident happened . . . at the [Théâtre d'] Orleans," Wharton wrote in his journal. "Part of the upper galleries gave way— killing . . . at least five people. . . . This fact pleads eloquently against the desecration of the Sabbath by the wretched custom here of keeping the theatres open."

A sickly man, Wharton consumed a cure-all of the time called "blue mass," which contained an injurious amount of mercury and probably caused far more harm than benefit. Still, he was able to walk long distances through the city to appraise and sketch its development with an architect's eye, and he reliably logged weather conditions, including "thermometrical observations taken at 9 A.M., 12 P.M., and 4 P.M. . . . [from] an instrument placed in a selected, shady place at the . . . New Custom House."

On the night of August 9, Wharton was disturbed from his sleep by what he called a "high wind in the night." It swished through the trees, causing their limbs to scratch against the sides of his house. Outside his bedroom window, the bend and sway of the branches was illuminated by the glow of gas streetlamps. Early in the morning on Sunday, the pounding of a "sudden dash of rain" awakened him again.

Wharton had a busy morning ahead and tried to drift back to sleep for more rest. He planned to purchase goods for his family at the open-air market near the riverfront and then proceed to church, where he was scheduled to lead a Sunday-school class.

Days earlier, Wharton had noted in his journal that, with many people having left New Orleans for the summer, "I have taken charge of Mr. Payne's Bible Class in his absence." Through the week he had pondered a meaningful lesson to teach and settled on one that would prove strangely prescient.

{ 8 }

Formidable
and Swift

*It was something formidable and swift, like the sudden
smashing of a vial of wrath. It seemed to explode all around
the ship with an overpowering concussion and rush of great
waters, as if an immense dam had been blown up to wind-
ward. In an instant the men lost touch of each other. This is
the disintegrating power of a great wind: it isolates one from
one's kind. . . . A furious gale attacks him like a personal
enemy, tries to grasp his limbs, fastens upon his mind,
seeks to rout his very spirit out of him.*
—JOSEPH CONRAD, TYPHOON (1903)

By 6:00 AM Sunday, Captain Thompson had sensed the strengthening wind and growing seas for over twenty-four hours. He stood
on the open deck and probably hoped, if not expected, that the storm
would dissipate. He was an experienced sea captain who had undoubtedly encountered many tempests, but none quite like this.

During the night, after emerging from the protection of Ship
Shoal, Thompson had given up on his seventy-mile dash to the mouth
of the Mississippi River. That course had required him to steam along
the shore with his vessel more or less parallel to waves approaching
from both land and sea, which sent the *Nautilus* rolling dangerously
side to side. He had no choice but to order the helmsman to turn into

the larger waves from the sea and to try to cut through them. The strategy was to maintain this heading and wait the storm out, but it was not working.

A half-hour past sunrise, Thompson could barely view the scene around him. Dull sunlight diffused through heavy clouds, while foam and spray whipped through the air. The waves attacking his ship from the sea had changed further. Many different lengths and heights and approach directions had jumbled together to create crests that were no longer well defined. Isolated peaks of water now rose high above Thompson's perch, then plummeted below the ship's waterline, leaving gaping holes in the sea. The helmsman had great difficulty keeping the vessel's bow nosed into the waves. Peaks and holes appeared suddenly ahead, then abeam, pummeling the vessel. The *Nautilus* was in the midst of what a nineteenth-century scientist called "a tremendous, cross, confused, outrageous sea, raised in pyramidal heaps by the wind from every point on the compass."

Captain Thompson could now view his cargo of livestock crowded onto the forward half of the main deck. The cows and horses and mules slid astern as waves lifted and overtopped the bow. White water streamed through their hooves. The animals stumbled forward as the bow fell into holes, and side to side as the vessel rolled. Some had fallen to the deck and been trampled by those around them. In the respites between waves, the animals that were still standing raised their heads and opened their mouths in screams swept away by the wind.

Thompson's assessment of the livestock's plight was more practical than humane. Aboard the main and lower decks of the *Nautilus* were 176 animals. Each full-grown cow or horse weighed more than one thousand pounds and was sliding back and forth unconstrained. Another vessel caught off the Mississippi delta that day faced a related danger. "At the most critical moment, [their cargo of] railroad iron broke adrift between decks, and at every roll of the ship, which were rapid and hard, the iron rolled from side to side, threatening to go through the sides of the ship." At the risk of life and limb, seamen rushed into the hold and saved that vessel by securing the iron, with extreme difficulty.

Captain Thompson knew that the animals would not bust through the bulkheads of the ship as readily as railroad iron, but he also knew that their slipping and sliding posed another danger that was just as deadly. The ship could become unbalanced in heavy seas. Yet Thompson's crew had no way to secure their cargo.

Michael Schlatre awakened at first light and ventured onto the beach, leaning into the wind. He looked along the shore toward Muggah's Hotel, struggling to shield his eyes from raindrops that now were driven horizontally through the air. If the *Star* had arrived in the darkness after the ball, it would have moored at the landing behind the hotel, but Schlatre detected no sign of its three decks and dual stacks. The vessel was now eight hours past its scheduled arrival. Schlatre felt even more certain that the captain had decided to remain on the mainland and not risk the transit to Isle Derniere.

Turning toward Caillou Bay and looking across the island, he saw bay water encroaching on the horse stables, carriage houses, and slave quarters clustered behind the main houses. With the marsh fringe on the bay side of the island completely submerged by water, the village now stood on a mere ribbon of land whose width had decreased from over a mile in places to just several hundred feet. The only prominent features of this ribbon were the buildings, the main houses soaring two stories above a sand surface that rose no taller than a man's height above the sea.

Still, Schlatre remained unconcerned, thinking that his house and the others on the island could withstand a severe blow with few difficulties. He had no idea that the island was about to take another step in its evolution—a step that would not occur smoothly and continuously over decades and hundreds of years, but abruptly and violently, in only a few hours.

At first light Sunday morning, a celebration erupted in the pilot-house of the steamer *Star*. Captain Abraham Smith and Thomas Ellis had just sighted the mainland marsh less than a mile away. For hours after Ellis recognized that the steamer was in danger of being blown into the deep water of the Gulf of Mexico, the *Star* had crept back toward the mainland. Its rear paddle wheel had strained to gen-erate enough thrust to overcome the resistance of the wind blowing against the vessel's layer-cake-like decks.

Now, as they drew close to shore, Smith and Ellis looked for rec-ognizable features that would signal their location on the mainland, but the unfamiliar scene must have left them stunned. The same north wind that had pushed a surge onto the bay side of Isle Derniere had also pushed bay water away from the mainland carpet of grasses, exposing a broad band of dark mud along the shore. Meandering channels, like the one Emma's steamer had followed across the marsh toward the island, lay drained and nearly empty. Their intricate branching patterns ex-tended across the normally submerged and otherwise featureless band of mud flats like canyons carved into a barren, arid land.

In spite of the unusual scene before them, Smith and Ellis soon recognized the marker at the mouth of Grand Caillou, a major bayou emptying from the mainland marsh into Caillou Bay. This waterway and its approaches cut deep into the mud and hence still contained sufficient water for the shallow-draft steamer to navigate inland. Ellis advised the captain to steam up the bayou and wait for the weather to calm. He wrote later, "There was at this time every indication of a se-vere storm brewing."

Captain Smith refused. The people on Isle Derniere had expected his vessel to arrive the previous evening. He knew that some of those men and women and children were wary of the weather and viewed the *Star* as their only means of escape. Smith ordered his crew to press on, and the steamer continued eastward, hugging the mainland shore. In the swirl of cloud and rain, the captain could not see the island that lay miles to the south across the bay. Acknowledging Ellis's greater experience, Smith proposed that they steam along the shore until they encountered known landmarks opposite the Village of Isle Derniere. They would turn south there and run with the wind and waves across the bay to Village Harbor.

Ellis knew that the waves would grow large and hazardous as they steamed away from the mainland. The vessel would be moving with the waves, slipping down their faces and courting the constant danger of losing control. He knew that it would be far safer for the *Star* to seek refuge in the protected waterways of the mainland and wait out the storm, but like Smith, he also knew that the people on the island were feeling isolated, even abandoned.

"Yes," he finally said. "It might be done."

Thomas Ellis considered only what those waves would do to the vessel, not what they were doing to the island. For days the persistent north wind had not only flooded the island's bay side but also driven waves against its shore. The waves had chewed into the mud, ripping away root-bound chunks and eroding the bay shore seaward. At the same time, the large waves from the sea had pounded the beaches on the other side of the island, transporting sand away and eroding the Gulf shore landward.

As the *Star* continued to steam along the mainland shore, the island was losing its lifeblood—its sediment. Some sand might be returned naturally after the storm, but not enough to account for the losses. Isle Derniere was diminishing, narrowing.

Emma awoke that Sunday morning to the rumble of a waterfall that had penetrated the consciousness of the people of Isle Derniere for over a day. Now, however, it was louder, more oppressive.

Looking from the front gallery of her home that morning, she must have thought that the sandbank on which her house stood seemed tiny and insignificant before a wild sea. It may have occurred to her then, as it would later, that the island "was one of the last places in the world where one would wish to be during a storm." The power and violence of the surf was overwhelming, and Emma longed to return to the mainland, despite the recurring epidemics of yellow fever, despite the recurring floods of bayou and river.

The deteriorating weather raised other concerns for Emma and her family. The health of Althee's three-month-old baby had not improved. The day before, Dr. Duperier had prescribed some medicine and promised he would come to their house and examine the child today. What would the family do if the storm prevented the doctor from traveling the half-mile down the beach from where he was staying at the hotel? What would they do if the baby's condition worsened and they had no medical assistance?

During breakfast, Emma saw the tension etched deep into the faces of Althee and Homer, her mother, the visitor staying with them, Mrs. Rommage—and most alarmingly, her father. She depended on him for assurance, confidence, and protection, but the look on his face offered none of that. At first, she may have thought he was deeply concerned for his infant grandchild. Then she watched him start at every shudder of the house and saw his eyes dart about the room, to the ceiling, the walls, the floor, as if he expected them to fly apart at any moment. She knew his concern was less for his grandchild than for the storm, as if it were stalking him—not the family, just him.

The *Nautilus* pitched and rolled wildly, erratically. The helmsman struggled to maintain control of the vessel in waves that were more peaks and holes than ridges and troughs. The seventy passengers huddled in cabins below decks, where they were shielded from wind and water but not from being thrown about like rag dolls.

Also below was steward Jim Frisbee, who suddenly felt the vessel lurch. Coming off a steep pitch, the *Nautilus* had heeled over in a tight turn, the bow moving away from the wave peaks. "The vessel [had] headed to the sea as long as possible," Frisbee said later, "and finding no other recourse, Capt. T. attempted to put the ship before the wind."

Alarmed, Frisbee knew it was a maneuver of desperation in the face of waves that had become too large, too confused, too unpredictable. The captain was trying to save his ship by putting its stern into the mountains of water, letting the vessel move with the waves rather than trying to cut through them, in a frantic attempt to stay afloat. Frisbee's alarm turned to fear when he felt the *Nautilus* suddenly stop after completing only one-half the rotation necessary to reverse course. This left it broadside to the largest waves, the most dangerous position for a ship in high seas. The vessel had, according to Frisbee, "got into a trough of a sea [and] would not wear."

Jim Frisbee scurried up ladders and burst onto the main deck, where the wind and rain pounded against his body. The mainmast, the tallest of three masts for rigging auxiliary sails on the oceangoing steamer, had crashed to the deck and hung off the starboard side. Destabilized, the vessel listed to starboard. Above the howl of wind and the crash of waves, Captain Thompson screamed for his crewmen to cut the mast away. "The bulkhead in [the] centre of the ship was knocked away by [the ship's] lurching," Frisbee later reported. "The foremast [positioned closest to the bow was] blown away at the same time." Huge waves now approached the ship broadside and loomed high above the vessel, as if they were rearing up before pouncing on their quarry.

Frisbee grabbed on to a railing on the port side. Passengers emerged from the cabins and spilled onto the main deck, grabbing on to rails and bulkheads to stay erect. "I then looked forward and saw Capt. T. coming aft," Frisbee said, "as if to notify the passengers that the ship was in danger." With the steep list, Thompson had to climb along the rails hand over hand to keep his balance. He could not see his son Powell among the passengers; the young man had remained below with the sick reverend.

Everyone on the main deck watched in horror as a pile of cows and horses and mules that had accumulated on the starboard side of the vessel grew larger. They were slipping down the steep slope. The animals below decks were also sliding, a total of 176 head piling up on the ship's starboard side, more than 150,000 pounds of living, squirming, unconstrained cargo.

The *Nautilus* now tilted at such an extreme angle that the starboard portholes on its lower decks were underwater. During previous days, the crew had been able to lower the port covers, but in the angry sea they could not latch them. Now water was spewing through some of the portholes, dousing the writhing knot of animals below and adding to the unbalanced weight on the starboard side of the vessel.

The list steepened. Frisbee's perch on the opposite side of the ship from the animals was thrust higher; his grip around the railing grew tighter. As the deck approached vertical, the pile of livestock disappeared under the sea. Many passengers and crew lost their grips and fell. Some slammed against bulkheads and others became tangled in rigging, but most splashed into the water.

Below, inside the captain's cabin, Powell Thompson and Reverend Twichell were thrown against the starboard bulkhead. Charts and books and all other unsecured items in the cabin rained down on top of them.

The lanterns that had been dangling from hooks smashed against the ceiling, sending glass flying; some of the flames were extinguished, and some flared spilled fuel. There may have been enough light for the reverend and Powell to regain their bearings—which way was up, which way was down—but direction would have been difficult to perceive because the cabin kept turning.

Then it stopped.

The reverend and Powell now lay on the ceiling, but may not have known it. They continued to feel gyrations, but the pitching and rolling of the *Nautilus* had been oddly reduced. The vessel gradually settled. Water began to intrude through open hatches and passageways. The ship became increasingly bottom-heavy, sinking lower.

They could not see the seawater filling their cabin. Any remaining lantern flames were doused, leaving them in complete darkness. Reverend Twichell and Powell Thompson could only feel the water wetting their clothes, creeping up their prone bodies. Their screams were lost in a cavity of air that diminished in size minute by minute.

{ 9 }

Extreme Jeopardy

We were shut up with no possibility of flight, on a narrow neck of land betwixt two unbounded seas. In a strife of the elements like this, there would have been disaster even in midland; here on this sea-girt sand-bank it would be tame to say that we were in extreme jeopardy.
—Reverend R. S. McAllister,
Southwestern Presbyterian, April 9, 1891

On Sunday morning, August 10, Michael Schlatre strode across the parlor toward his front door to see who was banging his fist against it and disturbing the Lord's Day. Schlatre was a pious man who after breakfast with his wife and seven children had held Mass for his family. He grabbed the knob and flung open the door expecting to discover some emergency, but he found none, just his next-door neighbor and relative, Thomas Mille, demanding to know whether the weather was putting him and his family in danger. Schlatre was well aware that this was Mille's first venture to the island and that the man had never experienced a storm on the Gulf of Mexico before, never heard the roar of surf. Yet he was more amused than annoyed by Mille's timidity and met the man's query with cool assurance. "There is no cause for worry," he said, perhaps through a sardonic smile. "We have had storms here before."

This did not assuage Mille's burgeoning alarm, and through the day the Frenchman returned to Schlatre's house, or sent other family members and servants there, to inquire whether conditions had worsened and whether they were in peril.

Schlatre decided to stoke the Mille family's flames of concern into an inferno. Finally, he sent them the joking message that "they had not seen the worse yet."

Schlatre later wrote, "But too true this proved."

The *Star*'s rear paddle wheel churned through Caillou Bay, propelling the vessel to the east along the marshy mainland shore. From the pilothouse, Captain Abraham Smith and Thomas Ellis kept their eyes trained a few hundred yards to their port side, scouring the monotonous wetlands for unique signs that would tell them their location relative to the island. Ellis knew the region and its terrain better than Smith and would have recognized the particular sign they were looking for: perhaps an odd-shaped bayou, or an unusually large bank of oyster shells, or a stake of driftwood driven vertically into the mud—something indicating the vessel was abreast the Village of Isle Derniere. They knew the island lay to the south, to their starboard side, about five miles distant but shrouded in rain and low clouds.

About 10:00 AM, Smith and Ellis determined as best they could that the *Star* was opposite the village. The captain gave the order to turn starboard ninety degrees and head due south across the bay, a course that they hoped would take them to the entrance of Village Harbor and the steamboat landing behind the hotel. If they had misread the signs along the shore or were blown off their course in the bay, both Smith and Ellis knew the *Star* could miss the barrier island and again steam unawares into the open Gulf of Mexico and its raging seas. In the building gale, they might not survive another navigation mistake.

As the *Star* emerged from the lee of the mainland and experienced the full force of the storm against its stern, the vessel became difficult to control. The steamer was traveling with the wind and waves, the wind now pushing it forward, not holding it back. The vessel's flat bottom became a surfboard teetering on the crests of waves before slipping and plunging down their steep faces. As the *Star* slid down each wave, it gained speed—"veering and hauling, 3 or 4 points first on one tack and then on the other"—making it difficult for the two helmsmen to steer the steamer, even though, Ellis noted later, they worked "the wheel for all it was worth."

Then, as they steamed farther across the bay, Smith and Ellis sensed the vessel rising particularly high on a crest. It appeared to rest there for a moment, then plunged forward and accelerated, causing the men's stomachs to drop. The vessel skimmed across the water, its bow starting to slip sideways despite the helmsmen's frantic spinning of the wheel. The steamboat caught an edge, like an inexperienced surfer. The *Star* broached, leaving it broadside to the waves—the same treacherous position the *Nautilus* had been in just a few hours earlier in the Gulf.

Knowing the steamboat was seconds from disaster, Captain Smith gave frantic orders to bring more steam and turn the vessel's bow back with the waves. At the same time, he and Ellis could look to the north through a side window of the pilothouse and see a pack of waves bearing down on them. They willed their steamer to regain speed and begin its turn, but to no avail. Smith and Ellis were helpless. The steamboat wallowed in a trough, its low gunwale directly exposed to the waves.

A wave hit broadside, and water surged over the gunwale and pounded against the first deck of cabins. The three-story-high steamboat heeled steeply sideways.

Through the window that looked north from the pilothouse, the men could see the horde of waves rushing to give the vessel a final push over the edge.

About the time the *Star* turned away from the mainland and began its run across Caillou Bay, W. W. Pugh was in the hotel on Isle Derniere. He was forty-five years old, with intense eyes set deep in a thin, almost skeletal face. Like Michael Schlatre, he was a deeply religious man; earlier that Sunday morning, he had either presided over prayers for his family or attended services with them at the hotel. He was a Welsh, Anglo-Saxon Protestant from a storied family. They had amassed huge sugar plantations, buying up small subsistence farms of French Acadians along Bayou Lafourche (pronounced *Lafoosh*). Known as "rigid and grave," the Pughs had risen to prominence among the "easy-going, easy-humored" Acadians to become one of the richest and proudest families in antebellum Louisiana.

Earlier that morning, Pugh, his wife and seven children, and many other hotel guests had gathered for breakfast in the hotel's dining room. The men and women at Pugh's table discussed what was unfolding outside. Everyone believed that the storm would be challenging, but that it would not prove dangerous for them and their families.

By midmorning, however, the guests had gathered around windows in the hotel building to witness something disturbing. Around the main structure, the Muggah brothers had built small cabins for visitors who desired accommodations with more privacy than could be had in the individual rooms in the main hotel. Now the cabins were disintegrating. At first the wind ripped pieces from walls and roofs. Then whole roofs lifted and tumbled through the air. People emerged from what was left of the structures and ran wildly across the sand to the safety of the main hotel building, crowding into the entranceway and parlors. The destruction outside continued as the walls of the cabins twisted and bowed and fell.

Pugh still had little concern for the safety of himself and his family, rationalizing that the cabins were flimsy and not constructed to survive a strong wind; their loss was expected. The hotel was well designed and strong—"a long low building," according to Pugh, "covering a good deal of ground, and supposed to be safe during a storm."

The others in the hotel that Sunday shared Pugh's confidence, but perhaps with glances now and then out the windows or with starts as gusts unexpectedly rattled the roof and walls of the main building. People stood about the first floor of the hotel, chatting in small groups. Some took their minds off the weather by playing billiards or cards at gaming tables. W. W. Pugh viewed these activities on the Sabbath with disgust. Many Protestants of the time expected their families to spend the Lord's Day in penance, abstaining from revelry and pleasure and spending the day praying and reading scripture.

Pugh's Sunday rules softened, though, when it came to his youngest child. Only one year and four months old, little Loula, like toddlers of any time, was intent on exploring the world around her. She wobbled through the hotel's parlors with no regard for the niceties of culture or religion, and no concern for wind and sea. As Pugh followed his daughter's unsure steps or ordered a house slave to do so, he may have re-examined the building and reinforced his confidence that it was solidly built. In fact, Pugh wrote, there were many well-constructed houses on Isle Derniere that could "resist anything short of a cyclone."

For precarious moments, the *Star* lay vulnerable to capsizing like the *Nautilus*. Disaster was averted when the vessel regained headway and swung its bow back to continue following the waves, rather than wallowing broadside to them.

In the pilothouse after the recovery, Captain Smith turned to Ellis, shaken, well aware that he had come close to losing his vessel. He asked whether they should come about and beat their way against the waves back to the mainland.

"No, sir," Ellis replied emphatically, "our only chance is to make it to the island."

Both Captain Smith and Ellis recognized that the two helmsmen were too inexperienced in handling the top-heavy vessel in heavy winds and seas. At Smith's request, Ellis stepped to the wheel, saying to the pilots in a friendly tone, "I [will] handle the spokes for a while." The pilots backed away more relieved than insulted.

Thomas Ellis surfed his way across the bay in what he called the most "memorable run that a high-pressure steamboat never made before or since."

By 10:00 AM, Sunday, when the hotel's cabins were flying apart on Isle Derniere, the sailing ship *Manilla*, carrying casks of wine from Bordeaux, was adrift in high seas. The ship had been disabled; its sails hung in shreds from its masts. The previous morning, steam-powered towboats had attached hawsers to the *Manilla*'s bow and attempted to haul her across the bar at Southwest Pass, but heavy breakers and shallow water drove them back offshore. Captain Rogers had chosen not to sail for another port or to duck into one of the shallow bays behind Louisiana's barrier islands. Rather, he had retreated from Southwest Pass to deeper water, where his crew deployed anchors and set them as firmly as they could into the seabed.

There, for the previous twenty-four hours, Rogers, his crew, and fourteen passengers had endured the growing wind and waves, hoping and praying for them to calm, but they did not. The sea became increasingly confused, pitching and rolling the vessel in unpredictable ways, repeatedly stretching the anchor lines so taut, so violently, that the bow seemed in danger of snapping off.

Then, at 8:00 AM on Sunday, with the storm still increasing in intensity, Captain Rogers had ordered his crew to get under way. They climbed into the rigging to raise the ship's sails and slipped the two anchor lines. Rogers knew that remaining at anchor was likely to end in disaster, but he also knew that running for safer waters posed its own extreme dangers. Sails were not designed for the hurricane winds of

Beaufort Force 12 and would likely be shredded. The *Manilla* was a cornered prey trying to evade a far quicker, far more nimble predator. Still, Rogers had no choice. He had to make a run for it.

Within two hours, the ship could no longer be maneuvered. It lay exposed and vulnerable before the elements, helpless, hopeless. The *Manilla* drifted with the currents and winds; it was ravaged by waves. The ship flailed in its death throes.

At 11:00 AM, Michael Schlatre looked into the wind across the sands of Isle Derniere toward Caillou Bay, whose surface was covered in white water. His eyes were drawn to something that in the swirl of spray and rain and clouds must have been difficult to discern from afar. As it drew closer, he distinguished the layers of decks and a rear paddle wheel beating through the froth. Two soaring stacks billowed columns of smoke that the wind streamed ahead of the vessel. Schlatre recalled later, "What was my astonishment to see the *Star*."

Schlatre grew concerned as the vessel pitched and rolled wildly, crazily, like a cork floating on rapids. He knew that a helmsman usually had to navigate with great care through the throat of Village Harbor to avoid running aground; in places, the channel was extremely shallow. Not this day, however. The north wind had continued to overfill the waterway with storm surge that for days had been creeping up the bay side of the island.

Twenty-four hours earlier, Schlatre would have seen tips of marsh grasses emerging above the surge. Now the water had been pushed higher against the island, submerging most of the tall grasses. The helmsman would have aligned the vessel for its approach to the island with the hotel that stood next to the steamboat landing. On this day there would have been little chance of running aground, except on the sand of the beach, the only part of the island still exposed.

Schlatre knew that the wind posed another concern for the steamboat's safety. It pushed hard against the vessel's superstructure, forcing

it to go one way even if the helmsman spun the wheel to go in another. Landing against the wooden dock behind the hotel would be
difficult and hazardous. He expected the *Star* to avoid the landing and
nose into the sand. He rushed the half-mile down the beach to watch.

Thomas Ellis felt pride for bringing the *Star* safely to the mouth of
Village Harbor. Thinking that everything was in order, he turned
the helm back to the pilots for them to make the landing and went
below to prepare to disembark.

As it turned out, he gave the wheel back to the helmsmen too
soon. From below, he watched as the steamer approached the dock
and made its turn, becoming broadside to the wind. The pilots were
able to hold the vessel at the end of the pier for only a few moments, and
several male passengers leapt to the pier's deck. They dashed across
the landing to the hotel with wind and rain beating against their backs.

As the men ran across the planks, a portion of the pier collapsed
behind them and the steamer was borne away by a gust, but anchors
were quickly thrown, and they caught hold in the bayou bottom, jerking the steamer's bow into the wind.

It was then, Ellis said later, that "the storm was upon us in all
its fury."

James Frisbee, the steward aboard the capsized *Nautilus*, was thank-
ful to be alive, but he was concerned about the prospects of staying so. His last memory aboard the *Nautilus* was of Captain Thompson
hurrying across the main deck toward a gathering of passengers to
warn them of the danger. Then, like a log in a stream, the vessel rolled
180 degrees, hurling everyone on the main deck into the sea and en-
tombing everyone below in the passageways and in the cabins.

Frisbee swam free of the ship and somehow avoided entangle-
ment with its rigging. These lines would have dragged him under as
the masts fell through the water's surface and pointed toward the

seabed. While treading water, he looked back to the *Nautilus* and saw the bottom of its hull rising and falling in waves that must have been forty feet or taller. He watched as passengers and crew emerged from the water and scrambled up the sides of the hull. Most slid back into the sea, their bodies raking across the sharp shells of barnacles that shredded the flesh of their hands and knees.

Again and again, the now-desperate survivors tried to claw up the sides of the hull. "Some six or eight persons succeeded," Frisbee recalled later. "Immediately after a heavy sea struck her sweeping them off."

Frisbee detected other survivors around him, twenty-five to thirty people adrift, floating on pieces of wreckage from the *Nautilus*. He recognized many of them—the purser, the first mate, the second engineer, the second clerk—but there was no sign of Captain Thompson.

For half an hour after the *Nautilus* capsized, Frisbee struggled to keep his head above water. Life jackets (then called swimming belts) made from cork were available by the 1850s and were used, for example, by England's Life Boat Institution. There is no evidence, however, of these swimming belts being aboard the vessels off Louisiana in 1856. To keep his body afloat, Frisbee depended on buoyant wreckage—and his wits. But the debris he clung to was too small.

The white water of the waves washed over him, submerging him. He drifted near Mr. Johnson, the vessel's chief engineer, who had latched on to a larger fragment of the wreck. Frisbee joined him on the more substantial raft. Over the howl of the wind, Frisbee screamed to Johnson, asking whether he had seen Captain Thompson. Shaking his head, Johnson replied that he had not. Frisbee would never see the captain again.

Frisbee and Johnson floated together in the open Gulf of Mexico, their arms snaked around and through the floating debris to keep their bodies from being swept away by the powerful waves. They were breathing, drinking in seawater—choking, coughing it back. They struggled to keep their heads above water and hoped that they would not have to endure these conditions for long.

Surely rescue vessels would soon put to sea and find them and the other survivors among the waves. After all, they were close to land, close to the mouth of the Mississippi, and close to a major port.

In New Orleans, Thomas Wharton had risen early that Sunday morning as planned and strode through the streets to the market, where he purchased food for his family's traditional large midday meal on the Sabbath. The weather seemed threatening, but he was not alarmed. He found "the air somewhat chill, and clouds drifting heavily from the eastward."

About the time Frisbee and Johnson floated together in the Gulf and Schlatre watched the *Star* arrive on Isle Derniere, Wharton walked from his home to the nearby Episcopal Church of the Annunciation to teach Sunday school. On his way, he observed that "the wind rose . . . and rain set in." He had no knowledge of what was transpiring on the Gulf shore. His lesson that morning was what he considered to be a "striking parable" from Luke 6:49:

> But he that heareth [my sayings], and doeth not, is like a man that without a foundation built a house upon the earth; against which the stream did beat vehemently, and immediately it fell; and the ruin of that house was great.

{ 10 }

Gravity Suspended

For all terrene forces, which are usually in operation were,
for the time being, merged into wind, and the law of
gravitation itself superseded. Nothing could fall. Everything
that was in motion went horizontally.
—REV. R. S. MCALLISTER,
SOUTHERN PRESBYTERIAN, APRIL 9, 1891

The swirling storm moved relentlessly toward the barrier islands of central Louisiana, its eye lurking just offshore by 12:00 PM Sunday, August 10. It had slowed its forward progress since Saturday evening, halving its movement from about fourteen miles per hour to about eight, as if it had paused to steady its aim and gather strength to deliver a mortal blow. The storm had become a monster, perhaps feeding over a pool of warm water in an eddy shed by the Gulf's Loop Current. Sustained wind speeds now ripped to 150 miles per hour— within six miles per hour of category 5 on today's Saffir-Simpson Scale. In the 1850s, the hurricane's winds, whether at 100 or 150, would have made it Force 12—a "sail-splitter"—with no further distinction deemed necessary.

The storm still had no name. Official names were not given to Atlantic Basin hurricanes until the early 1950s. Women's names were used starting in 1953, and men's named were added to the lists in 1979. In earlier times, only great storms were christened, and then only after landfall, when their level of devastation became clear. Some of these were named for saints, like Hurricane Santa Anna, which devastated Puerto Rico in 1824. Some were named after the year of their occurrence, like the Great Hurricane of 1722 that struck New Orleans shortly after the city was founded. And some were named after the locale where the death and destruction took place—such as the Isle Derniere Hurricane.

It was "simple as hurricanes go," the climatologist of Louisiana would say of the Isle Derniere tempest a century and a half later. It had "no circuitous curlicues in its path or diversionary changes of course, no lofty African pedigree." It was "just a homegrown killer coming of age off the western tip of the Florida Keys." To the survivors of the disaster, however, the storm would have seemed more devious than simple. At noon on August 10, the wind on Isle Derniere continued to blow from the land.

Eighteen years earlier, William Reid, in his *Attempt to Develop the Law of Storms,* used William Redfield's observations of the pattern of downed trees to describe conditions mistakenly attributed to northers on the Gulf coast. "Some of the violent north winds which blow in the Gulf of Mexico," Reid wrote, "are now clearly proved to be the left-hand side of rotary gales," or hurricanes. Such was the case for the system nearing Isle Derniere.

The storm had moved to the northeast across the Gulf of Mexico toward the northern Gulf coast, its track at about a forty-five-degree angle with the east-west trending shore. During this movement, the forward or left part of the storm's counterclockwise swirl had enveloped the island, bringing winds that blew persistently from the land like a winter norther.

But now, on August 10, 1856, the rotary had crept close, bringing its eye just offshore Isle Derniere, and the wind blowing from the land was about to change.

At 1:00 PM, Michael and Lodoiska Schlatre and their seven children sat around the dinner table in their beachfront house. Michael bowed his head and said a prayer to bless his family's midday Sunday meal. All were still dressed in their Sunday best from attending the Mass read by Michael in their home earlier in the day.

Around the table, house slaves bustled to and fro, delivering platters stacked high with food, filling glasses with rainwater that had run down the roof of the house and channeled into the cistern, a large tank or barrel to capture freshwater. With the beating rain, the cistern must have been near full and the slaves drenched. They had to venture outside to retrieve the collected water and to shuttle food to the main house from the kitchen, which stood in a separate structure to prevent the spread of fires. In the nineteenth century, with meals cooked over open flames in buildings constructed of highly flammable materials, such fires were commonplace. The slaves took care not to drip when they leaned over the dining table or family members to serve food and fill glasses, but it was a losing battle to keep the house dry.

"Already the rain began to come through the roof on the upper floor," Schlatre wrote later, "and thence found its way down into the bedrooms." He drilled holes in the second floor to keep the water from accumulating and placed buckets on the first floor under the holes to capture the flow from above. Forty-four years later, on Galveston Island, Texas, men would chop holes in their floors, not to let water out, but to let water into their homes to keep storm surge from floating the structures off their foundations.

There was no such desperation in the Schlatre house. "I had no apprehension of danger," Michael wrote. With the worsening conditions, his wife and oldest children were likely growing nervous, although no one dared to question the judgment of the head of the family. In an atmosphere of forced calm, they all watched the darkening of the sky and listened to the deepening howl of the wind.

After his family had finished their meal and his house slaves had cleared away the food and dishes, Schlatre noticed that some of the

tubs on the floor had filled to near their tops. The rain was now torrential and pouring through his roof. Schlatre's son Louis was ill and
was put to bed in a room. To keep from becoming drenched, he had
to be covered with a slicker.

At about 2:00 PM, Schlatre began showing signs of his own jan-
gled nerves. He repeatedly glanced out a window, checking on the
Star, which was moored behind the hotel. Michael was concerned
that the storm would drive the vessel from its mooring. With some relief, he affirmed, and reaffirmed, that "she still stood steadily."

Thomas Ellis rushed outside onto the *Star's* hurricane deck and
into the midst of the gale, trying to stop Captain Smith from making a mistake that would put the vessel's passengers and crew in jeopardy. In the pelting rain, Smith and the crewmen were struggling to
run ropes over the vessel's decks to keep them from being torn away
by the wind. The vessel was old and tired. Its decks bowed with every
gust, as if they were about to peel off one after another.

Many passengers were still trapped aboard the *Star*. Only a few
had risked limb and life to jump onto the wooden dock and run toward
the hotel when the steamer made its rough landing. After anchoring
in Village Harbor, the crew was unable to safely launch a skiff in the
violent gusts to ferry the rest of the passengers ashore. They remained
stranded in cabins onboard, including "quite a number of ladies," according to Ellis, "all very much frightened and a few had fainted."

Ellis shouted to the captain above the scream of the gale that the
lashings would not save the vessel. The wind was still increasing, and
soon the multiple decks with cabins full of people would be blown
away regardless of the straps. Ellis argued that everyone aboard should
go below the main deck of the vessel and into the solid hull, where
they had at least a chance to survive.

Captain Smith did not agree with Ellis. Perhaps he had tired of the
constant advice on how his vessel should be run. After all, the responsibility for crew and passengers, for vessel and cargo, lay ultimately

with him, not Ellis. So, while continuing to tighten ropes around the hurricane deck, the captain shook his head and shouted back to Ellis that the cabins were the safest place for the passengers. Further, he yelled, if they were sent down into the hull, the men and women and children would be exposed to the wind and rain on the main deck before they could climb through a hatch into the hold.

Ellis did not belabor the argument and rushed down two levels to the main deck, convinced that the upper decks would be blown away at any moment. He was also concerned about the wind pushing hard against the vessel and stressing the anchor and its lines. If the lines parted or the anchor's flukes dragged through the mud, the steamer would be driven seaward by the wind. The vessel would run aground on the bay side of the island, where it would stay—but only if the island remained above the sea.

If storm surge completely inundated the island, the *Star* and its crew and passengers would be blown across the Isle Derniere and into the Gulf's surf.

Many of the people on the island had fled their homes and trudged across the sand to seek refuge at the two-story hotel, which was considered one of the strongest structures on Isle Derniere. Wet and windblown, they huddled with the hotel guests in the parlor and game rooms and worried about the progress of the storm.

Among the refugees was Dr. Lyle, one of the few men who had jumped from the main deck of the *Star* onto the pier during the failed landing. Most of the passengers were still on the steamer moored behind the hotel. From a rear room in the building, it would have been difficult to see the *Star* even if the windows were not covered with shutters. The glass faced into the wind and would have been smeared by a film of rain and spray and foam.

The people who had gathered on the more protected sides of the hotel had better views through windows or cracked-open doorways of the conditions outside. Based on what he saw, W. W. Pugh lost the confidence that he had felt just a few hours earlier. "About 12 o'clock in the day," he wrote later, "the storm had [become] so violent, as to rush the waters from the rear part of the island up towards the most elevated points while the waves from the Gulf rolled against the front part with terrific fury."

With the deteriorating conditions, Dr. Alfred Duperier would have been pleased with the arrival at the hotel of Dr. Lyle, who could help tend to the medical needs of anyone injured during the storm. Duperier, like Pugh, was losing confidence that the islanders would emerge from the gale unscathed. "The water about 2 P.M.," Duperier said later, "commenced rising so rapidly from the bayside that there could be no longer any doubt that the island would be submerged."

The nearby *Star* gave the people in the hotel an option for escape. If the water rose dangerously high, they could seek refuge aboard the vessel. They likely felt uneasy, however, about not being able to confirm whether the *Star* was still safely at anchor.

Early in the storm, the Mille family had wanted to abandon their house and seek shelter at the hotel, as some of their neighbors had done. They did not leave their house, however, because of Althee's anxiety over her sick child. Moving the family to the hotel would have required a half-mile transit down the beach. She did not want to expose her baby to the wind and rain and risk making the illness worse.

Through the day on Sunday, the weather conditions deteriorated. The Mille slaves had to evacuate their quarters, which were being blown apart. The slaves gathered in the main house with the family except for one, Richard, Thomas Mille's body servant.

Richard confronted his master outside the main house, trying to convince him to order his family members and slaves to seek shelter in a nearby stable that Richard believed was the strongest structure on the island. Its walls were held vertical by pilings driven deep into the sand. The walls might rip away, but the pilings would remain erect and in place.

Mille refused. He and his family and the other slaves remained in the main house. Richard headed for the stable.

The Mille family felt far from safe, however. "When we looked out," Emma recalled, "and saw the steamboat, the *Star*, being tossed about on the sands in front of the big hotel, we were frightened."

Emma turned to her father, but found no comfort or reassurance. His fear had flashed into panic. She could see it in his expression— the look of prey when trapped.

"My father lost courage. We waited for the worst."

A half-mile down the beach from the other houses, Reverend McAllister looked out at the storm from the oceanfront boarding-house. Although only twenty-five years old, he was sickly and on the island for convalescence. "The daylight, even before noon," he wrote, "became very obscure, the blow increased to a furious tempest and the waves rising higher and higher seemed intermingled and fiercely contending with each other."

The five boarders in the house sat down to a midday Sunday meal with the host couple and their three children. The roar of wind and surf intruded from outside, dominating the atmosphere around the table. The three young women boarders spoke few words. Roland Delaney and Reverend McAllister were subdued as well, although, McAllister recalled, "no one was as yet willing to give expressions to his fears."

One of the young women was petite, with the fragile frame of a china doll. Earlier in the summer, she and Roland Delaney had spent time together. His advances had been welcomed. Now, even though they were thrust together at every meal, she paid no attention to him, treating him as if he did not exist, adding to the tension around the table.

By three o'clock that afternoon, the wind seemed to be roaring toward a peak. "For many days [the storm] had been, with imperceptible accretions, gathering power," wrote McAllister later, "and now it seemed all the aerial currents in creation had been turned upon us, one would not think the blast could have been stronger."

Not only could they hear the storm and feel it shudder their abode, but now they could see it. Reverend McAllister described the scene. "Fiery lightning almost constantly illuminated the heavens, and deafening thunders, peal upon peal, shook our circumscribed islet to its center."

Even though common in the midst of Louisiana's summer thunderstorms, lightning was not as routinely observed in the midst of hurricanes. A century and a half later, meteorologists would find in several studies that lightning in eyewalls over water tends to occur near or during storm intensification. The lightning outbreaks observed from Isle Derniere in August 1856 may have been a sign of such hurricane strengthening.

Though they would not have known this implication of what they were witnessing, those at the boardinghouse now felt deeply afraid and totally at the mercy of the storm. McAllister thought their minds had "almost reached the conclusion that nothing [could] be done."

The people of New Orleans went about their Sunday oblivious to what was unfolding on the Gulf coast. Thomas Wharton had taught Sunday class at his Episcopal church, attended formal services there, and then returned to his home on Camp Street in the lower Garden District, fifteen blocks upriver from the French Quarter. There he shared midday dinner with his wife and son. "At 1 P.M.," he wrote in his journal, "the [wind] increased to a gale, blew down a large China tree in the next garden, tearing up the pavement and crushing the fence on which it fell . . . and covered the street around us with fragments of Shade trees." Thomas, a meticulous man who took great pride in his home, was probably planning to remove the debris and clean his surroundings once the weather cleared.

In the nearby St. Charles Hotel, across Canal Street from the Quarter, there was little thought of the weather as a business meeting was brought to order as planned. The large, boisterous crowd of planters and merchants who had gathered the previous day under the hotel's rotunda for the weekly slave auction had long ago dispersed. The hotel was now quiet, as was usually the case on a Sunday. The meeting was small and included principal investors and property managers who were excited about a new development on the central Louisiana coast with enormous profit potential.

They felt that the project was timely because the transportation hurdle between New Orleans and the Gulf's barrier islands had finally been overcome. Travelers no longer had to depend on steamers to carry them the entire distance, winding down narrow bayous through swamps and marshes for many tens of miles. The recently completed Opelousas Railroad now whisked them close to the coast. It was an engineering marvel, its tracks transiting spongy marsh and mucky swamps for seventy-five miles from Algiers—located across the Mississippi from New Orleans—to near Brashear City. A flotilla of packet steamboats, including the *Star*, would then shuttle passengers down the Atchafalaya River into the Gulf and then eastward along the shore to Isle Derniere. The island was considered by investors "in many respects more desirably situated than any of the other home resorts then in favor."

With the opening of the railroad, the investors at the meeting believed that additional accommodations would be necessary for the projected increase in visitors to the island. Muggah's Hotel was not large enough to handle even one-third of the anticipated number of new customers.

Everyone crowded around a conference table to view just-completed drawings for the project. The size of the planned structure was stunning. It would be "the largest resort hotel in North America during the antebellum period," according to Bethany Bultman, "with luxuriant accommodations for 1,250 guests, . . . and 1,250 feet of double-decker galleries overlooking the Gulf and the bay." The investors rapidly approved the plans and instructed the management team—Mr. Hall and Mr. Hildreth—to push the project forward on a fast track, with construction beginning after the 1856 summer season.

It was unlikely that any of the participants in this meeting attended Thomas Wharton's lesson at the Episcopal church about the man who "without a foundation built a house upon the earth."

Even if they had, none of them knew that as they met at the St. Charles the sandy strip of sand on which they planned to build their "house" was deteriorating.

{ 11 }

Merciless
Waters

*The struggle for life commenced, and horror was painted on
every face, no one exposed could withstand the force of the
waves, and all who were caught without shelter or something
to hold on to fell victims to the merciless waters.*
—W. W. PUGH, *"A HISTORICAL SKETCH OF
ASSUMPTION PARISH, 1820–1860"* (1896)

At 3:30 PM, Michael Schlatre sensed danger for the first time. He watched the wind tear his separate kitchen building apart and tumble the remains close to the main house, where he and his family huddled. Earlier, his servants' quarters had been destroyed, but he had not been alarmed by the loss of those frail structures. The kitchen, however, was solidly built, and its failure gave him pause. Equally unsettling was an unusual scene that developed outside about an hour later. "The chickens in the yard were squatting in all directions, cows and calves lowing. . . . The air was darkened, and filled with sand and water, the wind howling the like of which I never heard."

On the faces of his family and servants Schlatre could see the fear simmering, and he knew he had to keep it from boiling over into panic. He had ordered his slaves inside the main house for their protection. Outside, fragments of destroyed buildings were flying through the air like missiles. He told his wife that even though he now saw danger, "all must keep cool, not to be frightened for that would do no good." He also tried to put a positive spin on what he thought would happen next, telling her that their house would be thrown off its stubby blocks down to the sand where they would be safer.

At 5:00 PM, Schlatre ventured outside onto the front gallery that faced an angry sea. He was protected on this side of the house from the northeasterly wind and could safely walk to the end of the porch and inspect the next-door house of Thomas Mille. He saw the wind thrust Mille's home forward toward the Gulf about five feet. The front edge fell to the ground; the rear remained elevated, propped up on four-foot-high blocks, leaving the house sloping seaward.

Then he said to himself, *Now for us.*

Seconds later his house too was thrust forward. It slipped off all of its blocks and came to rest lying flat on the sand.

Schlatre rode the house down without being injured. His gallery and home remained intact. As the structure fell, he heard a voice cry out from his family. He wrote later, "One scream and all was hushed within."

Inside the Mille home, Emma, her family, Mrs. Rommage, and their slaves tried to recover. They had all assembled in a single room when Emma heard a crash and flew through the air. The house jerked forward, and one side plunged down to the sand. Everyone and every-thing tumbled and slid down the tilting floor. They came to rest in a jumble against the wall at the base of the incline. Debris rained down on them. A timber fell against Emma's head and split it open.

Emma remained conscious and aware. She could feel the gaping wound with her hands and see the blood gushing down onto her white muslin dress, staining it red. She knew she was seriously injured and needed help. But Thomas Mille had disappeared.

At the secluded oceanfront boardinghouse farther down the beach from the Schlatre and Mille homes, Reverend McAllister and the other inhabitants were frightened; they felt trapped on a remote island with no chance of escape. They edged toward panic, but remained rational.

"Is there some undiscovered faculty in man," McAllister wrote later, "which comes to his aid when reason is paralyzed? I can scarcely believe that our intellect argued us into the notion that the central part of the house was the safest." There, the dozen inhabitants of the boardinghouse crowded together into a hallway.

From above, they heard a loud bang as the roof of the two-story building was peeled off its beams and carried away. Then the exterior walls, one after another, were blown free of the foundation. The interior walls that partitioned rooms in the house went next, bowing and swaying and then flying off into the air. Amazingly, none of the people huddled in the central hallway were crushed by falling debris. Rather than inflicting harm, the extreme winds protected them. The building remains were whisked away and not allowed to fall, as if "the law of gravitation itself was superseded," wrote McAllister.

Now the inhabitants stood on the floor in the open, exposed to the elements. All were overwhelmed with fear and consumed with despair. They bent down before the wind; some lay on the floor cowering. They felt there was nothing more they could do to save themselves. It was up to Providence. Many prayed, and one confessed.

The confessor was a servant, a cook. Before the storm, the mistress of the boardinghouse had discovered items in the house missing and accused the cook of taking them. The cook had denied it vigorously. Now, however, she "came forth in a voice which the howling tornado could not drown," recalled McAllister, "a full and itemized confession of the coffee, lard, sugar, hams, etc., which she had purloined." In spite of their peril, the self-indictment brought smiles of disbelief to the reverend and the others.

With walls no longer sheltering them, their eyes were battered by a wind-driven mixture of sand and water that made it difficult to see beyond the remains of the boardinghouse. The reverend could sense far enough, however, to determine that water was inundating the island.

"The Gulf on one side and the bay on the other," he wrote, "were advancing upon us. Higher and higher the two seas were rising, and would soon cover the denuded floor upon where, . . . we had hoped to hold our own."

Aboard the anchored *Star*, Thomas Ellis stood outside on the main deck and lashed himself to what remained of the vessel to avoid being blown overboard. He was a solitary figure atop a barren deck; the vessel's three stories of superstructure were gone. The wind had ripped them from the hull and swept them away.

Before the steamer began to disintegrate, the passengers and crew, including Captain Smith, became convinced that Ellis was right about the danger of remaining in the cabins on the upper decks. In a confused, disorderly retreat, men, women, and children had funneled down ladders and burst onto the main deck. Hunched over to protect their bodies from the driving wind and rain, they made their way to the hatch where, one by one, they scrambled down into the protection of the vessel's cargo hold.

After the superstructure had been stripped away, Ellis emerged from the hold and into the elements to determine whether the *Star* was dragging its anchor seaward. At first he tried to fix their position relative to the hotel, which he knew had to be near. But he could not see more than a few yards through the flying rain and spray.

Ellis looked out as far as he could from the stern of the vessel. He knew he was facing the Gulf, although his eyes could not detect its proximity. The wind had aligned the *Star*, whipping its hull around so that the anchor line attached to its bow was pulled rigid like a steel rod. The bow nosed into the northeast wind, and the stern pointed toward the surf of the Gulf of Mexico.

Ellis leaned over the stern railing, his safety lashing keeping him from tumbling into the water or blowing away. He lowered a heavy lead weight from the water's surface until it settled onto the sand below. The length of line he paid out told Ellis the depth of water. He then repeated the measurement, again and again, to determine whether the depth was changing—that is, whether the wind was driving the vessel across the island and toward the deadly surf beyond.

His measurements were definitive—the *Star* was on the move.

After his house fell to the sand, Michael Schlatre rushed from the front gallery into his home. He found his family and slaves afraid but uninjured. Schlatre wrote later, "The inmates stood still with fear."

His youngest son, Louis, was sick and crying. The little boy was scared that his parents were going to abandon him. Michael and Lodoiska tried to comfort the boy and reassure him that he would not be left alone.

Then Schlatre started from a terrific crash coming from above their heads. The roof had been torn from the house by the wind. Debris dropped around the seventeen people who had gathered on the first floor. Michael demanded that everyone crawl under the first-floor beds. There they would be protected by mattresses and bed frames from falling timbers.

With his family and servants under the beds, Schlatre stood alone on the floor and looked through cracks in a window shutter to the Mille house next door. The structure was gone. He could not see any part of the home; only the cistern still stood in the back. He now knew that his family had little time before their own house was blown apart.

Schlatre kept his composure and began preparations for his family's escape from the island. He called above the roar of wind for Ceily, one of his house slaves, to crawl out from under the bed and help him. Inside a large steamer trunk, they quickly stuffed clothes and a moneybox containing about $500. They sealed the trunk tight and placed it, along with some food, on top of one of the beds. Schlatre thought the trunk would remain dry and be available to them when they departed.

The storm shrieked and ripped. His family and servants cowered under the beds, crying and screaming. Schlatre demanded they be quiet. Then his attention again jerked upward to another crash. The second floor of his home had disappeared.

In the same instant, he was staggered by the impact of a gust of wind. The shutters that covered the first-floor windows had blown through. The wind now invaded in a rush, flipping a mattress off a bed and exposing Lodoiska and their children to falling debris.

Schlatre struggled with the mattress, whose large surface made it act like a kite about to be launched. With great difficulty, he returned it to the bed to shield his family from wreckage flying like shrapnel through the room.

In the midst of the chaos, he was shocked to see Thomas Mille, who "came into my house from somewhere, [w]ringing his hands, and laid down on the floor."

Thomas Ellis hustled down through the hatch in the main deck and into the hold where passengers and crew had congregated, their bodies shielded from wind and rain by the solid hull. Ellis announced to Captain Smith that the *Star* was dragging its anchor across the island and toward the surf. If this continued, they decided to scuttle the vessel in the shallow water over the island. They hoped that the hull and anchor dragging through the sand together might stop the vessel's march toward the sea.

Ellis rushed back to the main deck and again lashed his body to the vessel. Hunched over to protect himself from wind and rain, he continued his soundings off the stern. Although effectively blind, he sensed the wild surf just a few hundred feet in front of him. With the wind at his back, he could not feel the breakers' spray, but he heard the low-pitched rumbles of surf between high-pitched shrieks of wind. Looking over the side of the vessel, he may have been able to see the bay water rushing seaward into the Gulf, pushing against the hull.

His soundings told him that the *Star* was still being driven toward the surf. They were running out of time, and Smith had not yet ordered the crew to sink the vessel in the shallow water. It might not even help. They had few good options. If the *Star* slipped over the beach and into the breakers, staying aboard would be a death sentence. If they abandoned the vessel and sloshed across the beach toward where he thought the hotel stood, the current could overpower them and sweep them into the sea.

Ellis still could not see the largest structure on the island and did not know that the flooded beach between the vessel and the hotel had been transformed into a killing field.

Within one hundred yards of the *Star*, the wind tore pieces from Muggah's Hotel and whipped them through the air. W. W. Pugh led his wife, seven children, and house servants out of the rear of the disintegrating hotel in a mad dash to a small cabin behind the main structure. Soon after entering the cabin, they felt it shudder and sway and saw the roof peel back. Pugh again was forced to lead his family into the open.

Hunched over to protect themselves from the stinging rain, they waded back through the storm surge to the remains of the hotel. There they sought sanctuary behind the destroyed dining room where the hotel's cistern was still solidly in place. They gathered behind it, using the cistern as a shield from the wind.

The water from the bay rose incessantly into what was left of the hotel and drove the remaining inhabitants into irrational flight. "The women and children who first imagined themselves safe indoors," Pugh wrote later, "soon were compelled to leave their tenements, and the buildings rolled about, demolished, and their fragments scattered among the waves."

Chaos reigned on the beach. People stumbled this way, then that, but had nowhere to go that would be safe. The wind-driven rain pummeled their faces. They could not see the nearby hulk of the *Star*. They tried to run toward the highest elevation on the island to keep their heads above the rising surge. But they did not know where it was.

Shrapnel flew through the clusters of disoriented people. Everything was in motion—not only pieces of buildings but also pots and pans, forks and knives, books and glassware, chairs and tables, anything the wind could grab and hurl. The people were impaled by spearlike planks and dismembered by cannonball rubble. "Many persons were wounded," according to Dr. Alfred Duperier, "some mortally."

Those who survived the fusillade faced the threat of the water rising up their legs. Their dash across the sand slowed to a frantic slog. Giant tree trunks left on the island during previous storms had now refloated. They rammed the fleeing men, women, and children, crushing many of them.

Dr. Duperier tied himself to a large piece of wooden furniture. Around him, others clambered aboard logs and furniture and lumber, anything that would float. They were all swept seaward into the surf. Those on the beach who could not mount a raft, and those impaled or disabled by projectiles, disappeared under the breakers.

In the bedlam, the Pugh family had become separated. W. W. Pugh counted the heads that were crouched with him behind the hotel's cistern. His stomach dropped when he confirmed that three of his children were missing. He feared most for his youngest; at a little over one year old, she would be helpless under the conditions. Pugh had last seen a slave nurse holding the toddler in her arms, and then he lost sight of both of them.

He prayed that nothing had happened to his little Loula.

Michael Schlatre fumed at Thomas Mille, who was lying on the floor of Schlatre's house, quaking with fear. There was nothing wrong with the man that Schlatre could see, apart from his unseemly behavior. "I told him it was no way to act—to go under the bed with the others if he wanted." Mille docilely complied, crawling under a mattress and bed frame where some of Schlatre's children and slaves were huddling.

Disgusted, Schlatre turned and walked away through pools of water that now soaked the first floor. Rain penetrated the interior of what remained of his home; the roof and second floor had been ripped off, leaving the first floor with its walls intact but exposed to the elements from above. The driving rain fell against Schlatre's body and drenched his clothes. The surviving walls afforded him and his family some protection from the wind, although he knew that without the roof and second floor, the walls had little structural support. It was just a matter of time before they gave way.

The east side of the house went first. The gable plummeted onto several of the beds that protected Michael's family and servants. Worried that the frames could not support the rubble and would soon collapse, Schlatre ordered everyone from under the beds and to another room farther from the wind's frontal assault.

Once they were clustered into this new space, Michael Schlatre's eyes fell again on Thomas Mille, who lay in the midst of the women and children and slaves. Schlatre approached his neighbor coldly, asking him what had happened to his family. Mille answered that he had no idea. He expressed no interest in where they might be, and no concern about what might have happened to them.

Schlatre marched to the front door and threw it open, as if he were going to search for Thomas Mille's family himself. He looked toward the Gulf's surf and saw a woman sitting on the sand in front of his house. Bay water streamed around her, running off the island and into the Gulf.

She was Mrs. Rommage from New Orleans, and she had been living with the Mille family in their home. Schlatre told Mille that he was going to bring her into the shelter of his house. Mille objected, arguing that conditions were too severe to do anything for her. Ignoring the remark, Schlatre ventured outside toward the woman. After a few steps, the wind at his back hurled him forward onto the ground. Without reaching Mrs. Rommage, he turned around and crawled to the outside of his house, seeking shelter from the wind in the lee of the still-standing west gable.

Mille had watched Schlatre's rescue attempt. He then jumped up, ran outside, and joined Schlatre next to the gable. Schlatre must have been shocked when the man appeared next to him, and even more so when he agreed to help with another attempt to retrieve Mrs. Rommage from the water. Schlatre now planned to use a rope. One of them would tie it around his waist and venture out to Mrs. Rommage; then the other would pull the rescuer and the lady back to the house.

Schlatre was crouched behind the west gable when it was pushed by the wind and plummeted onto the right side of his chest and his right leg, lacerating the ligaments in his knee. He was trapped and could not move.

Thomas Mille emerged from the collapse of the wall unscathed. He crawled to near the fallen Schlatre, who was crying out for help. It was impossible for Mille to stand erect; whatever protection the house had provided from the wind and flying debris had vanished. All of the walls were gone. Out of the chaos appeared Thomas Mille's twenty-three-year-old son Homer. There was no sign of anyone else from the Mille family. Father and son grabbed the edge of the fallen gable and freed Schlatre from its clutches.

The unforeseen courage of Thomas Mille was contagious. The house no longer existed—only the wooden floor remained. On it was scattered bedding and pieces of furniture. In spite of this dire situation and the deteriorating weather, Lodoiska crawled forward to help her husband. She motioned for the other women to gather at his side, and they dragged him onto a mattress that was lying on the wood floor. "My wife hearing my cries for help came out to me," wrote Schlatre, "that moment I will never forget. She now took command, yes she the heroic one."

Meanwhile, Thomas Mille, buoyed by the regaining of his nerve, ventured away from the floor and into the storm, toward where his house once stood. He soon reappeared through the swirl of rain and spray with his wife in his arms. He laid her carefully on the mattress next to Schlatre. She had a "dreadful cut over the eye from a piece of timber," Schlatre wrote, "and though in her senses, said not a word."

Despite the pandemonium around them, Thomas Mille must have felt at least a fleeting mix of pride and despair. He had overcome his fear and saved his wife's life, at least for the moment, but he had found no trace of his other children. He knew of the well-being of only Homer, his oldest, but had not found Emma, Althee, or Althee's baby.

Michael Schlatre felt only despair. Since the wind had become a gale, he had been imbued with confidence that there was no danger. Now everything he knew was in upheaval. He lay severely injured, and people all around him were dying.

Schlatre was a man who valued courage and who looked down on other men who cowered in fear. Now, however, he faced his own mortality.

Emma Mille was still bleeding profusely from her head when bay water rushed through the remains of her home. Caillou Bay was spilling over the crest of the beach and into the sea in a torrent. Somehow Emma had both the presence of mind and the strength to grab a piece of lumber. It floated her body as the current swept her toward the heavy surf of the Gulf.

The water had also grabbed Althee and her infant and propelled them ahead of Emma. Althee tried desperately to grab for a timber with one arm, while struggling to keep her infant's head above water with the other. But she was unable to mount the large timber. It swung toward her, and she shrieked, "Don't crush my baby!" Those were the last words Emma ever heard from Althee. Mother and child were carried into the Gulf and its raging surf, where a breaker buried them. They vanished in the white water.

Emma was swept toward those same breakers. They pounded her, submerged her, and twisted her underwater. Somehow she hung on to the piece of wood and kept popping back to the surface for brief gasps of air between poundings. She was being driven across the surf into deeper and deeper water. And the farther she went into the broad expanse of breakers, the larger the waves became. At any location in the surf, the tallest waves were roughly the same height as the water was deep: in three feet of water they were roughly three feet high, and in six feet of water they were six feet high. When Emma reached a depth of twelve feet, the total vertical reach of the waves from the seabed was above the height of a two-story building.

Through every wall of white water that rumbled over her, she kept her arms wrapped around the piece of lumber in a death grip.

The wind and current had driven the *Star* to near the high point of the island when the clouds parted and visibility suddenly improved. Thomas Ellis was still on the stern sounding the depths. For the first time he could see the devastation around the vessel. It was as if the *Star* had been transported to a different place. The hotel had vanished. None of the houses were visible. The island appeared swept clean of everything built by humans.

Conditions continued to improve. He could stand; the wind had eased, almost to a calm. Ellis then spied a few dozen people standing next to some fence posts, fifty to sixty yards away.

He yelled into the hold to Captain Smith that there were survivors standing in the water. Smith and the crewmen bounded up through the hatch and onto the main deck, hauling a coil of quarter-inch line. One end was tied to the hull. Ellis grabbed the other end. With several crewmen, he leapt overboard into the shallow water and slogged to the cluster of people, paying out the line behind him. They pulled the line taut and tied it to one of the fence posts. Ellis and the crewmen guided the battered people in a procession through the water. Slowly, deliberately, they followed the line to the *Star*'s hull.

Both survivors and rescuers must have felt relieved that the worst of the storm was over. The wind no longer blew, the rain no longer fell, and debris no longer rocketed through the air. Overhead, blue sky appeared in patches.

They did not recognize the stadium of clouds that completely encircled them. It was deadly, and it was moving slowly, relentlessly, over them.

{ 12 }

Landfall

At 6:00 PM on Sunday, August 10, the hurricane had maintained its intensity for six hours with sustained winds of 150 miles per hour. This wind speed made the storm a category 4 on today's Saffir-Simpson Hurricane Scale, exceeding the sustained winds at landfall of many of the devastating hurricanes of the modern era, such as Ivan, Katrina, and Ike. The track of the storm had not wavered appreciably; it headed toward the northwest and came ashore at about a forty-five-degree angle with the east-west-trending barrier island. With the counterclockwise swirl of the storm, this track brought the extreme northeast winds that battered Isle Derniere before the storm's eye made landfall.

While the relative calm of the eye was over the island, the hurricane continued to crawl forward at about eight miles per hour. If the people on Isle Derniere had looked to the south over the Gulf, they would have seen a wall of dense clouds. As this eyewall drew closer, they may have detected these clouds roiling, churning with powerful motion.

Ellis and the crewmen of the *Star* were wading in the water, transporting the last survivor to the hull of the vessel. She was a woman with a broken leg. The men gingerly carried her through the current that still ran across the island from bay to sea. Even though the flow had subsided, each of the men still wrapped one hand around the taut line to keep from being swept away. They finally reached the vessel and were lifting the woman onto the barren main deck when a blast of wind assaulted them from the sea.

One moment the air had been calm; the next the eyewall rolled over them and delivered the strongest winds yet felt on the island. "The gale broke out from the S.W. [southwest] with greater force than it had at any time before," wrote Ellis, "and we now had not only the wind but the seas from the Gulf breaking over us."

Concerned that they would be swept overboard by wind and waves, the crew rushed the injured woman down through the hatch and into the confines of the hull. A total of 160 souls now crowded within the remains of the vessel. Only Thomas Ellis stayed on the main deck exposed to the elements. He again lashed himself to the hull and sounded over the gunwale with a lead line. He was now concerned that the wind blowing from the sea would drive the hull landward into Caillou Bay. The best chance of survival for the people aboard was for the *Star* to stay on the island. The hull would founder in the waves on Caillou Bay, as well as in those on the Gulf.

The wind and breakers were driving floating debris past the hull toward the bay. Ellis could see well enough to determine that the drift contained more than pieces of buildings; some of what floated by was living, breathing. There were horses struggling to swim, straining to keep their mouths, their nostrils, above water. Carriages floated among the animals, as if an entire stable had been destroyed and the current had carried away its contents. Many of the steeds were losing their battle; waves washed over their heads, choking them.

They were not alone. People were propelled bay-ward by what must have seemed like a river in rapids. "Several persons came surging by," Ellis observed. "Nothing in the power of man could save them and they passed out of sight into the bay."

Michael Schlatre expected to die. He lay on a mattress on the floor of his home. There was no roof over him; there were no walls around him. He could not move his right side. With the wind now coming from the sea, he asked his wife if the Gulf was washing across the island. Lodoiska answered that it was beginning to cover the sand. His family clustered near; some of the children were in tears. Lodoiska stared out at the surf as if waiting for the waves to engulf them. Terror filled the faces of Thomas and Homer Mille.

From the mattress, Schlatre faced Governor Hebert's home, which was on the opposite side of his house from Thomas Mille's. After his and Mille's houses fell to the sand, the home of the Governor had remained intact and supported on its stubby pilings. Now, however, Schlatre saw that the roof was gone and only one gable was still erect. He watched as the Gulf's waters churned under the remains and the structure rose, twirled around, and moved bay-ward. He expected the same to happen to his house when the Gulf came, and he knew that the waters would take him first.

Schlatre was wrong.

An intact roof floated by the remains of his home and knocked Lodoiska to the ground. It was the last Michael saw of her.

The Gulf then went after the rest of his family. The water floated the wooden floor, with everyone sitting or lying on it, and propelled it toward the bay. Then the huge raft lodged behind a cistern. "The waters now maddened by resistance came rushing over the floor," wrote Schlatre. Everyone and everything was swept into the surging Gulf.

Schlatre's little girl screamed and leapt onto her father, wrapping her arms tight about his neck. Together, they flailed in the soup of waves and foam and wreckage.

"I now rolled over and over," recalled Schlatre, "drinking in the hated fluid by great mouthfuls[,] the dear child still fastened to me, when I thought (for reader I could still think) that I must be near gone."

Schlatre justified what happened next on his dire circumstances. He expressed sorrow for the consequences of his action, but accepted no responsibility for it and admitted no shame.

"I put my hands to those of my child and broke her hold of me[.] God only knows what became of the dear one[.] Being relieved I now arose to the surface."

The boardinghouse that had stood alone a half-mile west of the village was destroyed, flattened, although the inhabitants were spared. Instead of falling on the people, the walls were propelled away from them by the wind. As they watched the Gulf invade the island, Reverend McAllister, Roland Delaney, and the others knew that the wooden floor on which they huddled would soon join the bay-ward current. They were left with only one option.

A small levee ran from the boardinghouse one hundred yards down the beach. At the far end of the levee was a wooden whirligig, a carousel that children used for entertainment. The four-sided platform spun around a central shaft that was sunk deep into the island. Together, the inhabitants of the boardinghouse decided to abandon the exposed floor and make their way to the whirligig, where they would have a chance to stay above the rising waters. Getting there, however, would be treacherous.

The levee had been heaped up into a ridge with a narrow crest that, in the wind, could not have been walked by a person standing erect. Already the Gulf's waves were lapping over the top of the levee and would soon wash it away. One after another, the people crawled on all fours along the levee crest for a length that today would measure a football field. "To anyone far off looking at us," wrote Reverend McAllister, "we must have presented the appearance of a number of monkeys marching single file."

One of the three young women boarders refused, however, to join the procession. She was the petite and fragile woman who had spent time with Roland Delaney before spurning his further advances. While other boarders pleaded with her to come with them, Roland walked up to her. With no argument and no waste of time, he simply scooped her into his arms and carried her safely across the levee. As he did so, the reverend wrote later, Delaney wore a smile of great satisfaction.

Once everyone had reached the carousel and stood upright on its frame, night fell over the island. The dim light of a stormy day turned impenetrably black. They could not see the waves coming at them but could feel the water hitting and washing through their legs. They could not see the persons next to them but could reach out and touch them to make sure they were still there. The sounds coming from the blackness were ungodly—shrieks and roars and screams.

"Our faith was staggered," recalled McAllister; "our hopes sunk; we were at our wits end."

By nightfall, Emma had been driven seaward through the punishing surf and then into the open Gulf of Mexico. Even there white water still prevailed. The wind both sheared off wave crests and over-steepened them so they broke. The resulting white water swept across her body, driving seawater into her mouth and nose, making her cough and gag. She kept her fingers wrapped tightly around the timber that floated her. At any moment, the surging flows could rip it from her body.

The roar of wind and waves blocked out all other sound. She tried to listen for the voices of her family members. She thought that they had also been driven into the water. But she could hear only the ever-present roar. She was alone in the darkness.

Suddenly, from somewhere, she heard her sister-in-law scream, "Look at Mama!" Emma saw her mother before her, "standing on wreckage in the water."

At the time it seemed real to Emma, but later she realized that it was only a vision, only her imagination running wild.

Still, she did not panic; she did not give up. Through the night she clung to the floating timber, calmed by an innocence and belief that life would go on. "I did not fear that anyone in my family would be killed, nor did I think any of them had been killed. I had no fear, no thought."

She did not know that she had been driven far into the Gulf. After the eye passed over the coast and the wind began to blow from the sea, she did not know that her makeshift raft was being pushed in the opposite direction along the same course.

Emma was driven back toward the island by Redfield's progressive whirlwind, and it ultimately saved her life.

For ten hours, Jim Frisbee, the steward of the *Nautilus*, had floated on a large piece of wreckage about seventy miles east of Emma and twenty miles from Southwest Pass, where his vessel had been bound before capsizing. Lying with him aboard the makeshift raft was the ship's chief engineer, Mr. Johnson. They were adrift over the relatively deep water seaward of the mouth of the Mississippi, where they rose and fell on huge waves. Churning crests of white water repeatedly washed over the two men.

Frisbee and Johnson struggled to maintain their grip on the raft and to keep it from tumbling over or breaking apart. With land so near, they knew they had a good chance of rescue after the wind and waves calmed, but they had to survive the storm first.

No rescue ships would have put to sea that day, and any ship already offshore in the Gulf had either sunk like the *Nautilus* or was fighting for its life.

Such was the situation aboard the sailing ship *Manilla*, which was carrying a load of wine and passengers from Bordeaux to New Orleans. The sailing ship drifted uncontrolled and helpless in the darkness. It had been anchored off Southwest Pass, but with conditions deteriorating, Captain Rogers had ordered his crew to set sail and run for calmer waters. The *Manilla*'s sails were soon shredded by the Force 12 winds.

All day Sunday the drifting vessel absorbed hard blows. In the midafternoon, a wave streamed across the vessel's exposed decks, ripping away the wheelhouse and longboat. Captain Rogers was twice swept overboard during the day, but he must have been tethered to the ship, because each time he was able to climb back aboard.

The captain undoubtedly feared that his vessel would soon be lost during the storm. The giant and confused seas were not the only hazards. When he had first slipped his anchor cables, the wind was still blowing from the land. If his vessel ran into problems, this north wind would push it offshore. Although the *Manilla* would encounter enormous waves there, the captain would not need to worry about being driven onto the beach. Offshore, they at least had a chance of remaining afloat.

When the eye passed Southwest Pass, however, and the wind switched, Captain Rogers knew their fate. The *Manilla* was being driven incessantly through the darkness toward central Louisiana's barrier islands, toward their shoal water and heavy surf. There was nothing he could do about it.

Michael Schlatre struggled to keep his head above water. After breaking the hold of his little girl and swimming free, he had grabbed on to several loose planks to keep himself afloat. He lay on them with lungs heaving, muscles spent. Schlatre could see around him to the faces of three of his sons struggling in the water. He watched them drown.

Schlatre was thrust toward the bay by the strong flow. The planks he clutched were too small to reliably float his body. When a larger piece of wooden debris drifted close to him, he abandoned the planks and climbed aboard the new raft.

He looked ahead into the deepening darkness to where the current was taking him. With his head turned toward the bay and his eyes protected from the punishing gusts from the sea, he spied Thomas Mille standing about one hundred feet ahead. Schlatre's raft was being driven straight toward him.

Schlatre had no idea how Mille had gotten so far ahead. They had been together, in the remains of Schlatre's house, when the surge had lifted and propelled his wooden floor bay-ward. Somehow Mille now was standing in a clump of marsh grasses in water that rose up to about his knees. Waves reached up to his waist.

The raft swept close to Mille, and he leapt onto it, as if it was his last chance for survival. Together, Mille and Schlatre surged toward Caillou Bay and the mainland. The raft swept over the flooded beach, crossed Village Harbor, and then got caught behind a bush whose upper branches emerged above the water. Schlatre knew that the bush would not hold them long. The fierce current pushing against the raft would soon overwhelm the branches. Schlatre and Mille would be thrust into Caillou Bay, where Schlatre knew the waves would be murderous.

A more substantial raft suddenly appeared next to them. It had also been caught behind the bush. Schlatre and Mille quickly abandoned their frail raft for the new one, which was a portion of an exterior wall of a destroyed home. Measuring eight feet by twelve feet, it was weather-boarded on one side and veneered with planks on the other. They climbed onto the smooth plank side and clutched the sash and frame of the window opening in the wall's center. Its glass had been broken out. Minutes after boarding, Schlatre could see that their new raft was on the move; it had shed the branches and was gaining speed toward Caillou Bay.

Unseen around them in the dark waters of the Gulf and bay, their wives, nine children, and one grandchild were gasping for their next breath or had taken their last.

Michael Schlatre thought he and Mille would soon be dead as well. With five miles of open water before them, "it never entered my mind," he wrote later, "that we could live to cross the bay."

Reverend McAllister and the eleven others from the boardinghouse stood on the frame of the carousel. Thus far, the waves on the island had reached high enough only to wash through their legs. They were well aware, however, that they faced a struggle to survive the night. In preparation, they distributed themselves around the periphery of the frame to balance it as best they could.

Three people stood on each of the carousel's four sides, with some of the taller positioned to help the shorter as the water rose. All of them wrapped their hands and arms around the upper spokes of the frame and readied themselves for the onslaught of the hurricane.

They stood there in silence, the only sounds coming from the storm. McAllister thought they had become mentally numb. For the past eight or ten hours, their minds had raced, trying to determine how to survive a hurricane on a low strip of sand. Now they were spent and their senses were under siege. Their hearing was overwhelmed by the roar of the storm, their sight cloaked by the onset of night. The sense of touch, however, seemed to have been enhanced. They were acutely aware of the feel of the water rising and falling on their legs, acutely aware that the waves were slowly reaching higher and higher on their bodies.

They felt pieces of floating debris knock against them. They thought they had become targets and there was no place to hide. The huge logs that had been deposited on the island during earlier storms rammed the carousel, threatening to destroy it and to knock the dozen people off the platform and into the raging surf.

At first the carousel was solid and still. Windblown sand had accumulated into a dune that had grown high enough to hold the frame firmly in place. That night, however, the waves beat against the dune, eroded it, and swept the sand away. The carousel began to spin. "The twirling and twisting, the dashing and splashing, the heeling and toeing, the flapping and floundering which ensued," wrote McAllister, "would at any other time have produced a first-class comedy."

At 9:00 PM aboard the *Manilla*, Captain Rogers felt a shock. His drifting ship, its sails long ago shredded, came to a jolting halt. Immediately, he felt more shocks. Waves pounded against one side of the ship. Stationary and broadside to the sea, the vessel heeled over in a steep list away from the breakers, as if trying to roll away from their punches. The *Manilla* could not escape, however, and wallowed back and forth in one place, inviting a knockout blow.

Rogers knew that they had been driven into the surf off one of Louisiana's barrier islands, but he did not know which one. They had drifted sixty miles to the west-northwest from the mouth of the Mississippi to Timbalier Island, within thirty miles of Isle Derniere. Rogers realized that the surf would soon rip his ship apart and that the crew and passengers had to somehow negotiate the giant breakers and make their way to the beach.

In the darkness, the captain could not see how far the beach was from the grounded ship. Whether close or distant, he knew the transit would be hazardous, even deadly, but they had no choice. He ordered everyone into the water. Earlier in the day, one of their launches had been lost overboard. Regardless, the breakers were far too large for any boat still stored aboard the *Manilla* to survive. They scavenged for anything onboard that was buoyant—empty barrels, loose boards—to use as rafts for the journey through the breakers.

Twenty-nine people entered the dark surf—the captain, fourteen crewmen, and fourteen passengers, including three women. Their only hope was to drift with the white water and not to fight it, until their feet touched sand. They then had to find the island's highest elevation to wait out the storm. It was possible that the island had been completely submerged by the storm surge. In that case, they would face a miles-long journey across the bay behind the island to the mainland marsh.

Passengers, crew, and captain slipped over the side of the ship to begin their journey before midnight, about three hours after running aground. Soon thereafter, waves broke the *Manilla* into pieces. Its cargo of wine casks drifted in the surf.

Hours into their voyage across Caillou Bay, waves swept over Michael Schlatre and Thomas Mille. Their raft pitched and rolled wildly. Their legs flailed back and forth. Each time their bodies were sent askew, they scrambled to return to their places on the raft. Schlatre moved slower than Mille, more deliberately, protecting the injuries to his chest and leg as best he could.

The waves twisted and flexed the raft, straining it, weakening it. Around midnight, Schlatre became alarmed when he sensed pieces breaking off. He inspected the raft as best he could, running his hands over it between waves. He discovered that the lost pieces had not been integral to the structure's strength; the important parts remained intact. For the first time, he thought they might survive the voyage across the bay. Michael began to feel some hope.

As the hours wore on, however, his fears intensified and wandered. Schlatre worried about their legs dangling behind the raft down into the bay. "I feared the sharks would cut off our legs every minute."

Through the night Schlatre and Mille vomited again and again. They were sick from the raft's gyrations and from ingesting seawater. Waves repeatedly and unexpectedly covered their heads with water; it was impossible not to inhale it, drink it. Schlatre tried to stay focused and keep his mind as alert as possible. The bay was full of debris, much of it large enough and sharp enough to injure or knock them from their raft. He tried to sense the approach of fragments and fend them off with his two hands and one working leg as best he could.

After Mille's performance early in the storm, Schlatre was surprised that he kept his grip on the raft under difficult, punishing conditions. "To do him justice he did hold on," Schlatre wrote, "for as often as I would look for him, after the passage of a wave larger than the others, I was sure to find him there, looking to see if I was washed away. I tell you this was no pleasant occupation, to see if each other were gone."

Isle Derniere was experiencing its own ordeal. When the wind switched direction and came from the sea, it pushed the Gulf against the island and raised a storm surge that was thirteen to eighteen feet above normal sea level. Since the island was only five to six feet high, Isle Derniere would have been completely and continuously inundated through the most intense part of the storm. With no large sand dunes lining the shore to contain the surge, the Gulf spilled landward over the low-lying beach. Breaking waves rode on top of the surge; the frothy walls of white water swept one after the other across the island. With the houses of Mille and Schlatre propped only about four feet above the ground, the breakers battered their external walls like wrecking balls.

The breaking waves also raised sea level in the surf on the Gulf side of Isle Derniere. This "wave setup" added to the storm surge. With the water on the Gulf side standing higher than on the bay side, seawater tumbled down slope across Isle Derniere from Gulf to bay. The current swept the wreckage of buildings, the bodies of people, and sand from the beach into Caillou Bay. By the end of the night, nearly every structure on the island had been destroyed and swept away.

The classic response of a barrier island to a storm is a simple shift landward. Waves lap over the top of the beach or dune and transport sand from the sea side of the island to the bay side, forcing a migration. The island keeps its form and may contain the same amount of sand, but the feature shifts to a more landward position.

This was not, however, what occurred during the 1856 hurricane. The waves did not simply lap over the island; rather, Isle Derniere was completely inundated by storm surge. The strong currents flowing bayward over Isle Derniere transported the sand farther landward than would have happened with waves periodically lapping over the top. This kind of inundation occurred on another Louisiana barrier island chain, called the Chandeleur Islands, during Hurricane Katrina in 2005. The islands were completely submerged by storm surge, and sand was stripped from the beaches and dunes, reducing the island's surface area by 80 to 90 percent.

During the 1856 hurricane, Isle Derniere was pushed beyond a tipping point from which it could not recover.

Survivors of the sinking of a ship adrift on a raft at sea

{ PART III }

THE
ISLAND
AND THE
AFTERMATH

Silence
Following
a Scream

We anticipate . . . that the storm has taken a wide range,
and that serious consequences have resulted. . . . There is a
painful rumor in town relative to Last Island, where a number
of our citizens are sojourning. The rumor is in fact too
terrible even for repetition.
—WEEKLY IBERVILLE SOUTH, AUGUST 14, 1856

In the early morning darkness of Monday, August 11, Reverend McAllister and the eleven others from the boardinghouse stepped down from the carousel to which they had clung through the night. The wind had calmed, the storm surge had ebbed, and what was left of the island now lay exposed. "Before daylight, I know not how long before," Reverend McAllister wrote, "the waters entirely abated and left us once more on dry land."

Soaked and chilled, they huddled together on the sand under a scavenged red quilt that was as drenched as they were. It offered some insulation and some comfort until dawn, when they could see the changed world around them. They were relieved, perhaps amazed, to be alive, knowing that they owed their survival to an amusement for children.

In the morning light, the whirligig was the only sign of human habitation that they could still detect around them. Where the boardinghouse had once stood, they saw only wave-smoothed sand, as if the structure had never existed, the wreckage swept away and disposed of in the bay.

They looked to the east along the beach toward the Village of Isle Derniere, toward the first cluster of buildings that should have been standing a half-mile away. Through the mist, they now saw nothing. Their relief over surviving the storm dissolved into concern for their fellow islanders. As a group, they started walking along the beach toward the village.

They soon passed bodies sprawled in the sand, the limbs contorted, the arms and legs strewn oddly, grotesquely. Then McAllister and the others jolted to a stop. Before them was a woman who was mostly buried. They could see only her "jeweled and lily hand . . . protruding from the sand, and pointing toward heaven."

Closer to the village, the reverend and the others froze again before the visage of a girl who was also partially buried. They could see her attractive face, her eyes looking up from the sand at them. They knew that only hours before she had been alive and well, enjoying life on the island with family and friends. Not far from her were a wife and husband lying together, positioned as if one was trying to save the other. What stunned them the most, however, was an infant they encountered wrapped in the now-rigid arms of its mother. Both were ghostly pale, as if the blood had run from their bodies.

The survivors from the boardinghouse must have felt terribly alone, wondering if the twelve of them were the only ones left alive on the island. "Sights like these suddenly presented," recalled McAllister, "gave a shock never to be forgotten, and called up certain feelings which no language can describe."

They pressed on toward where most of the people had lived. As they neared what they thought was the outer extent of the village, they confirmed that all of the fine two-story houses with their galleries were gone. The kitchens and stables and slave quarters were gone as well. They could see nothing remaining in the village, not even a foundation; the island had been swept clean. Everything and every-one was gone.

On their walk along the beach that day, McAllister and the oth-ers may not have noticed another change. The breakers and currents that had swept landward over the island during the storm had de-graded the beach. Before the storm, there had been small sand dunes scattered here and there along the shore, each standing a few feet high with a cluster of willowy beach grasses sprouting from its crest. Such grasses baffled the wind; the sand carried by the wind fell among the stems and built the dunes taller. On some of the barrier islands along the U.S. Atlantic and Gulf coasts, such dunes grew into promi-nent rims that ran parallel to shore just landward of the beach and served to contain the surge and waves of some storms, as levees con-tained some river floods.

Not on Isle Derniere, however. Its dunes were inconsequential before the hurricane, and nonexistent afterward. They had been flat-tened, eroded, like the small sand bank that had prevented the whirligig from turning before the sand was swept away. By wiping out any dunes and shaving the beach smooth, the waves and currents low-ered elevations below what they had been before the hurricane, leav-ing the strand vulnerable to further ravages.

A half-mile farther east from the edge of the village, the barren hull of the *Star* lay on the beach. The hold dripped with muddy, grimy filth that had collected over decades of carrying cargo along the waterways of Louisiana. Huddled in the midst of that filth were sur-vivors, about 150 of them, including W. W. Pugh.

He and members of his family had survived the night hanging on to the iron bands of a cistern behind the rubble of the destroyed hotel.

In the darkness of early morning, when the hurricane winds subsided and the sea retreated, Thomas Ellis left the *Star* and stumbled across the Pugh family. He led them back to the remains of the vessel, arriving after sunrise. With the heavy clouds lifting, they could see the destruction around them.

Only the largest timbers of the houses remained, scattered here and there across the sand. Everything else had been swept away. In the marsh on the bay side of the island, the wind and currents had laid the grasses flat, revealing numerous dead bodies.

On climbing down into the hold of the *Star*, Pugh was elated to see two members of his family who had lost their way in the storm. They had been among those whom Ellis and the crew had rescued from the water during the calm of the hurricane's eye.

Pugh's heart sank, however, after scanning the other faces crowded aboard the vessel's remains. There was no sign of his little Loula.

Near dawn, Michael Schlatre realized that he and Thomas Mille had survived the transit across Caillou Bay and were now floating over mainland marsh. They were lying side by side on the fallen wall that had become their raft. Around them, the tips of marsh grasses emerged above water that was about three and a half feet deep. Schlatre thought he knew where they were located from a pole he spotted soaring above the water. Such a pole marked the entrance to Turtle Bayou, a dozen miles landward of Isle Derniere, according to Schlatre.

Driven by the wind and current, the raft plowed through the flooded grasslands and then into a large lake, crossing it in an hour and a half before encountering the far shore and a submerged oyster bank. The raft scraped over the bank's crest and continued unimpeded. Schlatre knew they were again over marsh; tips had reappeared around them, the stems so pliant that they offered virtually no resistance to the craft's headway over a prairie tens of miles wide.

Schlatre began to worry again. They had reached the mainland, but if they were driven too far inland, rescuers would never find them. "It was death to go far up," he wrote later. He had no way to halt the raft's forward progress. Grabbing on to the tips of the grasses was useless: the raft was moving too quickly, too powerfully. On the other hand, if they stopped too soon, the storm surge could carry them back out into the bay when it retreated. He did not know which course was best for their survival. Even if he did know, he could do little to influence where the raft went. "Trusting Providence[,] we let it drive up the marsh at the Mercy of wind and current."

For three or four more hours, they were propelled inland, finally slowing about 10:00 AM. Schlatre was now able to reach his arm through the window opening in the center of their raft and grab handfuls of stems to first slow, then halt, their forward progress. Relieved, but too exhausted to consider their plight further, they slept for several hours.

When Schlatre finally awoke, he raised his head and examined the scene around them. "We were high & dry on the marsh on the most desolate looking spot that ever mortal saw, nothing but waste all around. Oh! Heavens I cried what is to become of us."

To many survivors, it seemed that every building on the island had been destroyed, but there was one that remained standing. It was the small stable whose walls were held vertical by pilings driven deep into the sand.

The stable provided a safe refuge for two survivors. One was an old horse that was nearing the end of its work life; the other was Richard, the body servant of Thomas Mille, who had failed to convince his master to send his family into the stable. "Had we gone into that outbuilding," Emma said later, "we would all have been saved."

Richard emerged after the storm to a barren island. A few people walked aimlessly through the sand, stunned, as if trying to fathom what had transpired.

Soon, however, a black woman, another slave, hurried up to him. She asked if he could assist an injured person on the beach who needed urgent attention. Richard set off across the sand in the direction that the woman pointed.

Michael Schlatre's raft was now aground and stationary in the marsh. His injuries during the storm made it impossible for him to rise to his feet. He could only lie on his left side; any pressure or jostling of his injured right breast and leg sent unbearable pain coursing through his body.

The weather remained miserable with rain and haze. Schlatre seemed oddly out of place still dressed in his Sunday clothes. They were soaked and soiled, his shirt ripped into shreds, exposing his upper torso to the elements.

Schlatre struggled to lift his head to detect where the raft had lodged. He pushed against the raft's wooden surface with his arms to elevate his eyes, but could rise no more than a foot and a half, not high enough to see above the marsh grasses that now soared around him. When the wind eased and the storm surge retreated back to the sea, the raft had nestled down into a stand of grasses. Stems now completely encircled the raft, rising above it three to five feet, as if the wooden wall had descended into a shallow hole.

Frustrated, Schlatre ordered Thomas Mille, who was sprawled next to him, to rise and report what he saw around them. Schlatre hoped to determine their location. He knew the shores of the bay and major bayous well, although he had little knowledge of the terrain away from the routes he typically steamed. He feared that they had been driven deep into the interior marsh where few people ever ventured.

Schlatre watched Mille struggle to his feet, dressed not in his Sunday best but in more durable bathing clothes, thick shirts, and boots that were better suited to the environment. Standing, Mille looked out over the grasses and tried to discern the surrounding terrain through the rain and haze. But he could not see far because his eyes had been blinded, he told Schlatre. The previous day, as the storm raged on the island, blowing sand had grated against his eyes, leaving the whites inflamed.

Schlatre pleaded with Mille to try harder, to try to make out any markers or distinctive features. He told Mille that their survival depended upon knowing their position in the marsh. Getting no results from Mille, Schlatre struggled again to see the terrain around them from his prone position. With his upper body propped up as high as possible, he peered through the surrounding grasses and was now able to discern two small isles he thought familiar. He pointed these features out to Mille, who cupped his hands over his eyes and was able to confirm the presence of the small islands. Schlatre concluded that he and Mille were well inland, some fifteen miles north of Isle Derniere.

Schlatre knew that no one would ever find them there, surrounded by an endless prairie of marsh. He noticed, however, that their raft had come to rest adjacent to a small bayou, like hundreds of others that meandered through these grasslands. Schlatre thought the thirty-foot-wide channel might offer them salvation; it appeared to drain toward Caillou Bay. He craned his neck to look down to the bayou's water, which was still dropping as the surge retreated, leaving the bed nearly dry. He told Mille that their only hope was to wait for high tide, then launch their raft into the channel and rely on the ebbing current to take them to Caillou Bay, where they might hail a steamer.

As they waited, the reality of being cast adrift set in. It had been twenty-four hours since their houses were destroyed and they jumped onto a raft together. During that time, they had taken nothing to drink. Mille cried out for water in anguish. Schlatre wrote, "A burning thirst now began to devour us."

The rain continued, and Schlatre considered how they might capture some of the water. He stuck out his tongue to savor a few drops, but soon found this was woefully unproductive. Schlatre wrote, "We longed for a piece of that ice they were using so prodigally in Plaquemine."

He then ripped a narrow shred of cloth from his shirt, wrung the salt water from it, and placed it at the lower end of a sloping board. The rain fell to the wood and ran down its surface to the cloth, saturating the material with freshwater. Taking the shred in his mouth, Michael twisted it, sucked it, generating a sip of water. He then showed Mille how to collect the rain and was struck by the satisfied expression on the man's face when he first drank from the rag.

Through Monday, they took turns with the rag, each one saturating and drinking from it three times, before passing it to the other. Schlatre recalled, "Heaven how good that water was."

In the Gulf of Mexico, steward James Frisbee and chief engineer Mr. Johnson had found no way to capture rain and satiate their thirst. They had been without water since the *Nautilus* capsized about thirty-six hours earlier. They had also been adrift about twelve hours longer than Michael Schlatre and Thomas Mille. The wreckage that had broken off the *Nautilus* and served as Frisbee and Johnson's lifeboat now rode easier in the Gulf as the heights of the waves slowly decreased and the time between waves slowly increased. The sea appeared less threatening, less confused. The jumble of waves during the storm was sorting out, transforming the water's surface into regular crests and troughs from the random peaks and holes to which the *Nautilus* had succumbed.

By now, Frisbee and Johnson would have been able to ease their grips on the raft. For the past day and a half, they would have had their fingers and hands clenched on to any hold available in a constant struggle to keep from being swept into the sea by wind and wave. During this period, they had had nothing to eat or drink. The lack of food would have depleted their strength, but it would not have soon threatened their lives. Some people have survived many weeks without eating. The lack of water, however, becomes life-threatening much sooner.

After thirty-six hours, Frisbee and Johnson would have lost significant amounts of body water. That they had no water available to replace the loss through drinking must have seemed odd; they were surrounded by a seemingly endless supply. But with its 3.5 percent salt content, seawater was poison—ingesting it would not have prolonged their lives but would have made them die sooner.

A 1 percent loss of body water triggers thirst. A 20 percent loss can cause shock. Assuming Frisbee and Johnson each weighed about 154 pounds and had a minimum daily loss from their bodies of a little over one quart per day—which unrealistically assumes that they would not lose any through sweating and exerting themselves to stay aboard the raft—they would be in shock and near death in about seven days. In the August heat, however, Frisbee and Johnson would have lost significantly more than one quart per day. If they were not rescued, they likely had fewer than seven days to live.

The prospects for rescue still seemed good, even though the weather remained ragged. An account from New Orleans for Monday, August 11, read, "The force of the gale . . . soon spent itself, tho' the sky continued murky as ever with sudden dashes of wind and rain." Unable to see the low-lying mainland, Frisbee and Johnson hoped the currents had not driven them far from the Mississippi. Surely there was a bustle of activity at the pilot station near the river mouth preparing search-and-rescue vessels to get under way.

As the hours wore on, their cravings for water grew. "The privation of water is justly ranked among the most dreadful of the miseries of our life," wrote a crewman whose ship sank in the mid-Pacific, leaving him adrift; "the violence of raving thirst has no parallel in the catalogue of human calamities." Ravaged by this violence, Frisbee and Johnson hoped and prayed for rescue, scanning the seas for the stack of an ocean steamer or the masts of a sailing ship.

But there was no bustle of activity on the mainland, no flotilla of vessels steaming through Southwest Pass and into the Gulf of Mexico to search for them.

Richard strode across the island in the direction that the black woman had indicated, toward the injured person on the beach. He passed corpses strewn about like garbage. In a world of rigidly defined classes of people, the remains were scattered indiscriminately, haphazardly. On this day, higher classes were no more favored over lower; slaves and planters lay side by side and sprawled on top of one another. "Both white and black in great numbers had been hurried to a sudden death," said one survivor.

Richard found Emma Mille sitting in the sand next to the water. Blood streamed down her face from a gaping head wound. Her left side bulged from internal bleeding, the blood pooling under her flesh. Though stunned by injury and her trial at sea, the eighteen-year-old woman was still conscious. She tried to pull together the tatters of her white muslin dress to cover herself as best she could.

Richard knew she was seriously injured. He could see that she was losing blood and knew she would probably die if he did not help her. He also knew that her father, his master, was missing, likely dead. The main house was gone, and except for Emma, there were no signs of survivors from the family. His master was not present to oversee his activities, to approve or deny his next move. The storm had shed his shackles and made him essentially a free man, leaving him able to make choices—and he made one.

Richard lifted Emma in his arms and carried her across the sand.

{ 14 }

Waiting

*The sea continued for days to lash about so angrily that no
vessel could come to our rescue; and the rain slacking only
at intervals, beat pitilessly upon us. We had no food. . . .
It is not worthwhile to try to convey an idea of the pangs of
hunger to those who have never felt them.*
—Reverend R. S. McAllister,
Southwestern Presbyterian, April 9, 1891

Before dawn on Tuesday, August 12, after drifting on a raft in the Gulf of Mexico for two days and two nights, the chief engineer of the *Nautilus*, Mr. Johnson, became irrational, deranged. In the darkness, James Frisbee tried to calm the man but was unable to bring him back to his senses. Both men were consumed by thirst. Their tongues had started to swell; their throats were dry.

Castaways commonly indulge in seawater to satisfy their thirst. Many of the crew of the USS *Indianapolis* who were thrown into the sea after the sinking of their ship during World War II went insane and then died after drinking seawater. Ingestion of salt can lead to hypernatremia, a medical condition with mortality typically greater than 50 percent. Victims are commonly stricken first by vomiting and then by mental changes, such as the delusions experienced by Johnson. Next, their breathing becomes labored, their seeing unfocused. Finally they slip into a coma.

Delirious, Johnson repeatedly tried to swim away from the raft, but Frisbee was able to stop him each time. When Frisbee later turned his back, however, Johnson escaped and disappeared into the waves, never to be seen again.

At dawn on Tuesday, Michael Schlatre could finally see that the tide had filled the channel next to where their raft had come to rest. He awakened Thomas Mille and ordered the man to use a sturdy plank as leverage to launch their raft into the channel. He hoped and prayed the ebbing tide would take them several miles out of the desolate reaches of the marsh and into Caillou Bay, closer to passing steamers.

With the rising sun illuminating the near-full channel, Schlatre was excited by the possibility of rescue. His hopes, however, were soon dashed. Picking up the plank, Thomas Mille made a feeble attempt to pry the weighty raft from the channel's margin and into the water, but he soon quit. Schlatre pressed the man to try again. Mille made another halfhearted attempt and then lay down and complained of pain in his stomach.

Schlatre lost hope. He now knew they were going to die in the marsh. He wrote later, "I . . . saw that I was counting on a broken reed."

Schlatre found a nail and inscribed his full name onto the side of their wooden craft. He then pulled off a shirt, tied it to the end of a plank, and drove the plank into the mud, leaving the shirt flying high as a flag. Should anyone pass by their location months or years hence, they would be attracted to the raft and would learn from the inscription on its side that some of the bones scattered on the wood and marsh belonged to him.

Through the remainder of the day, they lay on the raft side by side. As they rested, Mille pointed to a flock of birds in the sky. He told Schlatre that the birds would soon pick the remains of their dead bodies.

Schlatre was in constant pain from his injuries. When he had to shift position, he called for Mille to turn his injured leg. We were "two miserable creatures," recalled Schlatre, "half naked, starved, wounded, totally incapable of movement, . . . the rain pouring down on them in torrents, . . . the thunders rolled incessantly, . . . the tremendous claps . . . shook the very earth."

Schlatre now welcomed death to put an end to his agony.

On that Tuesday morning, the people of New Orleans still knew nothing of what had happened on Isle Derniere. During the storm the winds in the city had only reached Beaufort Force 8, which was described as a "fresh gale." At sea, such winds would push up moderate waves and, unlike Force 12, would be insufficient to split a man-of-war's mainsails. In New Orleans, the winds produced relatively minor damage, blowing down signs and ripping awnings.

Architect Thomas Wharton walked through the city, trying to assess the extent of damage. In the endless line of moored vessels along the levee's wharves, he spied the steamboat *Capitol*, whose dual stacks had been pushed flat by the wind. The steamer had limped into port from surrounding areas after the storm.

There were no reports of flooding in the city from Lake Pontchartrain, the broad, shallow body of water on the north side of New Orleans. Rather, the afternoon edition of the *Daily Picayune* reported devastation on the opposite side of the lake from New Orleans in the small community of Mandeville. There, surge and waves had swept away a dozen and a half bathhouses. This suggested that the center of the hurricane had passed to the west of the city, bringing winds from the south across the lake and driving a storm surge onto Pontchartrain's north shore. If the storm had passed to the east of the lake, the wind would have come from the north and blown water back into the city, a nightmare scenario that was realized 150 years later during Hurricane Katrina.

The *Daily Picayune* reported some loss of life during the storm, but on the river, not the sea. "Three Germans and two negroes, while attempting to cross the river during the storm . . . were all unfortunately drowned . . . a heavy sacrifice to elemental fury." As the days wore on, the people of New Orleans would learn that elsewhere the fury had been far more intense, and the sacrifice much heavier.

Thomas Wharton sensed this. As early as August 11, the day after landfall, he wrote in his journal: "The last thirty hours must have been a fearful time on the exposed Gulf shores, tho' in town we are so protected that we scarcely feel it."

There was no organized effort to investigate what might have happened along the coast. The weather continued on August 12 to be marginal: light rain turning heavy at night with some lightning. Even so, there were no clear preparations to launch a search-and-rescue effort once the weather cleared.

In the days after the storm, the editors of the *Daily Picayune* expressed shock that nothing was being done to assist those who had been stricken. "No boats had been sent out, and no relief of any kind had been provided by New Orleans . . . beyond . . . an occasional sailboat or inferior vessel, stocked with nothing to alleviate suffering or to satisfy hunger."

There was no response from city officials. No one took responsibility or command.

Emma Mille lay in the filth and sweat of the *Star*'s hold. Many others still clustered there as well, the wreck offering the only enclosed space on the island, the only shelter from the rain that would not quit falling. The vessel was half-buried in sand, its bow still attached to lines that stretched tight to anchors.

"I was very badly bruised," Emma said later. "I could not walk. I was very weak. Richard carried me to the hull of the *Star*—it was only a hull now." He also told her that she had lost her family. Everyone in her house was unaccounted for and feared dead except for Emma and Richard.

Dr. Alfred Duperier treated Emma's wounds. At the peak of the hurricane's winds, Duperier had escaped from the hotel as it flew apart. He took refuge for a short time in one of the surrounding small cottages, where he tied himself to an armoire. Before the wind switched, the storm surge from Caillou Bay inundated the island and the current flowed from bay to sea. Duperier was swept into the Gulf, where he spent twenty hours floating on the wooden wardrobe. After the hurricane's eye passed over the island, he was driven back to its sands.

Others floating in the Gulf were also miraculously returned to the island. "Towards [the *Star*] each one directed his path as he was recovered from the deep," recalled Dr. Duperier, "and was welcomed with tears by his fellow-sufferers, who had been so fortunate as to have escaped." In the hold, the survivors told stories of lost mothers and fathers, brothers and sisters, children and grandparents.

Although weak and exhausted, when Duperier reached the *Star* he immediately began caring for the injured. Many had been cut or impaled by flying debris; some had their legs or arms crushed by falling walls and roofs. Others needed only comfort; they were beyond help and would not see the next dawn. Through the day of August 12, however, Duperier returned again and again to Emma Mille.

He stitched her head wound and monitored her condition closely, concerned that she had lost a lot of blood and was weak. He had a deeper interest in the young woman, however, perhaps kindled by her sad circumstances. She was obviously distressed about the loss of her family. He wanted to help her in any way that he could. While Duperier tended to her, he began to feel the beginnings of a bond.

Some of the survivors who had sought shelter in the *Star* ventured outside into the gloom and rain to assess how many of their fellow islanders had succumbed to the storm. "The bodies of men, women and children were to be seen scattered all over the island," reported Alfred Duperier, "some in groups, some at a distance from each other, and many in positions indicating the ineffectual struggle they had made to save themselves, their relatives or friends."

The grim task of identifying the corpses and digging shallow graves in the sand had already begun. In the steamy late summer air, burial could not be delayed. The survivors believed that open decomposition would create the deadly miasma that many nineteenth-century physicians thought spread pestilence. Temporary signs marked the graves; the survivors anticipated that the bodies would be exhumed and their remains transported to the mainland for formal funerals and internments by their rescuers.

There were no indications, however, of anyone coming to their assistance. The survivors searched the bay behind the island for the telltale smoke streaming from the stacks of a rescue vessel, but detected only the whitecaps of rough water that would impede any approach to the island. They feared that they had been forgotten in the aftermath of the storm. Perhaps potential rescuers were dealing with other problems, or perhaps they thought it was still too dangerous to put to sea.

Whatever the reason, the survivors on the island, with little food and freshwater and many injured people among them, decided to do something to hasten their discovery. A small sailboat was salvaged from the debris, and two experienced seamen—the engineer from the *Star* and John Davis, the operator of a saloon on the mainland—volunteered to sail the vessel to Brashear City and find help. It is likely that they traveled a course taken by the *Star* on the steamer's regular run to the mainland. This route was hazardous for a tiny sailboat under conditions that remained rough, particularly for the transit across the open waters of the Gulf before ducking into Oyster Bayou.

On Tuesday morning, the survivors gathered along the shore of Village Harbor and wished the crew Godspeed before their sailboat departed. Many feared that the two men would become victims like so many others. Their fears were probably heightened when they quickly lost sight of the small sail among the bay's whitecaps.

About this time, survivors on Isle Derniere learned that they faced another unexpected danger. Those who were searching for bodies had discovered that the remains of some of their friends and family members had been plundered, some even mutilated. While identifying the island's dead, survivors reported, "you see the trace of fatal knife about the pockets of the victims, and a total absence of jewelry or other property." They rushed back to the *Star* to warn their fellow survivors that something on the island was terribly wrong.

Pirates had long prowled the central Louisiana coast. In the early 1800s, one of the most renowned, Jean Lafitte, had operated from Barataria Bay, a secluded location roughly fifty miles due south of New Orleans and about two-thirds of the distance along the coast from Isle Derniere to the mouth of the Mississippi. The bay opened into the Gulf of Mexico through an inlet wide enough for the passage of ocean-going sailing ships between two barrier islands—Grand Isle and Grand Terre. The rich marketplace of New Orleans had enticed Lafitte's band of privateers, known as Baratarians, to this coast that was relatively close to the city while being remote and wild enough to limit incursions by authorities.

Their center of operations was established on the sands of Grand Terre, not far from where the *Nautilus* capsized. From there they developed a lucrative business—plundering ships at sea and selling the stolen goods to New Orleans merchants at prices far below those of lawful suppliers. These goods included human beings. In 1808 a law was passed prohibiting the import of slaves into the United States; with supply suddenly limited, slave prices rose. Louisiana planters bought healthy black men for $800 to $1,000 apiece, while pirates bought them for $20 in Africa or $300 on the sugar plantations in Cuba. Overnight, slave smuggling became extremely lucrative, and the Baratarians fed the slave markets of New Orleans and the labor needs of sugar masters.

Although Lafitte and most of his Baratarians had left the Louisiana coast long before the 1856 hurricane, some of the original band remained. One of Lafitte's captains, Vincent Gambi, reportedly lived within thirty miles of Isle Derniere until the 1870s. Other accounts, however, maintain that Gambi was killed by his own men decades before the hurricane.

Regardless, after Lafitte departed, the swamps and isles of central Louisiana continued to harbor many who sought isolation from the legal authorities of the time. They included smugglers of goods and humans as well as wreckers, who preyed on shipwrecks and other disasters. In August 1856, some of these lawless men found their way to Isle Derniere.

They invaded the island in small boats and searched for the dead. They ripped earrings from the bodies of women and shirt studs from the bodies of men. Some of the victims were missing parts of their extremities. Their tissues had swelled as their bodies decomposed, making it difficult for the pirates to slip rings from fingers. The pirates simply clipped the fingers off. A female survivor saw some of the pirates at work. "One was actually seen to push the head of a person repeatedly down into the water, as if trying to take from him, and succeeded, doubtless, the speck of life remaining."

The islanders probably retreated to the *Star*, looking over their shoulders not only for the billowing smoke of an approaching rescue steamer but also for those who had plundered and mutilated the dead and who they feared might soon be coming for the living.

Aboard the *Star*, the retreating survivors would have told of something unusual they had seen on their forays along the island looking for bodies. Some searchers would have followed the route of the promenade to the east along the beach. After a few miles, though, they would have been forced to come to an unexpected halt. Before them was an expanse of water where none had been before the storm.

On the Coast Survey map of 1853, the island was continuous, extending uninterrupted for twenty-four miles. The new inlet opened just to the east of the Village of Isle Derniere, cutting through a narrow section of the island. The Isle Derniere had been severed into two parts, as if chopped by a meat cleaver.

{ 15 }

Rescue

Terror, grief and exposure had done the work of years; men of robust health and youthful appearance looked old and super-annuated; lovely, fascinating women were almost entirely bereft of youth and beauty; locks that rivaled the raven's wings were frosted with the snow of years; children forgot their joyous prattle, and put on the seriousness of mature age.
—ANNIE READ, LETTER TO THE DELTA
AFTER THE 1856 STORM

On Wednesday morning, August 13, heavy rain fell on New Orleans, continuing the series of downpours since Sunday's storm. It slacked off around midday, and the sun finally emerged—"to the great joy of our beclouded folks," according to the *New Orleans Commercial Bulletin*. That joy would be short-lived, however. By evening, the dense clouds and driving rain would return.

After days of wading to work and market through streets brimming with water a few feet deep, many residents of the city were frustrated. The services of New Orleans had been unable to alleviate the persistent flooding. Some of the steam-powered draining machines had failed to perform as designed and suck the standing water out of the city.

"That these machines should be out of order . . . just when they are particularly needed," wrote a reporter for the *Commercial Bulletin*, "is most provoking and calls for explanation." The disadvantaged, who lived in the low areas of the city away from the natural levees, suffered the most. The water was deepest in those areas, accumulating in lakes and ponds around tenements and leading to both inconvenience and disease.

Meanwhile, random bits of information about the past Sunday's gale were dribbling into the city. Many ships were overdue. The few that made it through the Gulf and up the river to New Orleans brought unsettling news that the storm at sea was far more intense than the conditions felt in the city. One of the arriving crewmen reported that "the 'rolling sweep' of the Gulf waves was extremely heavy" and had "convince[d] all of experience on board that a not far distant hurricane had produced it."

Another report from downriver of New Orleans closer to the Mississippi River mouth confirmed the severity of the conditions. "The storm that visited us . . . has proved the most destructive which has ever passed over this section of country. . . . The sea rose to a height that all the rice fields were four to five feet under water."

There were no newspaper reports of what had occurred on the Gulf coast barrier islands—although among the populace of New Orleans disturbing rumors had begun to circulate.

Rumors also swirled among the survivors on Isle Derniere, raising their level of anxiety. They chattered about a dead planter named Rochelle who had been found with a pocket sliced open and no sign of the $10,000 cash that he had carried with him, and about a young woman from New Orleans whose jewels worth $5,000 had been stripped from her lifeless body. Such stories were told in the filthy hold of the *Star*, where many of the survivors had sought shelter from the pirates as well from the rain and wind.

Far from the rule of lawful authorities, the pirates attempted to prey on the living as well as on the dead. "A negro and [a] white man came up boldly to the wreck of the *Star* and shook bundles of gold and valuables at the unfortunates," reported the *Daily Picayune*. They were trying to unnerve the survivors so they would surrender their valuables without a fight. Captain Abraham Smith emerged from the remains of the *Star* and stood defiantly in front of the pirates. They hesitated, and then retreated. Rather than attempt to overpower the captain and pillage those hidden inside the hull, they returned to the easier task of searching for booty among the dead.

The survivors wondered if the looters would return in force and try to rush the *Star*. They wondered if the two men dispatched aboard the small sailboat the previous day had survived the journey and sounded the alarm. They wondered if rescuers would arrive before the pirates returned.

The heavy rains added to the misery of Michael Schlatre and Thomas Mille. During Tuesday night they had given up and readied themselves for death—indeed, they welcomed it. Now, on Wednesday morning, Schlatre saw an opportunity that gave him a surge of strength. "I was now desperate, cared for nothing, pain in breast & broken leg were as nothing to compare to our helpless situation." The heavy rain had added to the tide. The water was above the muddy surface of the marsh and partially floated their raft. To lift the wooden wall higher, he rolled off its surface and into the water. He demanded that Mille roll off as well, to float the raft even higher. Then, using a plank for leverage, they were able to nudge the raft into the bayou where a wild flow ran toward the sea.

They scrambled aboard, and the raft shot downstream. It rushed onward, driven solely by the current for roughly a mile, and then suddenly slowed. Their exhilaration melted away; they had stopped three miles short of the open bay and passing steamers. Schlatre thought that rainwater funneling into the bayou had carried them downstream until it met the opposing flow of a rising tide. He knew that they had to wait for the tide to turn again—for the water in the channel to change direction and ebb toward the sea—before they could make further progress.

They felt stabbing pangs of hunger. It had been sixty-two hours since they had eaten, save for some grass that left a bitter taste in their mouths. When Schlatre rolled back into the water to grab more marsh grass, his fingers felt the hard, sharp edges of shells. They were mussels—many of them massed together along a bayou bank. He gathered dozens of them, threw them onto the raft, and crawled back aboard. Using his shoe as a hammer, he broke them open and, with Mille, greedily feasted on the meat.

While they waited for the tide to turn, Schlatre used his arms to raise his prone body above the raft so he could look for rescue vessels. First, he saw a sail, then the stacks of a steamer. He thought it was the *Star* leaving the mainland through the mouth of Oyster Bayou and entering the Gulf of Mexico.

Schlatre could now confirm their location: they were in Bayou Delarge on the mainland opposite the west end of Isle Derniere. He figured that they were a half-dozen miles east of the steamer, which he saw turn toward the island after entering the Gulf. He felt a surge of hope, and a sense of urgency. "I knew that the boat was taking the remaining people off the island, and once all were gone, she would return no more."

James Frisbee was comforted by the sight of other survivors from the *Nautilus* drifting around him. One of them rested on a large log, with roots that rose more than five feet above the water. By Wednesday, Frisbee's makeshift raft had begun to break up. When the large log drifted near, he swam to join the man lying across it, a passenger named John Wells who was from Brazos Santiago.

When Frisbee reached the log, however, he could no longer find Wells. The dehydrated man had gone limp and slipped away. "He went over before I reached him," said Frisbee, "and I saw him no more."

Frisbee tried to make himself comfortable on the log, pulling his body as far out of the water as possible, but every move made him wince. Long-term immersion in seawater would have left his skin marked with red sores, some no wider than the diameter of a writing pen, others spanning half the width of his back.

He had endured over three days with no freshwater, save for the few drops of rain that fell directly into his mouth or that he could capture in his hands. His body had dried out so severely that his tongue was parched and stiff, and he could no longer sweat or urinate. His thoughts were likely becoming cloudy, drifting toward confusion.

Earlier that Wednesday, long before dawn, a hotel in Brashear City had bustled with unusual excitement and activity. Normally in the early hours the building near the bank of the Atchafalaya River would have been dark and quiet to allow guests to sleep undisturbed. This morning, however, it blazed with lamplight and was filled with chatter. Inside one of its rooms, a message was quickly penned to the editors of the *Daily Picayune*. Later that morning, the letter would be handed to a conductor aboard the newly completed Opelousas Railroad for delivery to the newspaper in New Orleans.

BRASHEAR CITY HOTEL
WEDNESDAY, AUGUST 13, 1 AM

Eds. Pic.—John Davis has just got here from Last Island in a small sailboat, and reports Last Island entirely swept of all the houses by the storm of Sunday night, and that 187 lives were lost by the disaster. This is the amount hurriedly ascertained at present.

It had taken Davis and the engineer from the *Star* who accompanied him sixteen to eighteen hours to sail the winding route from Isle Derniere to Brashear City. Upon arrival, they roused the sleeping community with news of disaster on the island and of the survivors' dire need of assistance. This set in motion the first concerted rescue effort in the aftermath of the hurricane. Cries went out for the crew of the steamer *Major Aubrey*, moored at a nearby wharf, to prepare to get under way for Isle Derniere.

Near dawn, another brief note to the *Picayune* was dashed off, updating the breaking developments.

BERWICK'S BAY [NEAR BRASHEAR CITY]
AUGUST 13, 1856

In great haste. We have just sent the *Major Aubrey* to the assistance of the sufferers, who are now clinging to the hull of the steamboat *Star*. She starts hence in one hour, only waiting to wood [take on fuel] at this place. Respectfully Yours, Eugene Daly

The *Major Aubrey* fired her boilers and steamed down the Atchafalaya River. Upon entering the Gulf through Oyster Bayou, the captain turned the vessel to the east and churned along the mainland shore, toward Caillou Bay. From his raft in the marsh, Michael Schlatre thought he saw the *Star* entering the Gulf, but it was the *Major Aubrey* on its rescue mission to Isle Derniere.

When the *Aubrey* approached the bay side of the island, the captain would have scoured the horizon ahead for a landmark that would lead him to the mouth of Village Harbor. He was accustomed to seeing the long line of prominent buildings of the Village of Isle Derniere breaking above the horizon. His primary landmark was the most prominent building at the east end of the village, Muggah's Hotel. This day, however, the horizon was smooth, unbroken.

The captain found the proper course through trial and error. Nosing into Village Harbor, the crew saw some debris on the sand ahead, splintered and scattered. Amid this debris was the beached hull of an unrecognizable vessel. People emerged from its bowels and ran to the steamboat landing—or to what remained of the wooden piles and deck planks—to greet their rescuers.

The captain and crew realized the magnitude of what had happened here from the stench. For three days, bodies had been decomposing in the swelter—some were interred in porous sandy graves, while others were still unfound and hidden among marsh grasses.

On Wednesday evening and Thursday morning, Michael Schlatre and Thomas Mille lay together on the marsh, partially naked and nearly helpless. They had secured the raft and crawled into the marsh to sleep, although they found little peace. "The land crabs would pinch me every few minutes," recalled Schlatre, "causing me to shift position to avoid the infernal animals."

During the night it had rained, and Schlatre again drank from a rag that he placed at the low end of an inclined board to sop the collected drops. He worked at it for hours, gathering water, satiating his thirst. Mille, however, did not want to use the rag. He had an unsettled abdomen and no thirst—symptoms of severe dehydration. "He was no longer of further use to me," wrote Schlatre, "so soon as he would sit upright a moment, he would nauseate, complaining much of his stomach."

At midday on Thursday, when the tide began to ebb, the men crawled back on board their raft and nudged it into the channel to continue drifting with the flow toward Caillou Bay. Schlatre, despite his injuries, steered with a makeshift paddle, trying to keep the raft in the center of the bayou where the water ran most quickly. Mille lolled on the wooden surface, listless. On both banks of the channel, they started to see debris from Isle Derniere. Shattered lumber and pieces of houses littered the mud and grasses.

Soon, however, the raft slowed again, fighting a headwind and an opposing tidal current. Schlatre knew they were running out of time.

He began to paddle furiously, trying to make headway toward the open bay. "I thought that I had labored . . . on this raft, but [my efforts] were . . . nothing compared to the labor that I performed in the next two and a half hours . . . now prying, now paddling, now pushing, and the heavy thing moved like a snail."

With little help from the sick and complaining Thomas Mille, Schlatre coaxed the raft the final two miles down the bayou to near the open water of Caillou Bay. Exhausted, he secured the raft to a bank. He and Mille crawled into the marsh and lay down to rest.

James Frisbee's tongue was increasingly swollen, dry, and hard. His muscles cramped; he felt nauseous and weak. His system was approaching shock. He had drifted on debris in the Gulf of Mexico with virtually nothing to drink for more than four days. Still losing body water at a rapid rate in the hot weather, he was near death.

Then he spied a wooden door floating nearby. It must have been ripped from one of the wrecked ships. Summoning his remaining strength, he dragged the door onto the tree trunk and wedged it among roots roughly three feet above the water. He crawled onto the flat piece of wood and slept.

Frisbee had grabbed the panel door from the sea to improve his comfort. He did not realize that the door would be his salvation.

A full load of one hundred survivors, including the most severely injured from the storm, packed onto the decks of the *Major Aubrey*. With no more room on the vessel, over one hundred additional survivors had to remain behind to await the arrival of a second steamer. The *Major Aubrey* slowly backed off the bay-side beach of Isle Derniere and turned north to steam out of Village Harbor toward the mainland. Many of the survivors who crowded the vessel's open decks, passageways, and interior spaces wore bandages or slings. Some lay on litters;

others sat on the deck. They were disheveled and soiled after enduring the storm and days in the grimy, sweaty confines of the *Star's* hold.

W. W. Pugh was one of those aboard. His bony, angular face
had turned wasted, withered, his skin pallid, almost white, ghostly.
Dried blood and seawater had matted his hair into a tangled mass. He
and the others around him mourned the human losses during the
storm, but they also knew that many more of them would have perished if the *Star* had not returned to the island. The captains of that
vessel could have decided to remain on the mainland and wait out the
storm. But they did not, and many lives were saved.

With Dr. Alfred Duperier, Pugh organized a meeting of the survivors aboard the vessel. Votes were cast that affirmed a resolution
honoring Captains Thomas Ellis and Abraham Smith "for their noble
and humane efforts to preserve human life."

At 9:00 PM that night, the *Major Aubrey* docked at the terminus
of the Opelousas Railroad near Brashear City. Survivors who lived in
eastern Louisiana, like W. W. Pugh and his family and Reverend
McAllister, would board a special train to take them toward their
homes. An observer described Pugh as he disembarked the steamer.
"In his arms he held with a convulsive grasp the dead body of his infant [his little Loula], the only one out of seven which he had not been
permitted by an Allwise Providence to save."

The train stopped in Thibodaux (pronounced *Tib-a-doe*), a small
town thirty-five miles southwest of New Orleans, where Reverend
McAllister was the recently hired minister of the First Presbyterian
Church. McAllister was known as a sickly man who needed frequent
convalescences. That was why he had gone to Isle Derniere—he
thought it was a healthy place where he could grow stronger, and it
nearly killed him. After returning home, however, the reverend's per-
severance and resourcefulness during the storm became well known,
and he acquired new respect among his flock.

The Pugh family also left the train at Thibodaux; their Woodlawn plantation was about fifteen miles upstream from the town on Bayou Lafourche. Dirt roads ran along the banks of the bayou, allowing horse-drawn carriages to take the family to their home, but the trip was likely tedious. The road would have been blocked here and there by trees and branches that had fallen during the hurricane. The wheels would have mired in mud. The storm surge had traveled up the bayou and raised the water level in Thibodaux by four feet, spilling over the banks and turning unpaved roads into swamps.

Slaves would have cleared debris from the roadway and pushed the carriages through mud holes. When the Pugh family reached their Woodlawn plantation, the carriages would have stopped in front of the massive white columns at the front of their manor house. W. W. Pugh carried the lifeless body of his toddler around the side of the two-story mansion to his family's cemetery plot surrounded by an iron fence in the rear.

Loula was laid to rest among the prominent monuments and vaults of a dozen or more of her ancestors; eventually her grave was marked with an unassuming tombstone that, at two feet high and one and a half feet wide, matched her stature.

Today the mansion is gone, torn down, but the cemetery remains intact next to a sugarcane field. The engraving on the gravestone can still be read:

OUR LITTLE LOULA
Daughter of
W.W. Pugh and
Josephine Nicholls,
Born March 29th 1855
and perished during the
storm at Last Island
August 10th 1856

When the *Major Aubrey* arrived on the mainland, Dr. Alfred Duperier and the other survivors who lived in western Louisiana were transferred to a different steamer that took them to the rich sugar country along Bayou Teche (pronounced Tesh). Accompanying the doctor was his patient Emma Mille. Alfred had wrapped her stitched head wound in bandages. Emma recalled later that Duperier "learned that my parents had been lost and that I was an orphan. He asked if I would go with him on the relief boat to New Iberia to his mother's home." She agreed.

The steamer puffed to the west on Bayou Teche, which was described by Charles Dudley Warner in the late nineteenth century as "very picturesque by reason of its tortuousness and the great spreading live-oak trees, moss-draped, that hang over it." During the voyage, the survivors witnessed destruction unlike anything the inhabitants had ever seen along the Teche. Roofs had been stripped from buildings. Not one sugar mill was still standing. In fact, the hurricane had brought the sugar industry to its knees. The steamer passed field after field of prostrated cane: stalks had been bent flat to the ground by the wind. After the bumper sugar production of 1853, which coincided with the killer yellow fever epidemic in New Orleans, cane production during 1856 dropped 68 percent from the previous year, the lowest production in Louisiana in decades.

The steamer continued up the Teche for fifty miles, stopping at plantations and towns and delivering survivors to their homes and families and friends. At the end of the voyage was New Iberia, a thriving community composed of mostly small homes, a bustling main street, and a few majestic mansions covered in roses on the banks of the bayou. One of these mansions was called *Shadows on the Teche;* the bodies of two victims of the Isle Derniere hurricane would be buried there.

The steamer ultimately landed near the commercial center of New Iberia, where townspeople had gathered to meet the survivors.

Emma probably slept during much of the voyage, but after the vessel docked she would have been jostled awake as her chair was lifted from the deck. She may not have known what was happening, but when she twisted around she would have seen her doctor. He was carrying her, chair and all.

With Emma in his arms, Alfred proceeded down the gangway to the landing and toward the gathered townspeople. They would have been quiet, as if fearing news of a lost friend or loved one. The townspeople parted, making a walkway for Dr. Duperier to carry Emma to his family's home, a gray-stuccoed manor on the north side of the bayou. Here, Alfred's mother cared for Emma's wounds.

She "was so good to me," Emma would say years later. "My own could not have been kinder."

{ 16 }

Renewal

The house, which is now the convent near the bridge that
crosses the Teche, is where we first lived. My name is cut on
a window with my diamond engagement ring.
—Emma Mille Duperier, *Times*
Picayune, April 14, 1936

T hroughout south Louisiana, returning survivors of the hurricane
began to resume their normal lives, while hope for finding additional survivors diminished. The *New York Daily Times* reprinted a letter from Dr. Duperier, dated Thursday, August 14, reporting that Michael Schlatre and Thomas Mille were among the dead. Nothing had been heard from long overdue vessels like the steamship *Nautilus* and the sailing ship *Manilla*. An additional rescue steamer had followed the *Major Aubrey* to Isle Derniere and transported the remaining survivors to the mainland. Anyone who had been on Isle Derniere or on ships at sea and had not been confirmed alive were believed to be dead.

With the first survivors returning to their homes on the mainland, the stories of pirates preying on victims of the hurricane began to circulate through the plantations and towns and cities of Louisiana. The populace was at first shocked, then enraged. Within a few days, the *Daily Picayune* described the reaction of the people.

"EXCITEMENT ON THE LAFOURCHE—A gentleman informs us that there is much excitement on the Lafourche and the Teche, caused by the reported mutilation of the bodies of the dead, by the oystermen at Last Island."

The *Picayune* tempered its article by saying that the reports had not been confirmed and might contain exaggerations. Regardless, as the survivor stories were told and rumors grew and spread, plans began to take shape to mete out justice and retribution—not necessarily in that order.

At the same time, operations along the coast began to focus less on rescuing survivors and more on recovering bodies and goods. Some family members of the missing made grim plans to visit the Isle Derniere and search for the remains of lost loved ones. Underwriters planned to deploy a steam towboat, the *F. M. Streck*, to probe the remote bays and islands of the central Louisiana coast and recover as much cargo as possible from shipwrecks.

Except for financiers who would benefit from insurance settlements, the voyage of the *Streck* generated little interest among the public. Its departure from New Orleans was announced in a newspaper in a few curt sentences. The interest level would soon change, though, as would the presumption that there were no more survivors to be found.

Startled, Michael Schlatre suddenly sat up in the marsh. It was 3:00 AM, Friday, August 15, and he was trying to sleep. "Oh! God of heavens," he wrote later. "A stream of light from towards the island told me there was a steamer coming."

Schlatre roused Thomas Mille, but they had no way to signal the crew in the darkness. Helpless, they watched and listened to the steamer chug past.

Around dawn, Schlatre felt a renewed surge of excitement when he spotted another steamboat approaching, one he believed to be his own. With the size and shape of the *Blue Hammock*, it drew within three-quarters of a mile of them, close enough that Schlatre could see reflections of the furnace fire on the water. He knew the pilot was setting his course based on the point in the marsh shore near where they were marooned. "We cried aloud with our feeble voices hallowing with all our might, all in vain, she passed like a thing of life, her long black smoke streaming behind."

Schlatre's excitement turned to frustration, then anger. After almost dying of thirst, after struggling to reach the bay, the rescue boats, including his own, just steamed past them without even slowing. "We cried in the bitterness of our souls at the thought."

The two men crawled back aboard their raft, and Schlatre paddled them to a shell bank that stood two feet higher than the surrounding marsh surface. Here, he told Mille, they could die more comfortably than in the wet and muddy grasslands. Looking at Mille, Schlatre knew that death was not distant. Thomas Mille's eyes were set deep into hollows, and his breaths came too rapidly, too weakly.

As Schlatre settled on the shell bank, he pulled off the remains of his clothes and looked at his injured leg for the first time since the storm. From foot to hip, the skin had turned purple; dried blood covered his drawers. His kneecap floated as if the ligaments holding it had all been broken or stretched to their limits. In order to move his leg, he had to first use his hands to shift the kneecap into place.

After being immobile for days, he was somehow able to rise to his feet and limp about—and that was when he saw something small and white across the bay. Slowly, it grew larger. It was a sail.

Schlatre gripped a flag of clothing in his hand and frantically waved it back and forth above his head. Flying higher was another

light-colored flag that he had fixed to the end of a scavenged wooden
pole. As the vessel closed to within a half-mile, Schlatre felt an immense relief; he watched the crew lower and then immediately raise
their mainsail.

"You are seen they said to me."

On Sunday, August 17, two days after the rescue of Schlatre and
Mille from the mainland marsh, James Frisbee remained adrift
in the Gulf of Mexico, lying atop the door that was wedged flat among
the roots of the floating tree. He had been without freshwater for a
week, long enough to kill most men. This day, however, it had rained
hard, and he noticed water collecting in the recessed panels of the
door. He lowered his lips to them and, moving from one panel to another, consumed about a half-pint of freshwater, enough to help him
stay alive for another twenty-four hours.

The next day, August 18, Frisbee saw two vessels drawing near.
One was the steam-powered towboat *F. M. Streck*, searching for lost
cargo in the Gulf off Barataria Bay, near Jean Lafitte's former lair. The
other was a schooner that the *Streck* had under tow. Somehow Frisbee
found the strength to swim for the vessels. He reached the schooner
first and scrambled up its side like a man possessed. With few clothes
on his body, he jumped down to the main deck and raced across it for
the ship's water barrels. The officers on deck, who believed that too
much water, drunk too quickly, could be injurious to a dehydrated person, physically restrained him.

When the news was received in New Orleans that a crewman of
the *Nautilus* had been found alive, accusations flew. Authorities were
condemned for not doing enough to save those who survived the initial sinking. Two ship captains reported that, when she foundered, the
Nautilus was probably less than fifteen to eighteen miles from Southwest Pass. If rescue vessels had been sent to sea immediately after

the wind and waves calmed, they argued, many more crew and passengers would have been saved.

On Tuesday, August 19, the steamboat *Texas* steamed into Village Harbor and wound its way toward the destroyed landing behind where Muggah's Hotel once stood. Grim-faced men stood on deck with rifles cradled in their arms and pistols strapped to their sides. They had the eyes of hunters, and they scanned the sands of Isle Derniere, looking for the sudden flurry of game flushed from hiding. The search-and-rescue operations on the island had been brought to a close. All survivors and the bodies that could be found had been returned to the mainland. The hunters, however, were just starting their work. They were tasked with capturing and delivering justice to the pirates who had plundered the dead. "It is to be hoped," a letter-writer related to the *Daily Picayune*, "that these demons in human shape will meet with their just deserts."

While the armed men from the steamer divided into posses and fanned out across the island, a fifty-four-year-old man walked down the gangway with a different mission and a burden that his riches could not lighten. Samuel Stewart had overcome his Irish background to become one of the wealthiest men in New Orleans. He was a developer who had constructed the Pontalba Apartments and their famed cast-iron balconies that overlooked Jackson Square in the heart of the French Quarter.

Stewart's eldest son, Seymour, had been on Isle Derniere celebrating his twenty-first birthday. Samuel had waited for news of the fate of his son and prayed that he would be one of the survivors. But Seymour had not been among those rescued on Isle Derniere and brought back to the mainland. He was also not among the recovered bodies. There was no sign of him, no word about whether he was alive or dead.

The lack of news gave Samuel at least a glimmer of hope. He may have heard of the miraculous rescues of Michael Schlatre, Thomas Mille, and James Frisbee. Why couldn't his son have survived the storm and its aftermath as well?

Now, though, standing on Isle Derniere and sensing the pall of death that hung over the island, any hope that Samuel still harbored for his son being alive diminished. At best he might find evidence of what had happened to Seymour. He knew that search teams had scoured the island and did not find him. But Samuel had to try himself.

For many hours, under a baking sun, he walked the island searching for his boy. He was almost ready to give up when he came across a body in a secluded location.

It was bloated and degraded beyond recognition, but had about the same size and hair color as his son. Beyond those nonspecific characteristics, however, there was nothing that confirmed it was Seymour. Fortunately for Samuel, however, the pirates had not found and plundered the body. He examined the dead man's pockets and must have felt shock, mixed with profound relief, that his task had come to an end.

Inside were the twenty-one coins that Seymour had received from his mother in celebration of his birthday.

The armed men from the mainland tracked down and captured six of the pirates. They were now being held in secured rooms aboard the steamer *Texas* in Village Harbor. Posses still swarmed across the island, closing in on another group of the plunderers, while some of the men from the mainland searched and questioned the prisoners.

One of the captured pirates was discovered carrying a piece of jewelry, an expensive ring. After being whipped and threatened with hanging, he led some of the armed men to the hidden body of the woman from whom the ring had been stolen. It was Emma's sister-in-law, Althee Mille. There was no sign of her baby.

Incensed, the men nearly executed every captured pirate with no proceedings of justice. To them, the verdict was crystal clear: they had the evidence, and they had the guilty parties, so why waste time in a perfunctory court of law? "Those already taken had a very narrow escape from a summary disposition, so great is the exasperation against them," wrote the editors of the *Daily Picayune*. In the end, "calmer counsels prevailed and they remain for deliberate, though we trust not tardy or timid justice."

The editors' trust was satisfied; what happened next on the island was neither tardy nor timid. After two more pirates were captured and brought to the *Texas*, the steamer became not only a jail but also a courthouse. On the evening of August 19, the captain of the steamer selected a jury of twelve, and the proceedings got under way. Overnight, eight Swiss, Portuguese, and Spanish men were tried for crimes against the dead and helpless following the Isle Derniere hurricane. Two of them were found guilty as charged and sentenced to death.

In the mid-nineteenth century, the usual method of carrying out a death sentence was by hanging from a gallows or tree. Descriptions of the island suggest, however, that no large living trees remained, and after spending the night trying the accused, little energy was available to build even a makeshift gallows from debris. Hence, as Sothern suggested in *Last Island*, the sentences were probably carried out by a firing squad.

The two condemned men were dragged from the *Texas* and forced to march westward down the beach, past where the Schlatre and Mille houses once stood, past the wave-swept location of the boardinghouse where Reverend McAllister watched the waves build. An hour and a half after daylight, near the western end of Isle Derniere, shots rang out and the sentences of the court were fulfilled. The witnesses and executioners then trudged back to the *Texas* and were under way for the mainland by late afternoon.

Samuel Stewart was aboard the vessel when it left Village Harbor, accompanied by a metal coffin containing his son. In the days ahead, Seymour would be interred in a family vault under a monument at Metairie Cemetery, now known as Lake Lawn Metairie, near New Orleans. Samuel felt comfort in knowing that someday he would join his son in that vault, where their remains would rest side by side forever.

Also on August 19, Captain Rogers of the *Manilla* was recovering from a mangled right leg in New Orleans at Touro Infirmary, which is still open to patients today. He had broken the limb when his ship tried to run from the storm and lost its sails in high winds and heavy seas. After the vessel was driven aground on Timbalier Island on August 10, he was one of twenty-nine crew and passengers who slipped into the dark surf on makeshift rafts and struggled toward the beach through huge breakers. Nineteen survived the trip; ten drowned.

Fishermen found the survivors on Timbalier Island and transported Captain Rogers and the others to New Orleans in a small sailboat. After their ordeal, some of the passengers were too nervous to risk passage on such a small vessel and chose to wait on the island for a larger one to pick them up. The crew left behind a full cargo of undelivered goods that were released into the surf when the *Manilla* broke apart. Littered along central Louisiana's barrier islands from near the mouth of the Mississippi westward to Isle Derniere were casks of wines and brandies. Local lore maintains that for years after the storm fishermen were catching in their nets some of Bordeaux's finest.

The crew of the sailboat that discovered Michael Schlatre and Thomas Mille brought them to the home of the vessel's captain on the mainland. There, on Tuesday, August 19, despite receiving nourishment and hydration, Thomas Mille died.

Schlatre recovered some of his strength, and two days after Mille's death a steamer carried him to Plaquemine. At his nearby plantation on Bayou Jacob, physicians tended to his leg and chest injuries. Save for a persistent limp, he would fully recover.

Soon after his return to Plaquemine, though, questions were posed to Schlatre. The hurricane had killed his wife, six sons, and daughter, yet he survived. How did this happen? Could he have done more to save his family?

Within several months of returning home, Michael Schlatre wrote his account of the storm, likely in response to the nagging questions about the loss of his family, and perhaps to correct the perception that Thomas Mille had been a hero. One of the initial reports on the storm in Plaquemine's newspaper, the *Southern Sentinel*, had hailed Mille for coming to the assistance of the injured Schlatre on Isle Derniere.

In great detail, Schlatre recounted the deaths of his wife and children and the unseemly behavior of Mille. At the end of his account, he described himself as "a man in full health, a good constitution, a stout and courageous heart who puts his trust in the ruler above." He assumed no responsibility for what had happened to any of his family members during the Isle Derniere hurricane.

Schlatre gave the document to his wife's parents to answer their questions about the loss of their daughter and grandchildren. Whether they accepted his explanations was unclear. Later, his in-laws reportedly gave the manuscript to writer Lafcadio Hearn, who used it as background for his novel *Chita: A Memory of Last Island*, which was based roughly on the storm. Schlatre's verbatim account would eventually be published in the *Louisiana Historical Quarterly* in the 1930s.

As soon as he was physically able, Michael Schlatre went back to work on his plantation raising sugarcane, yet without much initial success; as elsewhere in Louisiana, the 1856 crop was destroyed, the cane prostrated, laid flat to the ground by the wind.

Eight months after the storm, Schlatre remarried and eventually had seven more children; like his first family, they were six sons and one daughter.

In spite of Schlatre's detailed account of the storm, the questions about what happened to his first family never stopped, but over time they turned to whispers—which still can be heard in Plaquemine today.

Emma's head wound healed slowly, although her condition improved enough that her brother-in-law soon traveled to New Iberia and brought her home to Milly Plantation on Bayou Plaquemine. On Emma's departure from the Duperier home, Alfred gave her a little book filled with religious poems. She opened it after arriving home and found a note hidden among the pages. She never forgot the words written by the doctor. "As Divine Providence saved us miraculously, it must be that we are destined for each other."

Also on arrival, Emma learned that her father had died after he and Schlatre were rescued from the marsh. Thomas Mille was laid to rest in Plaquemine in St. John's Cemetery under a large stone monument that still stands today. A nearby tomb contains the remains of Emma's sister-in-law, Althee Labauve Mille. The body of Althee's baby was not interred with her; it was never found. Neither was the body of Emma's brother, Homer. His name is engraved on the monument of his mother's tomb, also in St. John's Cemetery. With the deaths of her family members, Emma was left with only two sisters, one at the convent school, and the other married to the man who brought her home.

Two weeks after Emma returned to Milly Plantation, Alfred Duperier traveled there to call on her. "He said that he would never forget me," Emma recalled later. "He was a very handsome, prepossessing young man [and] said that he wished to marry me. . . . And, well, what could I do but accept."

They were wed on December 8, 1856, only four months after they were thrown together on the sands of Isle Derniere.

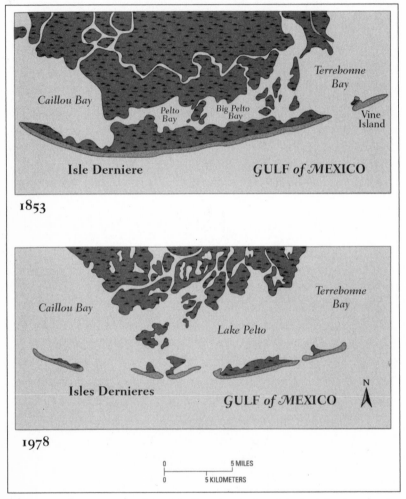

Long-term deterioration of the Isle Dernieres, showing the island narrowing and new inlets that were cut through the island during a span of 125 years

Forest
in
the
Sea

Just where the waves curl . . . you may discern a
multitude of blackened, snaggy shapes protruding
above the water,—some high enough to resemble
ruined chimneys, others bearing a startling likeness to
enormous skeleton-feet and skeleton-hands. . . .
These are bodies and limbs of drowned oaks.
—LAFCADIO HEARN, CHITA: A MEMORY
OF LAST ISLAND (1889)

On October 10, 1935, a reporter motored into New Iberia on assignment from the New Orleans *Times Picayune*. He parked his boxy automobile on West St. Peter Street in front of number 225, a stately home alive with children laughing and piano playing. He was greeted at the door and invited into the parlor to conduct an interview with the only survivor of the Isle Derniere hurricane who was still alive.

Emma Mille Duperier was celebrating her ninety-eighth birthday, playing melodies of her own composition at a rosewood piano, surrounded by a crush of friends and many of her two dozen children, grandchildren, great-grandchildren, and great-great-grandchildren. She still walked up and down stairs without help and worked tirelessly for charities and her church. Acquaintances and friends called her Tante (Aunt) Emma.

She had come to New Iberia as a bride and spent nearly eight decades there, the first five joyfully with Alfred, who passed away in 1904. She described her life since the storm as "happy years . . . raising a family and watching . . . [them] grow up."

Emma told the *Times Picayune* reporter the story of what had happened on Isle Derniere during the summer of 1856. She had been asked over the years whether Lafcadio Hearn's popular 1889 novel *Chita: A Memory of Last Island* was a true story. In that book, the Isle Derniere hurricane swept ashore during the ball at the hotel. The music played and people danced while the hotel and ballroom were torn apart by wind and waves. The storm actually came ashore about eighteen hours after the ball concluded. No one was dancing as disaster struck, although such a scene has long been part of Louisiana lore. Emma had been asked over and over whether she was Chita, the young Creole woman in Hearn's novel who was found after the storm and raised by fishermen. No, she would reply, that was not her. Her narrative about the storm was different and true.

It was also not complete. The story of the hurricane continued long after the rescue steamers brought the survivors and bodies to the mainland, long after the pirates were captured and the guilty executed. The Isle Derniere had degraded during the storm. And over the following century and a half, the deterioration of this land continued.

Three decades after the hurricane, Catharine Cole, the first full-time woman reporter for the *Times Picayune*, chartered a sailboat and visited Isle Derniere. She found it to be "the curse of God—where flowers bloom not, where no clean nor honest life is, and where even the bird hunters camp with fear and trembling, because of the ghosts of those who were drowned here during the storm of '56." Where a long line of elegant two-story homes had once stood she found only two depressing shacks thrown together from scavenged wreckage and perched above the sands on crude stilts.

Maps prepared by the Coast Survey in the 1890s, a few years after Catharine Cole's visit, showed an inlet east of where the village once stood, roughly the same location of the inlet that was carved during the 1856 storm. The map also showed that a second inlet had been cut through the east end of the island. Such inlets were not unique; the barrier islands lining the U.S. Atlantic and Gulf coasts were severed by hundreds of them, many wide and deep enough to serve as harbor entrances for oceangoing vessels. Virtually all of these inlets formed during extreme storms, commonly when a low and narrow part of a barrier island was submerged by storm surge, leaving the water on the island's bay and ocean sides at different levels. The resulting gradient in sea level forced water to run down-slope across the island and scour a narrow breach.

What was different about the inlets of Isle Derniere was that they were multiplying, transforming what had been a continuous, twenty-four-mile-long arc of sand into an island chain whose isles were growing in number. Many inlets through barrier islands fill with sand and seal shut in the weeks and months following the storm that cut them. In contrast, on Isle Derniere the inlets persisted; the tidal currents sweeping in and out of the openings were sufficient to keep sand from accumulating. By the 1890s, the Isle Derniere had become the Isle Dernieres, consisting of a chain of three islands.

In 1934, about the time of Emma's ninety-eighth birthday party, a newly published Coast Survey map of Isle Derniere showed that the islands were then severed by four major inlets and several minor ones. Scientists have compared this map to the 1890s map and shown that the Gulf shoreline had retreated landward one-third of a mile. While some barrier islands maintain their form and size as they migrate, the Isle Dernieres did not. They became progressively narrower. Between the 1890s and 1934, the islands lost 45 percent of their surface area, owing to both island narrowing and inlet carving. The location where Richard found Emma injured in the sand was under the Gulf's waves.

By 1988, the degradation was nearly complete. In the previous 101 years, the surface area of the Isle Dernieres had been reduced 78 percent. Further, the remains of the islands had migrated landward over two-thirds of a mile. Left stranded on their Gulf sides were outcrops of marsh in the beach and the trunks of thin trees in the surf, signs of a land in motion, a land degrading.

The Isle Dernieres were marching toward their destiny, toward the final step of their evolution. In 1991, scientists predicted that they would slip beneath the sea by 2015.

The islands survive today only by human intervention. The landmass has been restored, although not to its original character or configuration. Inlets have been filled and the islands built higher and wider with material dredged from nearby sources—mud and shell with little sand. The restored islands serve as a habitat for birds, including endangered species, and they maintain the bay behind the island as an estuary of mixed salt- and freshwater within which sea life thrives. The islands also help to protect the mainland from direct attack by storm waves and surge.

Island restoration is not, however, a solution to island degradation. The restored islands continue to erode as they have in the past.
Restoration is a form of maintenance that must be repeated again
and again to replace sediment removed by waves and currents. With
rising seas, the maintenance of barrier islands, whether in Louisiana
or elsewhere in the world, will become more difficult and more
expensive.

There are lessons in what has happened to the Isle Dernieres.
When the *Texas* steamed out of Village Harbor and across Caillou Bay toward the mainland on August 19, 1856, the permanent habitation of the islands came to an abrupt end. The plans to build a new,
huge hotel on the islands were never implemented; the homes and
businesses of the village were never rebuilt; and the packet steamers
from the mainland never returned.

"The lesson of the flood was not forgotten," wrote W. W. Pugh in
his 1881 "Reminiscences," "and will not be for many years to
come. . . . The resort was growing rapidly in public estimation, so it is
probable that a few years later, a storm of equal severity would have
been much more disastrous, the number of visitors being largely increased." The survivors appreciated that it was hazardous living on
such a low-lying strand as the Isle Dernieres.

This lesson was obvious to Catharine Cole when she visited
the islands three decades after the 1856 hurricane. "During storms
the waves will wash over Last Island, and few would venture to stop
there without a trusty boat near at hand."

Today, though, such lessons are forgotten or ignored. In the last
century and a half, the Village of Isle Derniere was one of only a few
U.S. seafront communities that were destroyed or severely damaged
during a storm and never rebuilt. The common practice is not only to
rebuild structures on devastated coasts but also to make them bigger
and more elaborate.

The west end of Dauphin Island, Alabama, is low and featureless, and like Isle Derniere, it has no natural prominent dunes. Its elongated village of homes was wiped out during Hurricane Frederick in 1979, but then quickly rebuilt. These new homes were devastated by Hurricane Elena in 1985, and again rebuilt. This destruction-construction cycle continued through Hurricanes Georges in 1998 and Katrina in 2005. At this writing, the island is being rebuilt for the fourth time in twenty-nine years.

The mainland community of Holly Beach in western Louisiana is at extremely low elevation and readily flooded even during a low-intensity hurricane. It was wiped out during Hurricane Audrey in 1957, rebuilt, and damaged severely again during Hurricane Carla in 1961. Then Hurricane Rita destroyed every structure in Holly Beach in 2005. The community of traditional Louisiana camps was being rebuilt with much larger homes when Hurricane Ike completely inundated the area again in 2008.

Hurricane hazards arise from the land changing and moving as well as from the direct impacts of the wind, surge, and waves. During Hurricane Katrina, many Gulf-front houses on Dauphin Island were lost because the island migrated past the structures, leaving only their barren pilings standing in the sea.

Changes in the position and size of the Isle Dernieres have occurred at rates among the most rapid found anywhere in the world. The coast was starved for sediment from the switching of the Mississippi River to a new course, and the sea rose relative to the land primarily from the sinking of the delta. These long-term processes made the islands vulnerable to devastating storms and extreme changes such as occurred in 1856.

Sediment starvation and sea-level rise are not, however, unique to deltas like the Mississippi. These processes can come about in ways different than river switching and land sinking, and they can impact all the world's sandy coasts.

In 2006 a panel of scientists sponsored by the National Academy of Sciences used a remarkable mix of different analyses to reach a consensus about the world's climate. Direct measurements of air temperature were available only for the past 150 years, so the panel combined various proxies for temperature that together spanned the past 2,000 years. The data, which came from different research groups and different sources, included ice cores, tree rings, corals, ocean and lake sediments, and borehole temperatures, as well as recent direct measurements. "With a high level of confidence," the panel concluded, "global mean surface temperature was higher during the last few decades of the 20th century than during any comparable period during the preceding four centuries."

Global warming is raising the levels of the world's seas by expanding seawater and melting grounded ice. The worldwide sea-level rise that many scientists are predicting for the twenty-first century and beyond could create situations along the world's coasts approaching what has occurred in the past on the Mississippi delta from the land's sinking. At Grand Isle in central Louisiana, between Isle Derniere and the mouth of the Mississippi River, measurements over the past half-century using a tide gauge show the sea rising relative to the land about 3.7 inches per decade, or about three feet per century. This reflects sea-level changes from both land sinking and the world's seas rising, the former being more than five times greater than the latter at this location.

In comparison, the 2007 report of the Intergovernmental Panel on Climate Change concludes that worldwide sea-level rise for approximately the twenty-first century could reach two feet, and uncertainties about ice sheet stability could raise it to within several inches of three feet. Recent research has shown that sea-level rise could be even greater, although estimates remain uncertain.

Should a rise of three feet or more occur, some of the barrier islands that line the Atlantic and Gulf coasts of the United States from

Rhode Island to Texas could deteriorate like the Isle Dernieres. The islands most susceptible to this process would be those that are sand-starved. The natural nourishment of the barrier islands along the Atlantic coast is restricted because the sand grains coming down the major rivers along that coast are trapped in broad estuaries, like the Chesapeake and Delaware bays, tens of miles from the ocean coast barrier islands. Further, huge quantities of sand are lost from the islands to shoals off capes, such as Diamond Shoals off Cape Hatteras. The coast is left with a deficit of sand, although conditions vary from island to island. Those barrier islands exposed to both rapid sea-level rise and extreme sand loss would grow lower and narrower and become increasingly vulnerable to hurricanes.

Since these storms will come ashore on rising seas, the surge and waves of hurricanes of the same intensity will reach progressively higher with time. Further, with the lowering of the land, the surge that inundates an island will be deeper. With the height of breakers in the surf controlled by depth, the deeper water over the island would be accompanied by larger waves. This could make the impacts of hurricanes of the future more extreme, even if wind speeds do not increase in a warmer world, as some tropical meteorologists predict.

We continue in the United States to develop extremely hazardous coastal locations, like the low-lying areas on the Bolivar Peninsula east of Galveston, Texas, that were wiped out in 2008 by Hurricane Ike. The extreme vulnerability of such locations today will only increase as the world's seas rise.

The Isle Dernieres are the canaries in the mineshaft, their demise warning us of what may happen along our coasts in a warmer world. It is a warning that we must heed. Our coastal lands are changing. And after future Katrinas and Ikes, we will face more and more destroyed communities that, if rebuilt, will likely be wiped out again, then again.

{ ACKNOWLEDGMENTS }

The staffs and holdings of the research libraries of the University of New Orleans, Tulane University, Louisiana State University, the University of Louisiana at Lafayette, the University of South Florida, the Library of Congress, and the Williams Research Facility of the Historic New Orleans Collection were invaluable in researching this book.

The beautifully restored plantations along the bayous and rivers of Louisiana illuminated plantation life of the 1800s. I toured the mansions and grounds of Destrehan (near New Orleans), Laura (in Vacherie), Magnolia Mound (in Baton Rouge), Shadows on the Teche (in New Iberia), and Madewood (in Napoleanville) plantations. Further understanding of nineteenth-century life was found in the exhibits and restored buildings at LSU's Rural Life Museum in Baton Rouge, the Iberville Museum in Plaquemine, the Louisiana State Museum at the Cabildo in New Orleans, and the Historic New Orleans Collection in the French Quarter.

The kind and gracious people of Plaquemine, Louisiana, shared knowledge of their ancestors and others who lived in or near this Mississippi River town in the mid-1800s. Some of these ancestors were on Isle Derniere on August 10, 1856. I particularly thank Tony Fama, the author of *Plaquemine: A Long, Long Time Ago* and *Plaquemine: A Glimpse of the Past*, who showed my wife and me the historic highlights of the town, including St. John's Cemetery where Thomas Mille and two of his wives are buried. I also thank the following residents of Plaquemine for their suggestions and insights on its history and people: Rita Lynn Jackson, who met with us at the Iberville Museum; Linda Migliacio, a descendant of Thomas Mille; Jeanette Schlatre, a descendant of Michael Schlatre who provided a copy of her family's history (see Hoffman in the sources section); and John W. Wilbert Jr., who discussed with us the Wilbert family history and sent me a copy of a newspaper article on the storm.

Through e-mail discussions, I appreciate the help of Gary Schlatre, a descendant of Michael Schlatre, for providing background information and a photograph of Michael and his son from his second marriage; and the help of Bryan Muench, a descendant of Emma and Alfred Duperier, for providing photographs of Emma and Alfred.

Also through e-mail discussions, I appreciate the help of entomologists Drs. Dawn Wesson and Amy Morrison in coming to a better understanding of the breeding of *Aedes aegypti*.

I thank Cathy Penland for putting me in contact with Bethany Bultman, who is a descendant of the Muggah brothers and who wrote "The Final Days of Isle Derniere," which appeared in *Louisiana Cultural Vistas*. Bethany was kind to discuss her ancestors and the 1856 storm with me in her nineteenth-century home in New Orleans near a portrait of two of her family members who died on the island.

I thank my longtime research collaborators Shea Penland of the University of New Orleans and Jeff Williams of the U.S. Geological Survey, with whom I have worked on the causes of the erosion of Louisiana's barrier islands off and on since the mid-1980s. Both offered encouragement and insights during the writing of this book. Shea left us too early, passing away during the spring of 2008.

I thank Michelle Tessler of the Tessler Literary Agency for efficiently and quickly selling the rights to my book, and Lindsay Jones of PublicAffairs for editing the book and offering many insightful and smart suggestions that have improved it.

My wife, Dee, and my sister, Ruth Bayard, offered great support and ideas. Dee read and commented on early drafts and spent far too many weekends and holidays and vacation days watching her husband write and rewrite. I hope to finish incorporating the copy-edits before she carries out her threat of throwing my laptop into the pool.

{ CREDITS }

TEXT

The author and publisher gratefully acknowledge permission to reproduce quotes from the following copyrighted material. While every effort has been made to secure permissions, we may have failed in a few cases to trace copyright holders. We regret any inadvertent omission.

"The Last Island Disaster of August 10, 1856: Personal Narrative of His Experiences by One of the Survivors" by Michael Schlatre, introduction by Walter Prichard. *Louisiana Historical Quarterly* vol. 20 (July 1937): 690–737. Used with permission of the Louisiana Historical Society.

"Survivor's True Romance of Last Island," June 10, 1928, and "Survivor of Last Island Dies," April 14, 1936. © 1928, 1936 The Times Picayune Publishing Co. All rights reserved. Used with permission of the *Times Picayune*.

"Account of the Storm on Last Island" by Captain Thomas H. Ellis. Special Collections, Louisiana State University Libraries, Baton Rouge, South Reading Room, Butler (Louise) Papers, folder 8, 1069, S-19-21. Used with permission of Louisiana State University Libraries.

"The Final Days of Isle Derniere" by Bethany Ewald Bultman. *Louisiana Cultural Vistas*, Louisiana Endowment for the Humanities, vol. 13, no. 4 (Winter 2002–2003). Used with permission of Louisiana Endowment for the Humanities and Bethany Ewald Bultman.

"A Historical Sketch of Assumption Parish for Forty Years—1820–1860" by W. W. Pugh. *Assumption Pioneer* (*Terrebonne Life Lines,* vol. 14, nos. 2 and 3). Bethany Ewald Bultman Papers, 2003:0085. Used with permission of the Historic New Orleans Collection.

ILLUSTRATIONS

Cover art: Modified from the 1861 drawing "Birds Eye View of Louisiana, Mississippi, Alabama, and Part of Florida" by John Bachmann. Courtesy of the Library of Congress.

First frontispiece: Modified from the 1861 "Map of the Alluvial Region of the Mississippi" by Chs. Mahon. Published by the Corps of Engineers. Courtesy of the Library of Congress.

Second frontispiece: Modified from the 1853 "Preliminary Chart of Ship Shoal Louisiana" by F. Gerdes of the U.S. Coast Survey. Courtesy of the National Oceanic and Atmospheric Administration.

Prologue: Appeared on the cover of the book of drawings *Elemental Warfare* by Ellsworth Woodward, circa 1900. Courtesy of Ogden Museum of Southern Art, New Orleans, La.

Part 1: Modified from the 1858 "Norman's Chart of the Lower Mississippi River" by Marie Adrien Persac. Published by B. M. Norman. Courtesy of the Library of Congress.

Part 2: First appeared in *Frank Leslie's Illustrated*, August 30, 1856. Courtesy of the Historic New Orleans Collection, accession no. 1974.25.4.65 and 1974.25.4.66, DETAIL.

Part 3: First appeared in *Frank Leslie's Illustrated*, October 17, 1857. Courtesy of the Library of Congress.

Epilogue: Appeared in S. Jeffress Williams, Kurt Dodd, and Kathleen K. Gohn, *Coasts in Crisis*, U.S. Geological Survey circular 1075, U.S. Government Printing Office, 1990. Courtesy of the U.S. Geological Survey.

{ NOTES }

See Sources for complete citations.

PROLOGUE: AN ISLAND CHANGED FOREVER

2   *In the summer of 1856, Emma Mille traveled with several of her family members to Isle Derniere:* Times Picayune, June 10, 1928.

2   *upriver from New Orleans:* With their civilization clustered along meandering waterways, Louisianans commonly expressed direction in terms of water flow: "upriver" means in the direction against the current, and "downriver" means in the direction with the current.

2   *Her father had owned a house on Isle Derniere:* Times Picayune, April 14, 1936.

2   *They likely rode in horse-drawn carriages:* The Mille plantation was on Bayou Plaquemine, which left the Mississippi River at the town of Plaquemine. In an interview, Emma told a reporter that her family boarded a boat in Plaquemine for Isle Derniere (*Times Picayune,* April 14, 1936). The family likely took carriages to transport the family several miles from their plantation to meet the steamer in Plaquemine.

2   *There they boarded the steamboat* Blue Hammock, *which made the scheduled runs:* Schlatre, p. 704, reported that the *Blue Hammock* made the scheduled runs to Isle Derniere. With the resort being relatively small (about four hundred people present in August 1856), I have assumed there was not an additional steamer making regular runs from Plaquemine, and hence the Mille family would have taken the *Blue Hammock.* The steamer *Star* also serviced the island, but from the railroad terminal near Brashear City.

2   *It was owned and often captained by Michael Schlatre Jr.:* Schlatre, p. 704, reported Schlatre's associations with the *Blue Hammock.*

2   *The seventy-four-ton side-wheeler:* Brasseaux and Fontenot, p. 170, describes a seventy-four-ton side-wheeled steamer named *Blue Hammock* that was in service at the relevant time and in the relevant area.

2   *During its journey to Isle Derniere, the steamboat would cross a remarkable sequence of diverse natural environments:* What follows this passage is a general description of some of the major natural environments and how they changed across parts of the delta that had been abandoned by the Mississippi River. The river had switched to a new part of the delta, leaving the area the Mille family transited to the coast starved for sediment. This is not a detailed description of a specific route across the delta. The steamer would have first encountered a major lobe of the delta about twenty miles downriver of Plaquemine.

225

3   *"It is a place that seems often unable to make up its mind"*: Kane, *Bayous of Louisiana*, p. 3.

3   *"The weird and funereal aspect of the place"*: *Harper's Weekly,* December 8, 1866.

5   *The vessel chugged from the marsh and into open water, a five-mile-wide bay*: In 1853, the bay width, measured due north of the mouth of Village Bayou to the mainland marsh, was about five miles. This is used herein as the bay width, although the width varied along the coast.

‹ 5   *"Isle Derniere may be readily known by the numerous houses on the beach"*: Gerdes, "Preliminary Chart of Ship Island Shoal, Louisiana."

5   *with its majestic homes tucked amid oleanders and a bustling hotel packed with guests*: *Times Picayune,* April 14, 1936.

5   *The highest ground on Isle Derniere was at the crest of its beach, where the sand rose only five to six feet above the sea*: Gerdes, appendix 21, p. 54*. The dimensions noted above are from the notes from the 1853 survey of the Isle Derniere.

6   *The island's lack of physical presence was a symptom that it suffered from the same affliction*: Specifically, the islands suffered from sea-level rise relative to the land and lack of sediment supply, as did, for example, the marshes. The detailed processes causing the deterioration of each environment were different, but the basic causes (i.e., sea-level rise and sediment supply) were the same. The cypress trees were likely stressed by saltwater intrusion forced by the sea rising relative to the land.

6   *except for a strange forest standing in the surf*: Such tree trunks in the surf are seen on the seaward side of some rapidly retreating barrier islands. The trees grow on the bay side of the island, and the island migrates landward past them, stranding them in the sea. Trees can also be stranded in the surf when the island deteriorates and loses surface area. For the Isle Derniere, both processes were operating. During trips there in the late 1980s and early 1990s, the author observed thin trunks of trees and shrubs rising above gentle surf.

6   *a hurricane that killed many of the most prominent residents of antebellum New Orleans and the sugar plantations of south Louisiana*: Sothern, p. 50, notes that relatively few victims of the storm were listed as residents of New Orleans. Some of the victims were likely part-time residents of the city. Thomas Mille, for example, was a plantation owner in the country and a merchant in New Orleans (see *New Orleans Commercial Bulletin*, August 16, 1856).

6   *a delta whose surface rose and fell*: Here I'm referring to the vertical building of the delta through deposition of organic detritus and inorganic sediments during river overflows, and the sinking of the delta through long-term compaction of detritus and sediments. These processes are discussed in later chapters.

7   *the Isle Derniere retreated landward about two-thirds of a mile while los-ing three-quarters of its surface area:* Average erosion rates for Isle Derniere are given in McBride et al., "Analysis of Barrier Shoreline," p. 45. Surface areas losses are given on p. 47.

CHAPTER 1: THE CITY OF THE DEAD

12   *the city's October to May business season:* Schafer, p. xv.

12   *a business as a merchant in the city: New Orleans Commercial Bulletin,* August 16, 1856.

12   *He was a Frenchman, born in 1800 in Cassis:* Mille's place of birth is engraved on his headstone at St. John's Cemetery in Plaquemine, Louisiana.

12   *born on October 10, 1837: Times Picayune,* June 10, 1928.

12   *She was a devout Catholic:* See Bultman Papers, folder 17, letter from Homer J. DuPuy to Bultman in regard to Emma Mille Duperier, February 12, 1999.

12   *When she was a child, there were no schools open to girls near her plantation:* The first girls' school opened in Plaquemine in 1857, after the Isle Derniere storm. See Fama, p. 92.

12   *Emma's younger sister was sent to the Sacred Heart Convent: Times Picayune,* June 10, 1928, reported that Emma's sister attended a convent school in St. James Parish. The Sacred Heart Convent School was operational in that parish in the town of Convent, Louisiana, during the time the sister would have attended school.

12   *"formal study, whether . . . Latin, history, science, or philosophy":* Crete, p. 112.

13   *the latest productions from Paris at the* Théâtre d'Orléans: Asbury, p. 122.

13   *opened in 1815 on Rue d'Orléans:* Zietz, p. 24.

13   *rectangular flatboats:* A flat-bottomed vessel up to one hundred feet long that floated downriver with the current, carrying goods to market. It was steered by crewmen with long oars called sweeps. These were one-way barges that were dismantled on arrival and their wood sold.

13   *This antebellum seaport rivaled New York's:* Wilson, Brady, and Adams, p. xx.

14   *"Their chief beauty":* Twain, p. 236.

14   *"Something of Southern Europe lives in the Garden District":* Star, p. 41.

15   *"The improvements are of the cheapest character":* Wilson, Brady, and Adams, p. 36.

15   *"Sandwiched":* E-mail from John Barry; also see Campanella, p. 52.

16   *"In high-river stage, in the New Orleans region":* Twain, p. 356.

16   *"excited my apprehensions":* Fenner, p. 15.

16   *"six deaths, four children and two adults"*: Ibid., p. 20.

17   *"dead-house"*: Ibid., p. 19.

17   *Drs. Stone, Choppin, and McGibbon, among others*: Ibid.

17   *"When informed of the first cases of yellow fever"*: Ibid., p. 4.

17   *"Five consecutive summers have now elapsed"*: Duffy, p. 7, quoting from *Cohen's New Orleans Directory of 1853*, p. v.

17   *Some outbreaks could be traced to a single infected person*: Duffy, p. 6.

18   *"Worse and worse . . ."*: Fenner, p. 10, quoting *The Delta*, June 22, 1853.

18   *"With deep regret . . ."*: Ibid., p. 4.

18   *his lower body was livid*: Ibid., p. 19.

18   *"partly the color of mustard"*: Ibid.

19   *"refused to save her honor"*: Duffy, p. 16.

19   *a second yellow fever death in his ward*: Fenner, p. 21.

20   *Last Island [Isle Derniere] Hotel*: *Planter's Banner*, June 1, 1853.

20   *Prior to the late 1840s, there were few structures on Isle Derniere*: Sothern, p. 28.

20   *In 1819 an expedition to discover wood resources*: Prichard, Kniffen, and Brown, p. 804.

20   *the steamboat* Meteor: Sothern, p. 19, quoting *Planter's Banner*.

20   *"Its southern shore looks out"*: *Daily Picayune*, July 28, 1852.

20   *(pronounced . . . Mac-auch)*: Bultman, "The Final Days of Isle Derniere," p. 76.

20   *Recognizing the enormous potential of Isle Derniere*: Ibid., p. 79.

21   *Mayor A. D. Crossman had ordered the firing of cannon*: Duffy, p. 74.

21   *moored less than one hundred yards from another vessel*: Fenner, p. 21.

21   *a poor, unpaved area—"a filthy pond"*: Ibid.

21   *"Our city has rarely been more completely deserted"*: Duffy, p. 27, quoting *New Orleans Bee*, July 2, 1853.

22   *snuffed 1,294 lives by the end of July*: Fenner, p. 46. Fenner provides a comprehensive list of the deaths certified by physicians.

22   *Dr. Fenner estimated the total cost of lives at 7,870*: Ibid., p. 70.

23   *ramshackle tenements that became surrounded with refuse*: Refuse disposal in the nineteenth century was a problem throughout the city of New Orleans. However, Wharton's description of the junkyard appearance of poor areas "pushed far into the swamp" and the care that he took in caring for his own home in the Anglo district suggests that there would have been more junk and potential containers in the poor part of the city.

23   *Aedes aegypti, a unique mosquito that carried the yellow fever virus*: Humphreys, p. 5.

23   *The clean freshwater in the vases not only kept the blooms vibrant*: Ibid.

CHAPTER 2: CHOCOLATE GOLD

25   *"thickly peopled by sugar planters"*: Hall, p. 352.

26   *"The great sugar plantations border both sides of the river"*: Twain, pp. 223–224.

26   *Schlatre, a descendant of German immigrants*: Schlatre, pp. 727–728.

26   *a ruggedly handsome man and unusually tall for the time*: Hoffman.

26   *"gold the color of chocolate"*: Barry, p. 97.

27   *the Mississippi annually carried a volume of sediment that would fill a container one mile square*: Twain, p. 2, citing a nineteenth-century article in the *New Orleans Times-Democrat* written by "able engineers."

27   *"the finest and most fertile . . . soil"*: Stuart, p. 284.

27   *they hoped to discover precious metals*: Cable, *The Creoles of Louisiana*, p. 13.

27   *wealthy or noble or had fatefully served the crown*: Sternberg, p. 60.

28   *"Every Saturday, they were seen floating down the river"*: Gayarre, vol. 1, pp. 354–355.

28   *Coast*: or *cote* in French, was used to describe settlements along Louisiana's rivers and bayous.

28   *The government provided them with the tools*: Gayarre, vol. 2, p. 131.

28   *Part of this region became known as the Acadian Coast*: In general, the people who occupied the Acadian Coast cultivated relatively small tracts of land. People of other cultures bought and combined these tracts into vast plantations and in that way affected the Acadian culture. This, of course, was not always the case, since some Acadians were plantation owners. Paulin Dupuy, who co-owned Milly Plantation with Thomas Mille, had ancestors from Acadia. See *Biographical and Historical Memoires of Louisiana*, p. 391.

28   *The grants were six or eight arpents along the waterway*: French, p. 289 (for a similar quote, see Sternberg, p. 61). Governor O'Reilly issued these regulations in 1770 when the Spanish administered the Louisiana colony. During French rule earlier in the century, a typical width of property along the riverfront was even less—2 to 4 arpents (384 to 768 feet), according to NationalAtlas.Gov (http://www-atlas.usgs.gov/about.html).

28   *small garden-crop farms*: Sternberg, p. 62. Sternberg is referring to the commercially successful crops of the German Coast that fed New Orleans in the eighteenth century. Settlers on the Acadian Coast grew "corn (maize), rice, sweet potatoes, and sugar cane primarily for their own consumption" (p. 63).

28   *fifty-four-year-old Etienne de Bore risked everything he owned*: Cable, *The Creoles of Louisiana*, pp. 111–113.

29   *king's mousquetaires*: Ibid., p. 111. France's Musketeers were personal guards of the French king, dating to the early 1600s. They were

disbanded for a decade in the mid-1600s, then operated continuously until 1776 (see Cohen, p. 77). Bore probably served in the Musketeers when he was in his twenties, in the 1760s. He left France for Louisiana in the early 1770s when he was thirty-two years old.

29 *sugarcane was difficult to grow in Louisiana*: Follett, p. 10.

29 *sold for $12,000*: Cable, *The Creoles of Louisiana,* p. 113.

29 *"The people were electrified"*: Ibid.

29 *In the 1840s, Michael Schlatre joined the charge*: Schlatre, pp. 735–736.

29 *he built a sugar mill*: Ibid.

29 *the core of sugar production*: Follett, p. 21, referring to the sugar plantations along the Mississippi River between New Orleans and Baton Rouge as a "core zone" of Louisiana's sugar production.

29 *An 1858 map showed on both sides of the Mississippi*: Persac, "Plantations on the Mississippi from Natchez to New Orleans, 1858."

30 *one of the highest producers of sugar cane in Iberville Parish*: "Sources Behind the Project: Documenting the Louisiana Sugar Economy, 1844–1917." This website lists sugar production during antebellum times for plantations in Iberville and other parishes, including one plantation co-owned by Thomas Mille and Paulin Dupuy. In Louisiana, a "parish" is equivalent to a county elsewhere in the United States.

30 *the fields around the big house*: Gore, p. 17, shows an example of the usage of the term "big house" as the manor of a plantation.

30 *"The green was so vivid"*: Latrobe, p. 38.

30 *slaves muscled aboard thousand-pound hogsheads*: a hogshead—a large wooden barrel capable of carrying one thousand pounds, according to Sternberg (p. 22)—was a standard shipping container for granulated sugar. Bolles (1878) reported a somewhat larger barrel capacity of thirteen hundred pounds.

30 *"like Satan's own kitchen"*: Twain, p. 64.

31 *"Verse . . . sweetens the toil of slaves"*: Bryant, *Letters of a Traveler,* p. 74.

31 *"We encourage their singing"*: Ibid.

31 *"some wild melody . . . that fairly made the old cane-shed shake"*: Richardson, p. 4.

31 *Emma Mille had a passion for music*: Emma's deep, lifelong interest in music was shown in the *Times Picayune* interview of April 14, 1936. She played her own pieces on the piano for her grandchildren and great-grandchildren.

31 *Laura Locoul of Laura Plantation practiced daily for hours*: Gore, p. 69.

31 *ragtime, music that the puritanical considered vulgar*: Sales, p. 52, referring to an editorial that appeared in Feather's *The Book of Jazz.*

32   *Dupuy emerged as a successful and wealthy planter:* Biographical and Historical Memoires of Louisiana, p. 391.

32   *a near-record crop of cane yielding 452 hogsheads:* "Sources Behind the Project: Documenting the Louisiana Sugar Economy, 1844–1917."

32   *Louisiana planters collectively produced the most sugar in their history:* Follett, p. 23.

32   *shipping 25 percent of the world's sugar exports:* Ibid., p. 22.

32   *"It was generally noted that yellow fever seasons":* Pugh, "A Historical Sketch," entry for Saturday, June 6, 1896.

33   *"Hardly had we started when our men saw":* Cable, Strange True Stories, pp. 55–56.

33   *Such violent water partially overflowed the channel:* "Sources Behind the Project: Documenting the Louisiana Sugar Economy, 1844–1917" refers specifically to Milly Plantation.

33   *reducing the sugar crop by one-third:* Ibid.

33   *Most had to borrow money to purchase and operate their plantations:* Frederick Law Olmsted, pp. 321–322.

33   *"The money-lender gyrated around":* Cable, The Creoles of Louisiana, p. 228.

33   *They were high-stakes gambles:* Frederick Law Olmsted, p. 321.

33   *By 1812, slaves and immigrant laborers:* Barry, p. 40.

34   *"If we make the river what it ought to be":* Tompkins, p. 215, quoting General Banks.

34   *"After the lapse of another century":* Harper, p. 256.

34   *"Time has shown beyond a doubt":* Pugh, "A Historical Sketch," entry for Saturday, May 9, 1896.

34   *"food for fever":* Irish immigrants were so susceptible to yellow fever in New Orleans that they were referred to as "food for fever" in English, p. 49.

35   *Slaves were too valuable:* Coogan, p. 316.

35   *These immigrants had no choice:* English, p. 49.

35   *"lived in the utmost squalor":* Gill, p. 38.

35   *"Wanted—a cook or chambermaid":* Wakin, p. 52.

36   *Industrial Canal, whose floodwalls would fail:* The walls failed during Hurricane Katrina in 2005, causing extensive flooding in New Orleans. See, for example, van Heerden and Bryan.

36   *"Ten thousand micks, they swung their picks":* English, p. 49, quoting an article in the New Orleans Times Picayune, July 8, 1837.

36   *"We found [the canal's] surface enlivened with the sails of vessels":* Lyell, Second Visit, p. 134.

37   *Geology at the time was a popular, lively topic:* Secord, p. xi.

37   *"The whole alluvial plain appears as a channel of an immensely large river"*: Harper, p. 258.

37   *"The great merit of the* Principles*"*: Secord, p. ix, quoting a letter from Charles Darwin to L. Horner, August 29, 1844.

38   *"Many geologists, when they behold the spoils of land"*: Lyell, *Principles*, p. 274.

38   *"But Mr. Bringier, the State surveyor"*: Lyell, *Second Visit*, p. 137.

39   *"We must conclude that the land has sunk down vertically"*: Ibid.

39   *"the ground was slowly raised, year by year"*: Lyell, *Principles*, p. 269.

CHAPTER 3: "THE SUMMER RESORT FOR THE SOUTH"

41   *"The Summer Resort for the South"*: Sothern, p. 25, quoting the *Planter's Banner*, September 4, 1852, referring to Isle Derniere.

41   *In about AD 1300*: Penland, Suter, and Boyd, p. 198, report that the Mississippi River switched to a new channel six hundred to eight hundred years before the present—that is, between approximately AD 1200 and 1400. Hence, the 1300 date has roughly a one-hundred-year uncertainty. See also Fraser.

42   *"Plaquemine culture"*: Sternberg, p. 2. See also Quimby.

42   *Their huts had roofs of leaves and walls of poles*: Sternberg, p. 2.

42   *hunted bears and deer*: Neuman and Hawkins.

42   *Native Americans would die by the tens of thousands*: Kelton, p. 21.

42   *Disease and slave raids combined to cause a collapse in the population*: Historian Dr. Paul Kelton, University of Kansas, e-mail to the author, March 7, 2007.

42   *its beginning coincided with an abrupt change in the environment wrought by nature*: This is not necessarily to argue that there is a causal relationship between the river switching and the emergence of the Plaquemine culture. Also, note that the switch occurred in the part of the channel between the Gulf and tens of miles below Plaquemine.

42   *One of these natural course changes took place between AD 1200 and 1400*: Penland, Suter, and Boyd, p. 198.

43   *Before the river switched course*: See ibid. for a discussion of the stages of transformation from a bird's-foot delta to a barrier island.

43   *The shore retreated at rates that would have been among the most rapid*: Modern studies of shoreline erosion of delta systems around the world have shown that when sources of sediments are limited, and the land sinks relative to the sea, the coast erodes at extreme rates. See, for example, results from the Mississippi delta, including Isle Derniere, in Williams et al.

44   *The Coast Survey's mandate was to produce accurate navigation charts*: Based on an act of Congress to provide for surveying the coasts of the

United States, signed by President Thomas Jefferson on February 10, 1807. See NOAA, "An Act."

44   *a mammoth undertaking:* Smithsonian Institution, *Annual Report,* 1872, p. 101.

44   *organized separate parties to survey the different parts:* Ibid., p. 100.

45   *ranging on rods held by assistants:* The plane table—the primary topographic surveying instrument used by the Coast Survey from its inception through much of the twentieth century—is a table, approximately thirty by twenty-four inches, mounted as a level surface at the top of a tripod. On the surface lies an alidade with a telescope that ranges on a rod held vertical by an assistant. The instrument allows the surveyor to scribe surveyed points—for example, along a shoreline—onto a paper map that rests on the plane table. See Shalowitz, pp. 159–160.

45   *"General Reconnaissance of the Gulf Coast of Louisiana":* Gerdes, "General Reconnaissance of the Gulf Coast of Louisiana."

45   *"Preliminary Chart of Ship Island Shoal, Louisiana":* Gerdes, "Preliminary Chart of Ship Island Shoal, Louisiana."

45   *Muggah's Hotel, a center of entertainment for visitors:* Sothern, p. 33. See also Bultman, "The Final Days of Isle Derniere."

46   *At one end stood the home of Paul Octave Hebert:* Bultman, "The Final Days of Isle Derniere," p. 80, reports that Governor Hebert's home was next to Michael Schlatre's.

46   *a visitor from New Orleans, Mrs. Rommage: Times Picayune,* April 14, 1936.

46   *The primary shipping lane between Galveston and New Orleans:* Bache, *1854,* p. 69.

46   *a slave was ordered to hail a vessel:* See Sothern, p. 27, who was quoting an article published in August 1854 in the New Orleans newspaper, the *Daily Delta.*

47   *unsightly blemishes, like a tan or freckles:* Clinton, p. 100.

47   *She had a broad, rounded face:* See photograph of Emma as a young woman in the *Times Picayune,* June 10, 1928.

47   *"This famous beach teems every evening with people":* Daily Delta, August 20, 1854.

47   *"Shell Road":* This smooth, firm road made of crushed white shells ran the six miles between New Orleans and Lake Pontchartrain parallel to the New Basin Canal. It was ideal for horse-drawn buggies, whose ride could be bone-jarring over the more typical potholed and rutted roadways of antebellum times. It was the road that Charles Lyell traveled to view the canal during his second trip to America.

47   *"If ever there were clothing to die for":* Bultman, "The Final Days of Isle Derniere," p. 79.

47   *blown-glass flycatchers:* Examples of these are on display at the Destrehan Plantation manor house on the Mississippi River near the New Orleans airport.

48   *From 1840 to 1865, the average height of women:* J. E. Murray, p. 123, reports height statistics from a Shaker commune in Pennsylvania of people of European ancestry. Interestingly, during antebellum times there was an odd decrease relative to earlier years (known as the "antebellum puzzle") in the average heights of both men and women, although this decrease may not have been reflected in the heights of planters' family members, like Emma. Explanations for the puzzle include a "deteriorating disease environment promoted by urban agglomeration" and the increase in the price of "protein-rich foods." The former idea may explain planters' heights, as they were not immune from disease, but the latter does not. See Sunder, p. 78, for a general discussion of the antebellum puzzle.

48   *today the average height of U.S. women with high incomes:* Worcester, p. 331; Worcester also notes that today low-income women have an average height of five feet, three inches.

48   *doorknobs of the eighteenth and nineteenth centuries were installed:* Such low door knobs can be observed today at the restored big house of Destrehan Plantation.

48   *"purity ruled appearance":* Clinton, p. 101.

48   *Toward the end of the 1850s, some of these dresses:* Volo and Volo, p. 146.

49   *deep interest in national politics:* Ibid., p. 197.

49   *"The senator from South Carolina has read many books on chivalry":* Sumner, p. 9.

50   *"Mr. Sumner was struck unawares over the head":* Copeland, p. 361, quoting a newspaper editorial in the *New York Tribune,* May 23, 1856.

50   *"For Mr. Sumner we have not the least sympathy":* Ibid., p. 367, quoting a newspaper editorial in the *Federal Union* of Milledgeville, Georgia, June 3, 1856.

50   *Debates swept the country and sometimes turned violent:* Volo and Volo, p. 197.

50   *attacking a hotel with cannon and fire:* Griffin.

50   *The abolitionist John Brown and his men:* Peterson, pp. 5–6.

50   *On a typical Louisiana sugar plantation in the early 1850s:* Follett, p. 24.

51   *"the water is clear and salt":* Sothern, p. 21, quoting from *Planter's Banner,* 1847.

51   *"[It is] certainly one of the finest places for promenading I have ever seen":* Ibid., p. 21.

CHAPTER 4: THE LAW OF STORMS

53   *the law of storms:* For background, see, for example, Reid, *An Attempt to Develop the Law of Storms by Means of Facts, and Piddington,* 2nd ed.

53   *No one knows the exact location:* See best track information for Storm 1, 1856, in, for example, Landsea et al. Because we lack comprehensive observations from this time, there is considerable uncertainty about the track and starting location of the storm.

53   *The seawater where the storm fired up was uncomfortably warm:* This and the other conditions cited are general requirements for the formation of a tropical storm.

54   *"17 souls of us":* Schlatre, p. 704.

54   *"hostile Indians lining both banks":* Ibid., p. 727.

54   *"feathers grew on trees":* Ibid.

54   *aboard the ship* Hope: Hoffman.

55   *They were a hardworking people:* Gayarre, vol. 1, p. 355.

55   *"Côte d'Or" or the Gold Coast:* Ibid.

55   *deciding that Missouri's climate did not suit him:* Schlatre, p. 734.

55   *navigation, surveying, and engineering:* Ibid.

55   *becoming both a steamboat captain and a sugar planter:* The position of steamboat captain was considered as romantic and exciting a position in the mid-nineteenth century as that of airline pilot would be considered today. And with their wealth and influence, sugar planters were at the top of the social hierarchy.

55   *The hoops held together large sugar containers:* Schlatre, p. 705. The hoops were metal straps that held wooden barrels, or hogsheads, together. Filled, hogsheads could hold one thousand to thirteen hundred pounds of granulated sugar.

55   *he had business on the mainland in Plaquemine:* Ibid.

55   *"it fell to my lot to witness":* Ibid.

55   *Other hands appeared in the reflected image before him:* Accounts confirm that Thomas Mille had a body servant with him on the island. *Times Picayune,* April 14, 1936.

56   *Mille had lived most of his fifty-six years in Louisiana:* Thomas Mille was married twice, the first time to Virginie Hebert in 1824. Since she was from a local family in Plaquemine, I have assumed that they met in Louisiana and were married there. Mille was born in 1800, hence my estimate that most of his life was spent in Louisiana.

56   *"retained a deep nostalgia for mother country":* Crete, p. 97.

56   *sherry in the evening:* Ibid., p. 103.

56   *"haughty bearing":* Ibid., p. 97.

56   *Creoles had different backgrounds from French Acadians:* Sparks, pp. 380–381.

56   *"the first blood and rank in France"*: Ibid., p. 380.

56   *Emma's mother, Pauline, after the death of her rich French father*: Schla-tre, pp. 729–730, reported that Pauline's father was named Flognier and that he was "tolerably wealthy." He mentioned that Pauline's sister, who was mentally disabled, inherited substantial wealth.

57   *"expended the best of their energies in trivial pleasures"*: Cable, *The Creoles of Louisiana*, p. 140.

57   *"Alluvial banks cave and change constantly"*: Twain, p. 56.

57   *"[the loss of] a quarter of a million dollars worth"*: Ibid., p. 44.

58   *Just a year earlier, on September 16, 1855*: For a general discussion of hurricane impacts, see Roth. For the track of the 1855 hurricane, see Partagas and Diaz, year 1855, fig. 6.

58   *"truly deplorable"*: *New York Times*, September 26, 1855, reprinted from the *New Orleans Crescent*, September 19, 1855.

58   *ripped from its mooring*: Roth.

58   *telling him of the confidence the storm had given her*: Bultman, "The Final Days of Isle Derniere." Schlatre's wife referred to a storm that hit Isle Derniere on August 29, 1855. Since available records show that only one tropical system hit the coast that summer, on September 16, 1855, I have assumed that the one referred to in the letter actually came ashore on September 16.

58   *glow of the repaired and reanchored lightship*: Roth.

58   *"Having been at the Island"*: Schlatre, p. 705.

58   *people on the island would have had difficulty standing erect*: The track of the storm showed that it came ashore near the mouth of the Mississippi River. At landfall, this track would position winds blowing from the land over Isle Derniere. For the track, see Partagas and Diaz, year 1855, fig. 6.

59   *"gossip, intemperance"*: Kett, p. xv.

59   *Flocking to their lectures were artisans, salespersons, factory workers, and clerks*: Postman, p. 40.

60   *With the opening of a Lyceum in New Orleans in 1844*: City of New Orleans, p. iii.

60   *During the War of 1812, the Great Louisiana Hurricane*: Miller and Rivera, p. 30.

60   *"We regret that the discussions which unavoidably arise among different investigators"*: Henry, *Scientific Writings of Joseph Henry*, pp. 212–213.

60   *Photographs show that he had a clean-shaven face*: See, for example, Youmans, p. 197.

60   *He was a social, enthusiastic person*: Ibid., p. 204.

60   *"the Storm King"*: Toomey, p. 110.

60   *Espy had the rare skill*: Youmans, p. 203.

61　*summarized in his 1841 book* The Philosophy of Storms: See Espy.

61　*"Thus the law will become general":* Ibid., p. 8.

61　*"Founded on the established laws of physics":* Ibid., p. 198.

61　*"France has its Cuvier, England its Newton, America its Espy":* Wilson and Fiske, p. 375.

61　*"It had been sneeringly said":* Espy, p. v.

62　*William C. Redfield had no university education:* Denison Olmsted, p. 4.

62　*he covered seven hundred miles:* Ibid., p. 6.

62　*Every evening he updated a log:* Ibid.

62　*the devastation of a great storm:* Ibid., p. 7.

62　*He noted that a violent wind from the southeast:* Ibid.

62　*the storm was a whirlwind:* Ibid., p. 8.

63　*"A stranger accosted me":* Ibid., p. 13.

63　*"a practical man little versed in scientific discussions":* Ibid.

63　*"practical evils arising from unfounded rules":* Espy, p. 253.

63　*"I cannot give to this alleged theory":* Smith, p. 464, quoting Robert Hare.

63　*"The grand error":* Redfield, p. 39.

63　*"I did not anticipate":* Toomey, p. 109.

64　*"Espy misquoted [me]":* Ibid.

64　*"progressive whirlwind":* Denison Olmsted, p. 4.

64　*the rotation of the earth gives the air "some spin":* Emanuel, p. 97.

64　*"Mr. Redfield insists":* Espy, p. v.

64　*preparing to open the Smithsonian building:* The first building of the Smithsonian was completed in 1855 and, with its distinctive design, is known today as the Castle.

65　*in the great hall of this building:* Fleming, p. 143.

65　*a unique map that showed weather conditions:* Smithsonian Institution, *Annual Report,* 1858, p. 32.

65　*By 1847 one major telegraph line:* Fleming, p. 144. Figure 7.1 presents a map of this telegraph line, dated December 1847 and labeled the Washington & New Orleans Telegraph Co.

65　*a small group of telegraph operators who signed on each day:* Cox, p. 55. Cox reports that the first public weather map was exhibited in the Smithsonian Institution in 1850, yet most sources report that it first appeared in 1856. Since the Smithsonian's "castle" building was completed in 1855, I use the 1856 date here.

65　*Over the years the network grew:* Smithsonian Institution, *Annual Report,* 1858, p. 32.

65　*A card of a specific color was hung at each station:* Ibid.

65　*meteorologists knew that winter storms:* See, for example, Fleming, p. 141.

65   *"Hot sunshine[,] West wind"*: Wilson, Brady, and Adams, p. 121, quoting Thomas Wharton, journal entry of August 7, 1856.

66   *It would be seven days hence: Daily Picayune*, August 13, 1856.

CHAPTER 5: SECRETS OF THE DEEP

68   *the wind was not blowing from the sea*: Schlatre, p. 705.

68   *"nothing extraordinary"*: Ibid.

68   *the "northers" that recurred every few weeks*: A norther is a winter storm associated with the passage of a cold front. Some of the nineteenth-century books on storms addressed northers, like Reid, *The Progress*, p. 296.

68   *"the billows [from the sea]"*: McAllister, quoted in Sothern, p. 35.

70   *"Though there were some trees lying about"*: Pugh, "A Historical Sketch."

70   *"Toward night"*: Ibid. I have added "[was not]" to the quote because that is what the context of the original phrasing seemed to imply.

70   *the* Atlantic, *a ten-ton bark*: A bark is a type of sailing vessel with at least three masts.

70   *"So little was thought of a storm"*: Pugh, "A Historical Sketch."

71   *Captain Thomas H. Ellis of the steamer* Star: Ellis.

71   *Ellis had just arrived at his hotel room*: Ibid.

71   *When he made his way back to the landing*: Ibid.

71   *these seamen were alarmed*: Ibid.

71   *None of them had ever seen the water level higher*: Ibid.

71   *They feared a bad storm and severe damage*: Ibid.

71   *The storm was as much as one and a half days away*: Ibid.

72   *Ellis respected the seamen and valued their opinions*: Ibid.

72   *"fright and persuasion"*: Ibid.

72   *paddle wheel set amidships*: Volo and Volo, p. 328.

72   *all of the key U.S. Atlantic ports had regular steamer service*: Ibid.

72   *his face covered with scraggly black whiskers*: Based on "The Loss of the Nautilus," *Daily Picayune*, August 25, 1856.

73   *at sea a few hours*: Ibid.

73   *"The appearance of Galveston from the Harbour is singularly dreary"*: Bixel and Turner, p. 1, quoting *Francis Sheridan's Journal*, 1839–1840.

73   *About the time of Sheridan's visit in the late 1830s*: Ibid., p. 2.

73   *a race between Galveston and nearby Houston for commercial dominance*: Larson, p. 12.

73   *the largest cotton port in the United States*: Ibid., p. 13.

73   *death and devastation in Galveston during a 1900 hurricane*: see, for example, Larson.

74   *The Nautilus had to deliver the U.S. mail*: Sothern, p. 62.

74   *In front of a secluded oceanfront boardinghouse on Isle Derniere*: McAllister. In a personal communication, Bethany Bultman, author of an

article on the Isle Derniere storm published in *Louisiana Cultural Vistas,* suggested that the boardinghouse where McAllister stayed may have been the one owned by the Pecot family and advertised in the *Planter's Banner,* although she felt that the evidence supporting this conclusion was not definitive.

74   *a half-mile farther down the island:* McAllister.

74   *"looked like things of life":* Ibid.

74   *"bewitching spell":* Ibid.

75   *Twelve people were spending the summer:* Ibid.

75   *"three ladies, young, single":* Ibid.

75   *"pale melancholy":* Ibid.

75   *"as to enjoy to the utmost an exhibition":* Ibid.

75   *revealing delicate, striking features:* based on a photo of Althee Mille in the *Times Picayune,* June 10, 1928.

75   *two of her stepsiblings from her father's first marriage:* Based on engravings of children's names and birth dates on the monument for Thomas Mille's first wife in St. John's Cemetery in Plaquemine. The monument reads at the top, VIRGINIE HEBERT CONSORT OF THOMAS MILLE. Two of Virginie's children were buried with her.

CHAPTER 6: FORCE 12

81   *Captain Francis Beaufort of the British Navy had jotted into his journal:* Huler, p. 70.

81   *system of abbreviations:* Ibid., p. 148. Through much of the nineteenth century, the method of visually estimating wind force was not referred to as "the Beaufort Scale" but as "Admiral Beaufort's system of abbreviations."

81   *"Hereafter I shall estimate the force of the wind":* Ibid., 70.

81   *Beaufort tinkered with the scale:* Ibid., pp. 73–74.

82   *"light air" that would be "just sufficient to give steerage way":* Ibid., p. 121, which presents a version of the scale from 1833. The other descriptions of different force levels are also from this 1833 version, except for Force 12 as a "sail-splitter," which is from an early version from the beginning of the 1800s (ibid., p. 74).

82   *"which no canvas can withstand":* Ibid., p. 121, from an image initialed by Beaufort from *The Nautical Magazine* of 1832.

82   *This numerical scale was first officially used:* Aside from Beaufort's initial use of his scale aboard the vessels he commanded, Huler, p. 123, notes that the voyage of the *Beagle* in the early 1830s was the first official test of the scale by another sea captain, Robert Fitzroy. In August 1853, at the First Meteorological Conference in Brussels, the Beaufort Scale was adopted for international shipping.

82   *In fact, at 7:00 AM that Saturday, August 9:* Ludlum, p. 166.

82 *"Beaufort turned the sailing ship into an anemometer"*: Huler, p. 245.

82 *The storm at this time had a sustained wind speed*: Landsea et al. Hurricane winds are seventy-four miles per hour or greater.

82 *"The air is filled with foam and spray"*: Huler, p. 256.

83 *"stadium of thick, white cloud[s] surrounding the eye"*: Emanuel, p. 8.

83 *"Imagine a Roman coliseum"*: Ibid.

83 *evaporation is one of the most important sources of heat*: Ibid., p. 57.

83 *"The amount of power dissipated by a typical mature Atlantic hurricane"*: Ibid., p. 61.

83 *feeding on ample warm seawater*: In general, the water temperature conducive for hurricane growth is greater than 80 degrees Fahrenheit (26.50 degrees Celsius). See, for example, Gray, p. 675.

84 *"the sea that was white with foam"*: Schlatre, p. 705.

84 *"blew hard but steady"*: Ibid.

84 *the vessel anchored eight miles offshore of his house*: Ibid.

84 *"brought home her anchor"*: Ibid.

85 *"who ventured in the water"*: Pugh, "Reminiscences," p. 74.

85 *"lowing in a plaintive way"*: McAllister reported hearing the lowing of cattle on the island on Saturday morning.

85 *Aboard were Major Nelson and the ladies*: Ellis.

86 *no larger than the water was deep*: When waves break in the surf, they become "energy-saturated" (see, for example, Guza and Thornton; Sallenger and Holman). Under this condition, the ratio of wave height to water depth is approximately constant. Idealized waves in the surf, for example, have been shown theoretically to be 78 percent of the water depth, regardless of how high they were offshore, whether 4 feet or 40 feet. Direct measurements of real waves in the surf have confirmed the dependence of height on local depth, and that dependence has been expressed in terms of a statistic of the distribution of waves. The highest one-third wave height in the distribution, called the significant wave height, was found to be roughly 50 percent of the water depth. Maximum waves in the distribution of breakers are roughly twice the significant height; hence, maximum waves are roughly equal to the water depth.

87 *The coast of western Louisiana was marked with five such ridges*: Gomez, p. 11.

87 *Their name was derived from chene*: Ibid., p. 9.

87 *"To see a chenier from afar"*: Ibid.

87 *His son, Powell, was with him aboard the* Nautilus: *Daily Picayune*, August 25, 1856.

88 *Aboard were 176 horses and cows and mules*: Ibid.

88 *approximately seventy passengers*: *Nautilus* steward James Frisbee in his statement in the *Daily Picayune* of August 25, 1856. Frisbee said

that there were thirty cabin and fifteen steerage passengers when the ship first left Galveston; they discharged about six, maybe a few more, on their return for ice, then took on an additional twenty-five passengers and another five or six steerage passengers for a total of about sixty-nine or seventy.

88   *weather was fine:* Daily Picayune, August 25, 1856.

88   *The change began at 3:00 AM, Saturday:* Ibid.

88   *Many early steamships were outfitted:* Volo and Volo, p. 328.

89   *Screw propulsion systems had been introduced:* Ibid., 329.

90   *seventeen passengers: three who had booked passage:* Daily Picayune, August 19, 1856.

90   *two steam-powered towboats chugging toward his vessel:* Ibid.

90   *"The commerce of [the Mississippi Valley] will, in time, certainly exceed":* Corthell, p. 3.

90   *"to an arm, of which the hand at the end":* Hall, p. 336.

91   *"All the inland wealth of agriculture and minerals":* Corthell., p. 6.

91   *"[drag] iron harrows over the bars":* Ibid., p. 17. These harrows were usually used as farm equipment and dragged behind a tractor to break up soil and smooth fields before planting.

91   *By 1853 the channel was eighteen feet deep:* Ibid., p. 18. A new appropriation was made during 1856 to build jetties on Southwest Pass to help control the shoaling of the channels. This was too late to keep the mouth open during the days leading up to the 1856 hurricane.

92   *In March 1859, thirty-five ships would be trapped:* Ibid., p. 7.

92   *Nineteenth-century charts of the U.S. Coast Survey:* Ibid., p. 10.

92   *pushed water away from the mainland coast:* The narrow shelf and close proximity of deep water to shore would have limited this set-down, or decrease in sea level due to the offshore push of winds. Yet even a small lowering of sea level would have made the water shallower over the bar and forced the waves to break harder and more completely.

93   *"both anchors ahead, and sent down royal and top gallant yards, fore and aft":* New Orleans Commercial Bulletin, August 19, 1856.

93   *reported financial losses of more than $7 million:* Corthell, p. 7.

94   *"I was never fond of dancing":* Times Picayune, June 10, 1928.

CHAPTER 7: THE OPENING ROAR

95   *Michael Schlatre and his wife of ten years:* Schlatre's account of the storm does not mention the ball, only that he walked "backwards and forwards" many times to the hotel that day. Since most of the planters and their families attended the ball, I have assumed that the Schlatres were among them.

95   *7:00 PM, Saturday, August 9:* The Times Picayune article of June 10, 1928, by Maurice Elfer reported that the ball was held on Sunday,

August 10, and that the people danced into the night as wind and waves ripped the hotel apart. All of the other first-person accounts confirmed, however, that the ball was on Saturday, August 9, and concluded about midnight, when everyone returned to their homes or hotel rooms, long before the peak of the storm hit. No one was dancing in the ballroom during the disaster, unlike the scene sketched in the popular nineteenth-century novel by Lafcadio Hearn, *Chita: A Memory of Last Island,* which was inspired by the Isle Derniere disaster.

95   *"backwards and forwards, to and from the hotel"*: Schlatre, p. 705.

96   *Lodoiska's confidence in the safety of the island*: Bultman, "The Final Days of Isle Derniere," p. 84.

96   *as though he were preparing to attend Mass*: The church that the Schlatre family attended is discussed in Fama, p. 261.

96   *A formal photograph taken several years later*: The description of Schlatre's formal dress and facial features is based on a portrait of Schlatre done after the hurricane and reproduced in Bultman, "The Final Days of Isle Derniere," p. 86. It was originally published in the *Baton Rouge State Times,* August 9, 1961.

96   *"blew with much the same force, strong and regular"*: Schlatre, p. 705.

96   *Schlatre was anxious about its scheduled return at 10:00 PM*: Ibid.

97   *south, or starboard, side . . . north, or port, side*: Starboard is the right side of a vessel, port the left side. Early in the nineteenth century, the left side was referred to as larboard, although by the 1850s this usage was in decline.

97   *He had not left the exposed main deck "from the time the gale sprung up"*: *Daily Picayune,* afternoon edition, statement of Jim Frisbee, August 25, 1856.

97   *At 7:00 or 8:00 PM Saturday evening*: Ibid.

97   *"It shoals suddenly to five feet on the inshore"*: Bache, 1854, p. 69.

98   *"At 6:00 PM [Saturday, August 9], it was blowing a strong gale"*: *New Orleans Commercial Bulletin,* morning edition, August 18, 1856. This was observed by the captain of the ship *C. D. Merwin.*

99   *Abraham Smith had taken command of the river steamboat Star*: Ellis, p. 3.

99   *There it offloaded passengers and took on board cargo and travelers*: Ibid., p. 2.

99   *"The weather [was] threatening"*: Ibid.

99   *"his hat gone, and looking frightened"*: Ibid.

99   *"It took but a moment to realize that the boat"*: Ibid.

100   *"as good and gallant [a] man as ever trod"*: Ibid., p. 3.

100   *"I told him he was looking in the wrong direction"*: Ibid.

100   *"was compelled to let the pole go"*: Ibid.

100   *The men wore formal coats with tails:* This description of the apparel worn that night is based on line drawings of dancers at balls during roughly the same period. See, for example, the online holdings of the Library of Congress (available at www.loc.gov).

101   *"the best people of the country"*: Pugh, "Reminiscences," p. 73.

101   *Dr. Alfred Duperier felt uncomfortable at balls:* See *Times Picayune,* June 10, 1928, where Duperier is described as "not a society man."

101   *The thirty-year-old physician worked toward his medical degree:* Biography of Alfred Duperier, collection 55, Weeks Family, Edith Garland Dupre Library, University of Louisiana, Lafayette. Fenner, p. 19, reported that a Dr. Stone was present at the autopsy of the first victim of yellow fever in 1853.

102   *Although orchestras usually played at balls:* Southern, p. 136.

102   *a good dance fiddler was heavily sought after:* Ibid.

102   *"I recall with sadness the skill and taste of the old German"*: Pugh, "Reminiscences," p. 74.

102   *suddenly came to life, stepping toward each other to switch places:* Blasis, p. 496, describes some of the dances of the time.

102   quadrille de contredanses: The quadrille evolved during the nineteenth century from two couples to four, with each couple forming the side of the square. In America it became the forerunner of the square dance, which is still popular today.

103   *a sought-after look induced by putting drops in the eyes:* Streatfeild, p. 119.

103   *"flowing, diaphanous"*: Crete, p. 115.

103   *"to the point of madness"*: Ibid., p. 116.

103   *His father was a builder in New Orleans:* See Hilliar for background on Seymour Stewart's father, Samuel, and his mother.

103   *Seymour had been exposed to the Creole philosophy:* Crete, p. 98.

104   *ordered a crewman to repeatedly lower a weighted line:* Surveyors of the mid-nineteenth century had recommended this safety procedure. "Vessels plying between [Ship Shoal] and the shore should be careful with their leadline"; Bache, 1854, p. 69.

105   *"Before the dance ended the wind arose"*: Pugh, "A Historical Sketch."

105   *"if the storm doesn't blow over by the morning"*: Bultman, "The Final Days of Isle Derniere," p. 83.

105   *"that the* Star *. . . would not venture out"*: Schlatre, p. 705.

105   *the dance ended around midnight:* Pugh, "Reminiscences," p. 74.

106   *the storm was getting stronger:* Pugh, "A Historical Sketch."

106   *"A very serious accident"*: Wilson, Brady, and Adams, p. 17, quoting Thomas Wharton, journal entry of February 27, 1854.

106   *"thermometrical observations taken"*: Ibid., p. 7.

106   *"high wind in the night"*: Ibid., p. 121, quoting Thomas Wharton, journal entry of August 10, 1856.

107   *"I have taken charge of Mr. Payne's Bible Class"*: Ibid., p. 120, quoting Thomas Wharton, journal entry of August 5, 1856.

CHAPTER 8: FORMIDABLE AND SWIFT

109   *"It was something formidable and swift"*: Conrad, p. 36.

109   *He had no choice but to order the helmsman*: Daily Picayune, afternoon edition, statement of Jim Frisbee, August 25, 1856. The article notes that the ship had been headed into the sea rather than directly toward Southwest Pass.

110   *A half-hour past sunrise*: Sunrise on August 10, 1856, in New Orleans, about one hundred miles north from the *Nautilus's* position, was at 5:25 AM, according to a calculator developed by the U.S. Naval Observatory.

110   *"a tremendous, cross, confused, outrageous sea"*: Piddington, 2nd ed., p. 176, quoting Dr. A. Thom's description of the seas created by "rotating gales."

110   *"At the most critical moment, [their cargo of] railroad iron"*: Account of the ship *C. D. Merwin* in the *New Orleans Commercial Bulletin*, August 18, 1856.

111   *with extreme difficulty*: Ibid.

111   *Michael Schlatre awakened at first light*: Schlatre, p. 705.

111   *Still, Schlatre remained unconcerned*: Ibid.

111   *his house and the others on the island*: Ibid., p. 706.

112   *sighted the mainland marsh less than a mile away*: Ellis, p. 3.

112   *exposing a broad band of dark mud along the shore*: During the passage of winter cold fronts, Smith and Ellis had both probably observed north winds exposing some of the mud along the shore. On the approach of the hurricane, however, these north winds would have been far stronger than those normally associated with cold fronts; hence, a wider band of mud would likely have been exposed.

112   *marker at the mouth of Grand Caillou*: Ellis, p. 3.

112   *"There was at this time every indication of a severe storm brewing"*: Ibid.

113   *"Yes," he finally said*: Ibid.

113   *For days the persistent north wind had not only flooded the island's bay side*: Such a process also occurs during the north winds associated with the passage of winter cold fronts, which had contributed to the long-term narrowing and deterioration of Isle Derniere.

114   *"was one of the last places in the world"*: Times Picayune, June 10, 1928.

114   *The health of Althee's three-month-old baby had not improved*: Ibid.

114   *The day before, Dr. Duperier had prescribed some medicine*: Ibid.

114   *visitor staying with them, Mrs. Rommage:* Times Picayune, April 14,
       1936.

114   *and most alarmingly, her father:* The description of Thomas Mille's grow-
       ing fear is an interpretation based on (1) Emma's statement in an inter-
       view published in the *Times Picayune* on June 10, 1928, that her father
       had "lost courage" and (2) Schlatre's personal account of the storm, in
       which he describes Thomas Mille's persistent nervousness about the
       weather and Mille's apparent unconcern for his family once the storm
       hit the island.

115   *"The vessel [had] headed to the sea as long as possible":* Times Picayune,
       evening edition, August 25, 1856.

115   *"got into a trough of a sea [and] would not wear":* Ibid.

115   *The mainmast, the tallest of three masts:* This is an interpretation of
       Frisbee's account in the *Times Picayune,* evening edition, August 25,
       1856. It was stated that the mainmast fell on the starboard side and
       the ship listed in that direction. It was also stated that the captain or-
       dered the mast cut away. I assume that he did this after the mast fell.

115   *"The bulkhead in [the] centre of the ship was knocked away":* Ibid.

115   *Frisbee grabbed on to a railing on the port side:* Ibid.

115   *"I then looked forward and saw Capt. T. coming aft":* Ibid.

116   *the crew had been able to lower the port covers:* Ibid.

CHAPTER 9: EXTREME JEOPARDY

119   *Michael Schlatre strode across the parlor:* This scene of Mille con-
       fronting Schlatre about the potential danger on the island is described
       here as occurring Sunday morning. In Schlatre's account, p. 706, he
       reported the "fears of the Milles [sic] family who constantly sent . . .
       to ask me . . . if . . . there was any danger." So evidently such scenes
       occurred through the day and, with the deteriorating conditions, prob-
       ably started early. Hence, this scene in the time sequence is placed
       earliest in the morning, followed by other scenes beginning at 10:00
       AM. That Thomas Mille himself queried Schlatre on Sunday as the
       wind grew stronger was verified in Emma's account in the *Times
       Picayune,* April 14, 1936.

119   *after breakfast with his wife and seven children:* Schlatre, pp. 705–706.

119   *"There is no cause for worry":* Times Picayune, April 14, 1936.

120   *Schlatre decided to stoke the Mille family's flames of concern:* Schlatre,
       p. 706.

120   *"they had not seen the worse yet":* Ibid.

120   *"But too true this proved":* Ibid.

120   *About 10:00 AM, Smith and Ellis determined:* Ellis, p. 3.

120   *In the building gale:* Ibid., pp. 3–4.

120   *experienced the full force of the storm:* Ibid., p. 4.

121   *"veering and hauling, 3 or 4 points first":* Ibid.

121   The Star *broached:* Ibid.

121   *A wave hit broadside, and water surged over the gunwale:* Ibid.

122   *W. W. Pugh was in the hotel on Isle Derniere:* Although his two pub-
       lished accounts do not explicitly report that Pugh and his family were
       staying at Muggah's Hotel, the texts imply that they were at the hotel.
       For example, he and his family sought shelter during the storm behind
       "the dining room," which, from the context of the account, was that of
       the hotel; see Pugh, "Reminiscences," p. 76.

122   *He was forty-five years old, with intense eyes:* This description of Pugh
       is an interpretation of an undated photograph of him in Bultman, "The
       Last Days of Isle Derniere," p. 82. At the time of the storm, he was
       forty-five years old, and the photograph is of a middle-aged man.

122   *"rigid and grave":* Kane, *Plantation Parade,* p. 217.

122   *Pugh, his wife and seven children:* Pugh, "Reminiscences," p. 74.

122   *Then whole roofs lifted and tumbled through the air:* Ibid., p. 75.

123   *"a long low building":* Ibid.

123   *"resist anything short of a cyclone":* Ibid.

123   *Captain Smith turned to Ellis, shaken:* Ellis, p. 4.

123   *"No, sir," Ellis replied emphatically:* Ibid.

124   *"I [will] handle the spokes for a while":* Ibid.

124   *"memorable run that a high-pressure steamboat":* Ibid.

124   *Then, at 8:00 AM on Sunday:* New Orleans Commercial Bulletin,
       morning edition, August 19, 1856.

125   *Within two hours, the ship could no longer be maneuvered:* Ibid.

125   *Michael Schlatre looked into the wind:* Schlatre's account, p. 705, sug-
       gests that he looked out into the bay and saw the *Star* making its land-
       ing on Isle Derniere before breakfast, while Ellis's account specifically
       states that the *Star* did not make its turn from the mainland until
       10:00 AM, and then had to cross Caillou Bay. Here I have assumed the
       accuracy of the timing reported from the steamer by Ellis; Schlatre's
       sighting of the vessel would thus have been about 10:30 AM or later.
       Schlatre also said that he saw the vessel across the bay, "close on the
       main shore" (p. 705). This seems unlikely given the weather condi-
       tions; the vessel must have been much closer to Isle Derniere when
       Schlatre first saw it.

125   *"What was my astonishment to see the* Star*":* Schlatre, p. 705.

125   *Schlatre grew concerned:* Ibid.

126   *He rushed the half-mile down the beach to watch:* Ibid.

126   *becoming broadside to the wind:* Ellis, p. 4.

126   *several male passengers leapt to the pier's deck:* Ibid.

126   *"the storm was upon us in all its fury":* Ibid.

127　*waves that must have been twenty-five feet or taller:* The *Nautilus* was thought to have capsized close to Southwest Pass, probably over the deep water near the shore there, where the waves would not have lost much of their energy as they progressed across a shallow muddy shelf that lies offshore much of Louisiana.

127　*He watched as passengers and crew emerged:* Times Picayune, evening edition, August 25, 1856.

127　*"some six or eight persons succeeded":* Ibid.

127　*twenty-five to thirty people adrift:* Ibid.

127　*Life jackets (then called swimming belts):* A version of such a belt was used by England's Life Boat Institution before 1858; see Royal Cornwall Polytechnic Society, p. xxx. Further, several versions of buoyant swimming belts by different inventors and manufacturers were listed in a catalog in 1851; see Royal Commission, p. 50.

127　*He drifted near Mr. Johnson:* Times Picayune, evening edition, August 25, 1856.

127　*more substantial raft:* Ibid.

128　*"the air somewhat chill":* Wilson, Brady, and Adams, p. 121, quoting Thomas Wharton, journal entry of August 10, 1856.

128　*"the wind rose . . . and rain set in":* Ibid.

128　*"striking parable":* Wilson, Brady, and Adams, p. 123, quoting Thomas Wharton, journal entry of August 17, 1856.

CHAPTER 10: GRAVITY SUSPENDED

129　*The swirling storm moved relentlessly toward the barrier islands:* Position, intensity, and other data on this storm are available as part of NOAA's Hurricane Research Division's Reanalysis Project. For documentation and discussion of the procedures used in acquiring these data, and the data of other early storms, see Landsea et al.

129　*The storm had become a monster:* Research scientists have hypothesized that the intensity of Hurricane Opal in 1995 grew explosively because it passed across a warm water eddy of the Loop Current before coming ashore on the U.S. northern Gulf of Mexico coast. Shay et al., p. 1366.

129　*wind speeds now ripped to 150 miles per hour:* Landsea et al.

129　*Official names were not given to Atlantic Basin hurricanes:* See National Hurricane Center.

130　*such as the Isle Derniere Hurricane:* Alluding to its impact, Ludlum, p. 165, refers to the storm as the Last Island Disaster. Blake et al. refer to the storm as "Louisiana (Last Island)" and through 2004 rated it the tenth most intense land-falling storm in the United States, tied with Hurricane Hugo.

130   *"simple as hurricanes go"*: Bultman, "The Last Days of Isle Derniere," p. 85.

130   *"Some of the violent north winds"*: See the discussion of Gulf of Mexico northers in Reid, *The Progress*, p. 296.

131   *"Already the rain began to come through the roof"*: Schlatre, p. 706.

131   *Forty-four years later, on Galveston Island, Texas*: Larson, p. 170.

131   *"I had no apprehension of danger"*: Schlatre, p. 706.

132   *The rain was now torrential*: Ibid.

132   *Schlatre's son Louis was ill*: Ibid.

132   *He repeatedly glanced out a window*: Ibid.

132   *"she still stood steadily"*: Ibid.

132   *In the pelting rain, Smith and the crewmen*: Ellis, p. 4.

132   *The vessel was old and tired*: Bultman, "The Last Days of Isle Derniere," pp. 81, 84, describes the *Star* as an old steamer that had been constructed in the 1840s.

132   *Many passengers were still trapped*: Ellis, p. 2.

132   *"quite a number of ladies"*: Ibid., p. 4.

132   *the multiple decks with cabins full of people*: Ibid., p. 5.

133   *which was considered one of the strongest structures on Isle Derniere*: *Times Picayune*, April 14, 1936.

133   *Among the refugees was Dr. Lyle*: Ellis, p. 4.

134   *"About 12 o'clock in the day"*: *Times Picayune*, July 13, 1919.

134   *"The water about 2 P.M."*: Ibid.

134   *They did not leave their house*: *Times Picayune*, April 14, 1936.

134   *The slaves gathered in the main house*: *Times Picayune*, June 10, 1928.

134   *trying to convince him to order his family members and slaves*: Ibid.

135   *"When we looked out"*: *Times Picayune*, April 14, 1936.

135   *"My father lost courage"*: *Times Picayune*, June 10, 1928.

135   *A half-mile farther down the beach from the other houses*: McAllister. The Coast Survey map of the 1850s shows the Village of Isle Derniere spread in a linear fashion along the shore to the west of the landing. Other sources, previously referred to, note that the cluster of houses belonging to Thomas Mille, Michael Schlatre, and Governor Hebert was a half-mile from the hotel. I'm assuming that the boardinghouse where McAllister stayed was another half-mile down the beach to the west, probably at the westernmost end of the village.

135   *"The daylight, even before noon"*: McAllister.

135   *The five boarders in the house sat down to a midday Sunday meal*: Ibid.

135   *"no one was as yet willing"*: Ibid.

136   *"[the storm] had been, with imperceptible accretions, gathering power"*: Ibid.

136   *"Fiery lightning almost constantly illuminated the heavens"*: Ibid.

136   *lightning in eyewalls over water:* Molinari, p. 520.

136   *"almost reached the conclusion that nothing [could] be done":* McAllister.

136   *"At 1 P.M.":* Wilson, Brady, and Adams, p. 121, quoting Thomas Wharton, journal entry of August 10, 1856.

136   *Thomas, a meticulous man:* Ibid., p. xvi.

137   *They felt that the project was timely:* Times Picayune, July 6, 1919.

137   *Muggah's Hotel was not large enough:* Ibid.

138   *"the largest resort hotel in North America during the antebellum period":* Bultman, "The Final Days of Isle Derniere," p. 80. Bultman provides a rendering by a present-day artist of what the building would have looked like.

138   *Mr. Hall and Mr. Hildreth:* Times Picayune, July 6, 1919.

CHAPTER 11: MERCILESS WATERS

139   *He watched the wind tear his separate kitchen building apart:* Schlatre, p. 706.

139   *he had not been alarmed by the loss of those frail structures:* Ibid.

139   *"The chickens in the yard were squatting in all directions":* Ibid.

139   *"all must keep cool, not to be frightened":* Ibid.

140   *He saw the wind thrust Mille's home forward:* Ibid.

140   *"Now for us":* Ibid.

140   *"One scream and all was hushed within":* Ibid., p. 707.

140   *They had all assembled in a single room:* Times Picayune, April 14, 1936.

140   *Thomas Mille had disappeared:* Emma stated in an interview that her father had lost courage (*Times Picayune*, June 10, 1928). After his house was knocked from its blocks, Thomas left the remains and wandered alone to Michael Schlatre's house next door, "wringing his hands"; Schlatre, p. 727.

140   *Reverend McAllister and the other inhabitants:* McAllister.

141   *"Is there some undiscovered faculty in man":* Ibid.

141   *From above, they heard a loud bang:* Ibid.

141   *"the law of gravitation itself was superseded":* Ibid.

141   *"came forth in a voice which the howling tornado":* Ibid.

142   *"The Gulf on one side and the bay on the other":* Ibid.

142   *the vessel's three stories of superstructure were gone:* Ellis, p. 5.

142   *men, women, and children had funneled down ladders:* Ibid.

143   *His measurements were definitive:* Ibid.

143   *"The inmates stood still with fear":* Schlatre, p. 707.

143   *Then Schlatre started from a terrific crash:* Ibid.

143   *Inside a large steamer trunk, they quickly stuffed clothes:* Ibid.

144   *"came into my house from somewhere":* Ibid.

145   *the* Star *was still being driven toward the surf*: Ellis, p. 6.

145   *they sought sanctuary behind the destroyed dining room*: Pugh, "Reminiscences," p. 76.

145   *"The women and children who first imagined themselves"*: Times Picayune, July 13, 1919.

146   *"Many persons were wounded"*: Ibid.

146   *three of his children were missing*: Pugh, "Reminiscences," p. 78.

147   *"I told him it was no way to act"*: Schlatre, p. 707.

148   *Mille had watched Schlatre's rescue attempt*: Ibid., p. 708.

149   *"My wife hearing my cries for help came out to me"*: Ibid.

149   *"dreadful cut over the eye"*: Ibid.

149   *Emma Mille was still bleeding profusely*: Times Picayune, April 14, 1936.

149   *The water had also grabbed Althee and her infant*: Ibid.

150   *"Don't crush my baby!"*: Ibid.

150   *At any location in the surf, the tallest waves*: As noted earlier, the waves were *roughly the same height as the water was deep.*

150   *Ellis then spied a few dozen people*: Ellis, p. 6.

CHAPTER 12: LANDFALL

153   *sustained winds of 150 miles per hour*: Landsea et al., p. 194.

153   *exceeding the sustained winds at landfall of many of the devastating hurricanes of the modern era*: Keep in mind that the destructive potential of a hurricane involves more than peak wind speed; the size of the storm and the speed of its forward movement are also important, as well as other factors. Researchers are investigating new ways to categorize hurricanes to reflect more accurately their destructive potential.

154   *She was a woman with a broken leg*: Ellis, p. 6.

154   *"The gale broke out from the S.W. [southwest]"*: Ibid. In contrast, Schlatre, p. 708, did not mention the calm of an eye. He wrote that around 5:00 PM the wind suddenly changed direction and broke out from the east-southeast. Since Schlatre was seriously injured when the eye would have moved over the island, I have depended on Thomas Ellis's observations of the conditions.

154   *The wind and breakers were driving floating debris*: Ellis, pp. 6–7.

154   *"Several persons came surging by"*: Ellis, p. 7.

155   *some of the children were in tears*: Schlatre, p. 709.

155   *"The waters now maddened by resistance"*: Ibid.

155   *"I now rolled over and over"*: Ibid., p. 710.

156   *"I put my hands to those of my child"*: Ibid.

156   *A small levee ran from the boardinghouse*: McAllister.

156   *"To anyone far off looking at us"*: Ibid.

157   *"Our faith was staggered"*: Ibid.
157   *"Look at Mama!"*: *Times Picayune*, June 10, 1928.
158   *"I did not fear that anyone in my family"*: Ibid.
159   *When the eye passed Southwest Pass*: *The New Orleans Commercial Bulletin*, August 19, 1856, reported that the wind near Southwest Pass switched direction, from winds coming from the north to winds coming from the south, at about 10:00 AM on August 10. On Isle Derniere, ninety miles to the west, Ellis, p. 6, reported a calm "between 5 and 6 PM" before "the gale broke out from the S.W. [southwest]." It appears that the eye passed near Southwest Pass about seven hours before making landfall on Isle Derniere. The track of the storm was at an angle to the coast; it approached Isle Derniere from the southeast and passed south of Southwest Pass. See Landsea et al.
159   *Schlatre could see around him to the faces of three of his sons*: Schlatre, p. 710.
160   *he spied Thomas Mille standing about one hundred feet ahead*: Ibid.
161   *"it never entered my mind"*: Ibid.
161   *Reverend McAllister and the eleven others*: McAllister.
161   *They stood there in silence, the only sounds*: Ibid.
162   *"The twirling and twisting, the dashing and splashing"*: Ibid.
162   *At 9:00 PM aboard the* Manilla: The timing of the *Manilla* going aground was given in the *Daily Picayune*, morning edition, August 19, 1856.
162   *from the mouth of the Mississippi to Timbalier Island*: Ibid. This article gave the location where the vessel "struck" the barrier island.
162   *Twenty-nine people entered the dark surf*: Ibid.
163   *waves broke the* Manilla *into pieces*: *New Orleans Commercial Bulletin*, morning edition, August 19, 1856.
163   *"I feared the sharks would cut off our legs"*: Schlatre, p. 712.
164   *"To do him justice he did hold on"*: Ibid.
164   *raised a storm surge that was thirteen to eighteen feet*: This is a rough estimate based on the range of storm surge elevations expected during a category 4 hurricane. Such estimates do not take into account, however, the unique shape of the shore and seabed of a particular location. They also do not include the breadth of the storm and other factors important in forcing storm surge. "Normal sea level" refers to the stage of the astronomical tide at the time of the hurricane's landfall.
164   *Since the island was only five to six feet high*: Gerdes, appendix 21, p. 54*.
164   *"wave setup"*: When waves break on a beach, they raise sea level in what oceanographers call "wave setup." For example, one set of measurements showed this setup at the shoreline to be about 17 percent of the deepwater significant (highest one-third) wave height; see Guza

and Thornton. Later work has shown dependence on other factors as well; see Holman and Sallenger. Wave setup would be added to the storm surge forced by wind, barometric pressure, and so on.

165   *This kind of inundation occurred on another Louisiana barrier island:* See Sallenger, Wright, Lillycrop, et al., and Sallenger, Wright, and Doran.

CHAPTER 13: SILENCE FOLLOWING A SCREAM

169   *"Before daylight, I know not how long before":* McAllister.

169   *they huddled together on the sand under a scavenged red quilt:* Ibid.

170   *As a group, they started walking along the beach:* Ibid.

170   *"jeweled and lily hand . . . protruding from the sand":* Ibid.

170   *her eyes looking up from the sand at them:* Ibid.

170   *"Sights like these suddenly presented":* Ibid.

171   *the fine two-story houses with their galleries:* Ibid.

171   *the barren hull of the* Star *lay on the beach:* Ibid.

171   *The hold dripped with muddy, grimy filth:* Ibid.

172   *the hurricane winds subsided and the sea retreated:* Ellis, p. 7.

172   *Only the largest timbers of the houses remained:* Pugh, "A Historical Sketch."

172   *Michael Schlatre realized that he and Thomas Mille:* Schlatre, p. 712.

173   *"It was death to go far up":* Ibid.

173   *"Trusting Providence[,] we let it drive up the marsh":* Ibid.

173   *"We were high & dry on the marsh":* Ibid., p. 713.

173   *the small stable whose walls were held vertical by pilings:* Pugh, "A Historical Sketch," wrote that only one building, a small stable, remained standing.

173   *the other was Richard, the body servant of Thomas Mille:* Emma Mille told a reporter that Richard survived the storm in an "outbuilding" that I have assumed was the same stable that Pugh referred to; see *Times Picayune,* June 10, 1928.

173   *"Had we gone into that outbuilding":* Ibid.

174   *a black woman, another slave:* Ibid.

174   *He could only lie on his left side:* Schlatre, p. 713.

174   *The weather remained miserable with rain and haze:* Ibid., p. 714.

174   *Schlatre ordered Thomas Mille, who was sprawled next to him:* Ibid.

175   *he could not see far because his eyes had been blinded:* Ibid.

175   *able to discern two small isles:* Ibid.

175   *"A burning thirst now began to devour us":* Ibid.

176   *"We longed for a piece of that ice":* Ibid.

176   *"Heaven how good that water was":* Ibid., p. 715.

176   *Some people have survived many weeks without eating:* Piantadosi, p. 36.

177   *A 20 percent loss can cause shock:* Ibid., p. 51.
177   *"The force of the gale . . . soon spent itself":* Wilson, Brady, and Adams, p. 121.
177   *"The privation of water is justly ranked among the most dreadful":* Philbrick, p. 116.
178   *"Both white and black in great numbers":* Pugh, "A Historical Sketch."
178   *Blood streamed down her face: Times Picayune,* June 10, 1928.
178   *the tatters of her white muslin dress: Times Picayune,* April 14, 1936.

CHAPTER 14: WAITING
179   *crew of the USS* Indianapolis *who were thrown into the sea:* See, for example, Stanton, pp. 172, 177.
180   *When Frisbee later turned his back: Daily Picayune,* August 25, 1856.
180   *"I . . . saw that I was counting on a broken reed":* Schlatre, p. 715.
180   *"two miserable creatures":* Ibid., p. 716.
181   *blowing down signs and ripping awnings:* Ludlum, p. 165.
181   *steamboat* Capitol, *whose dual stacks had been pushed flat:* Wilson, Brady, and Adams, p. 123.
181   *"Three Germans and two negroes": Daily Picayune,* afternoon edition, August 12, 1856.
182   *"The last thirty hours must have been a fearful time":* Wilson, Brady, and Adams, p. 123.
182   *"No boats had been sent out": Times Picayune,* July 20, 1919.
182   *"I was very badly bruised": Times Picayune,* June 10, 1928.
183   *"Towards [the* Star] *each one directed his path": Times Picayune,* April 14, 1936.
183   *Although weak and exhausted:* Ibid.
183   *He stitched her head wound: Times Picayune,* June 10, 1928.
183   *"The bodies of men, women and children were to be seen": Times Picayune,* July 13, 1919.
184   *The grim task of identifying the corpses:* Pugh, "Reminiscences," p. 78.
184   *A small sailboat was salvaged:* The *Daily Picayune,* morning edition, August 14, 1856, reported that John Davis and the engineer from the *Star* had set out for Brashear City in a "small sail boat."
185   *"you see the trace of fatal knife about the pockets of the victims": Daily Picayune,* August 20, 1856.
185   *Jean Lafitte, had operated from Barataria Bay:* Davis, p. 32.
185   *while being remote and wild enough:* Asbury, p. 155.
186   *One of Lafitte's captains, Vincent Gambi:* Asbury, p. 159; Sothern, p. 14.
186   *Other accounts, however, maintain that Gambi was killed:* Asbury, p. 167.

186   *"One was actually seen to push the head of a person"*: Fama, p. 172, quoting the *Southern Sentinel*.

187   *The Isle Derniere had been severed into two parts*: Times Picayune, July 6, 1919.

CHAPTER 15: RESCUE

189   *"Terror, grief, and exposure"*: letter to *The Delta* after the 1856 storm by Annier Read, reprinted in the *Times Picayune*, July 27, 1919.

189   *"to the great joy of our beclouded folks"*: New Orleans Commercial Bulletin, morning edition, August 14, 1856.

189   *"That these machines should be out of order"*: Ibid.

190   *low areas of the city away from the natural levees*: Ibid.

190   *"the 'rolling sweep' of the Gulf waves was extremely heavy"*: Daily Picayune, morning edition, August 13, 1856.

190   *"The storm that visited us"*: Daily Picayune, evening edition, August 13, 1856.

190   *disturbing rumors had begun to circulate*: In the *Daily Picayune* of Thursday morning, August 14, 1856, the first reports of the storm on Isle Derniere noted that "the rumor that prevailed yesterday . . . is probably too true."

190   *$10,000 cash that he had carried with him*: Fama, p. 171, quoting the *Southern Sentinel*.

190   *a young woman from New Orleans whose jewels*: Ibid.

190   *"A negro and [a] white man came up boldly"*: Ibid., p. 172, quoting the *Southern Sentinel*.

191   *"I was now desperate, cared for nothing"*: Schlatre, p. 717.

192   *save for some grass that left a bitter taste in their mouths*: Ibid.

192   *"I knew that the boat was taking the remaining people"*: Ibid., p. 718.

192   *One of them rested on a large log*: Daily Picayune, afternoon edition, August 25, 1856.

192   *"He went over before I reached him"*: Ibid.

193   *Long-term immersion in seawater*: Ibid., p. 182.

193   *his tongue was parched and stiff*: This description is an interpretation based on what happened to the men from the *Indianapolis*; see, for example, Stanton, p. 186.

193   *Brashear City Hotel*: Daily Picayune, morning edition, August 14, 1856.

194   *Berwick's Bay [near Brashear City]*: Ibid.

195   *"The land crabs would pinch me every few minutes"*: Schlatre, p. 719.

195   *"He was no longer of further use to me"*: Ibid.

196   *"I thought that I had labored"*: Ibid.

196   *Then he spied a wooden door floating nearby*: Daily Picayune, August 25, 1856.

197   *"for their noble and humane efforts to preserve human life"*: *Daily Crescent,* August 18, 1856. W. W. Pugh was elected president of the survivors, and Alfred Duperier the acting secretary.

197   *terminus of the Opelousas Railroad near Brashear City:* At that time, the railroad extended to Bayou Boeuf. This section of tracks had opened on March 1, 1856, about five months before the storm; see Rightor, p. 303.

197   *"In his arms he held with a convulsive grasp the dead body of his infant":* New Orleans Crescent, August 16, 1856.

198   *The storm surge had traveled up the bayou:* Times Picayune, July 20, 1919.

198   *Our Little Loula:* This inscription was obtained from the engraving on Loula's headstone.

199   *"learned that my parents had been lost":* Times Picayune, April 14, 1936.

199   *"very picturesque by reason of its tortuousness":* Warner, p. 88.

200   She *"was so good to me":* Times Picayune, April 14, 1936.

CHAPTER 16: RENEWAL

202   *"Excitement on the Lafourche":* New Orleans Commercial Bulletin, morning edition, August 19, 1856.

202   *reports had not been confirmed:* Ibid.

202   *the voyage of the* Streck *generated little interest:* New Orleans Commercial Bulletin, August 18, 1856.

202   *"Oh! God of heavens":* Schlatre, p. 722.

203   *"We cried aloud with our feeble voices hallowing":* Ibid., p. 723.

203   *"We cried in the bitterness of our souls at the thought":* Ibid.

204   *"You are seen they said to me":* Ibid., p. 725.

204   *One was the steam-powered towboat* F. M. Streck: *Times Picayune,* August 25, 1856.

205   *"It is to be hoped":* Daily Picayune, August 20, 1856.

205   *a fifty-four-year-old man walked down the gangway:* Hilliar reports that Samuel Stewart was born in 1801. Ancestry.com reports his birth date as November 24, 1801, in Down Patrick, Ireland.

206   *For many hours, under a baking sun:* Fama, p. 175, quoting the *Southern Sentinel*, August 30, 1856.

206   *Inside were the twenty-one coins:* The *Southern Sentinel* of August 30, 1856 (quoted in Fama), reported that an initialed watch in his pocket confirmed that the body was that of Seymour Stewart. Hilliar's family history reports that the twenty-one coins were used for identification.

206   *The armed men from the mainland:* Daily Picayune, August 20, 1856.

207   *"Those already taken had a very narrow escape":* Ibid.

207   *as Sothern suggested in* Last Island: Sothern, p. 75.

208 *Captain Rogers of the* Manilla *was recovering:* Daily Picayune, August 19, 1856.

208 *fishermen were catching in their nets some of Bordeaux's finest:* Sothern, p. 63.

209 *Plaquemine's newspaper, the* Southern Sentinel, *had hailed Mille:* Fama, p. 169, quoting the *Southern Sentinel.*

209 *"a man in full health, a good constitution":* Schlatre, p. 727.

210 *a little book filled with religious poems:* Times Picayune, April 14, 1936.

210 *"As Divine Providence saved us miraculously":* Ibid.

210 *"He said that he would never forget me":* Ibid.

211 *They were wed on December 8, 1856:* Ibid.

EPILOGUE: FOREST IN THE SEA

214 *West St. Peter Street in front of number 225:* The address was given in the Times Picayune, June 10, 1928. It is also noted in the census of 1930.

214 *a stately home:* The Duperier home was valued at $20,000 in the 1930 census, significantly more than most surrounding homes and a high amount for real estate at the time, indicating that it was certainly large and probably elaborate in design.

214 *Emma Mille Duperier was celebrating her ninety-eighth birthday:* Times Picayune, April 14, 1936.

214 *"happy years . . . raising a family":* Ibid.

215 *"the curse of God":* See Field, Field, and McLaughlin, p. 130. "Catharine Cole" was a pseudonym used by Martha Field, a reporter for the *New Orleans Times Picayune.*

215 *Maps prepared by the Coast Survey:* See the atlas by McBride et al., "Analysis of Barrier Shoreline Change," and the map by McBride et al., *Shoreline Changes of the Isles Dernieres,* each of which shows maps and changes to the islands and provides statistics about changes from the nineteenth century to the twentieth.

216 *the islands lost 45 percent of their surface area:* McBride et al., "Analysis of Barrier Shoreline Change," p. 47.

216 *the Isle Dernieres had been reduced 78 percent:* Ibid.

217 *"The lesson of the flood was not forgotten":* Pugh, "A Historical Sketch."

217 *"During storms the waves will wash over Last Island":* Field, Field, and McLaughlin, p. 130.

218 *The west end of Dauphin Island:* For background information on Dauphin Island, Alabama, see Sallenger et al., "Extreme Changes."

218 *The mainland community of Holly Beach:* For background information on Holly Beach, Louisiana, see Sallenger et al., "Hurricane Rita."

219 *a panel of scientists sponsored by the National Academy of Sciences:* National Academy of Sciences.

219 *"With a high level of confidence"*: Ibid.

219 *Recent research has shown*: For example, Stefan Ramstorf concluded in
a 2007 paper in the journal *Science* and in a separate review of the
2007 IPCC report that "a sea level rise [during the twenty-first cen-
tury] exceeding one metre can in my view by no means be ruled out."

220 *become increasingly vulnerable to hurricanes*: Culver et al. report geologic evidence of an earlier (1,100 years ago) collapse of barrier islands
along a portion of the North Carolina Outer Banks. They hypothesize
that this may have been triggered by a hurricane. Also, Sallenger et
al., in "Barrier Island Failure Modes," discuss the possibility of barrier
island failure using an example of the response of Louisiana's Chandeleur Islands both during and after Hurricane Katrina.

{ SOURCES }

Abrahams, Roger D., Nick Spitzer, John Szwed, and Robert Farris Thompson. *Blues for New Orleans: Mardi Gras and America's Creole Soul*. University of Pennsylvania Press, Philadelphia, 2006.

Asbury, Herbert. *The French Quarter: An Informal History of the New Orleans Underworld*. Alfred A. Knopf, New York, 2003 (originally published in 1936).

Bache, A. D. *Report to the Superintendent of the Coast Survey Showing the Progress of the Survey During the Year 1853*. Robert Armstrong, Washington, D.C., 1854.

———. *Report to the Superintendent of the Coast Survey Showing the Progress of the Survey During the Year 1858*. William A. Harris, Washington, D.C., 1859.

Barnard, F. A. P., et al. *Report on the History and Progress of the American Coast Survey Up to the Year 1858*. American Association for the Advancement of Science, 1858. Available at: http://www.history.noaa.gov/stories_tales/cs1858_1.html (last updated June 8, 2006).

Barry, John. *Rising Tide: The Great Mississippi Flood of 1927 and How It Changed America*. Simon & Schuster, New York, 1997.

Bergerie, Maurine. *They Tasted Bayou Water: A Brief History of Iberia Parish*. Pelican Publishing Co., Gretna, La., 2000.

Biographical and Historical Memoires of Louisiana. Goodspeed Publishing Co., Chicago, 1892.

Bixel, Patricia Bellis, and Elizabeth Hayes Turner. *Galveston and the 1900 Storm: Catastrophe and Catalyst*. University of Texas Press, Austin, 2000.

Blake, Eric S., Jerry D. Jarrell, Max Mayfield, and Edward Rappaport. "The Deadliest, Costliest, and Most Intense United States Tropical Cyclones from 1851 to 2004 (and Other Frequently Requested Hurricane Facts)." NOAA Technical Memorandum NWS TPC-1. Available at: http://www.nhc.noaa.gov/pastint.shtml (last updated July 27, 2005).

Blasis, C. *The Code of Terpsichore, the Art of Dance: Comprising Its Theory and Practice and a History of Its Rise and Progress, from the Earliest Times*. Edward Bull, Holles Street, London, 1830.

Blassingame, John W. *The Slave Community: Plantation Life in the Antebellum South*. Oxford University Press, New York, 1979.

Bolles, Albert Sidney. *Industrial History of the United States: From the Earliest Settlements to the Present Time*. Henry Bill Publishing Co., Norwich, Conn., 1878.

Brasseaux, Carl A., and Keith P. Fontenot. *Steamboats on Louisiana's Bayous.* Louisiana State University Press, Baton Rouge, 2004.

Britsch, Louis D. *Migration of Isle Dernieres: Past and Future.* Technical Report CERC-86-6. Coastal Engineering Research Center, U.S. Army Corps of Engineers, 1986.

Bryant, William Cullen. *Letters of a Traveler; or, Notes of Things Seen in Europe and America.* Kessinger Publishing, Whitefish, Mont., 2005 (originally published in 1850).

———. "The Hurricane," in *Poems.* Harper & Brothers, New York, 1840.

Bultman, Bethany Ewald. Bethany Ewald Bultman Papers, Williams Research Facility, Historic Collection of New Orleans, New Orleans.

———. "The Final Days of Isle Derniere." *Louisiana Cultural Vistas* (Louisiana Endowment for the Humanities) 13, no. 4 (Winter 2002–2003): 76–95.

Burke, James. *Circles: Fifty Round-Trips Through History, Technology, Science, Culture.* Simon & Schuster, New York, 2000.

Burrow, John W. Editor's introduction to *The Origin of the Species by Means of Natural Selection; or, The Preservation of Favoured Races in the Struggle for Life* by Charles Darwin. Penguin Classics, New York, 1985 (reprint).

Cable, George W. *The Creoles of Louisiana.* Pelican Publishing Co., Gretna, La., 2005 (originally published by Charles Scribner's Sons, New York, 1884).

———. *Strange True Stories of Louisiana.* Charles Scribner's Sons, New York, 1889.

Campanella, Richard. *Time and Place in New Orleans.* Pelican, 2002.

City of New Orleans, First District. *Catalogue of the Library of the Lyceum and Library Society.* R. C. Kerr, New Orleans, 1858.

Clark, Lewis, and Milton Clark. *Narratives of the Sufferings of Lewis and Milton Clark, Sons of a Soldier of the Revolution, During a Captivity of More Than Twenty Years Among the Slaveholders of Kentucky, One of the So Called Christian States of North America.* Bella Marsh, Boston, 1846.

Clement, William. *Plantation Life: On the Mississippi.* Pelican Publishing Co., Gretna, La., 2000.

Clinton, Catherine. *The Plantation Mistress: Woman's World in the Old South.* Pantheon, New York, 1984.

Cohen, Richard A. *By the Sword: A History of Gladiators, Musketeers, Samurai, Swashbucklers, and Olympic Champions.* Random House, New York, 2002.

Cohen's New Orleans Directory for 1853. New Orleans, 1853.

Coleridge, Samuel Taylor. "The Rime of the Ancient Mariner," in *Coleridge's "The Rime of the Ancient Mariner."* Educational Publishing Co., New York, 1906.

Collot, Victor. "Translation of General Collot's Description of de Bore's Sugar House and Comparison with the West India Cane." *Louisiana Historical Quarterly* 1, no. 4 (1918): 327–329.

Conrad, Joseph. *Three Sea Stories: "Typhoon," "Falk," and "The Shadow-Line."* Wordsworth Classics, Hertfordshire, U.K., 1998 (originally published in 1903).

Coogan, Tim Pat. *Wherever Green Is Worn: The Story of the Irish Diaspora.* Macmillan, New York, 2002.

Copeland, David A. *The Antebellum Era: Primary Documents on Events from 1820 to 1860.* Debating Historical Issues in the Media of the Time Series. Greenwood Press, Westport, Conn., 2003.

Corthell, Elmer Laurence. *A History of the Jetties at the Mouth of the Mississippi River.* John Wiley & Sons, New York, 1880.

Cox, John D. *Storm Watchers: The Turbulent History of Weather Prediction from Franklin's Kite to El Niño.* John Wiley & Sons, Hoboken, N.J., 2002.

Crete, Liliane. *Daily Life in Louisiana 1815–1830,* translated by Patrick Gregory. Louisiana State University Press, Baton Rouge, 1981 (originally published in French, 1978).

Culver, Stephen J., C. Grand Pre, D. Mallinson, S. Riggs, D. R. Reide, J. Foley, M. Hale, L. Metger, J. Ricardo, J. Rosenberger, C. Smith, S. Snyder, D. Twamley, K. Farrell, and B. Horton. "Late Holocene Barrier Island Collapse: Outer Banks, North Carolina, USA." *The Sedimentary Record* 5, no. 4 (2007): 4.

Davis, William C. *The Pirates Lafitte: The Treacherous World of the Corsairs of the Gulf.* Harcourt Books, New York, 2005.

Day, John, Donald F. Boesch, Ellis J. Clairain, G. Paul Kemp, Shirley B. Laska, William J. Mitsch, Kenneth Orth, Hassan Mashriqui, Denise J. Reed, Leonard Shabman, Charles A. Simenstad, Bill J. Streever, Robert R. Twilley, Chester C. Watson, John T. Wells, and Dennis F. Whigham. "Restoration of the Mississippi Delta: Lessons from Hurricanes Katrina and Rita." *Science* 315, no. 5819 (March 23, 2007): 1679–1684.

Depew, Chauncey M. *1795–1895: One Hundred Years of American Commerce,* vol. 1. D. O. Haynes and Co., New York, 1895.

Douglass, Frederick. *My Bondage and My Freedom,* with an introduction by Dr. James M'Cune Smith. Miller, Orton and Mulligan, New York, 1855.

Duffy, John. *Sword of Pestilence: The New Orleans Yellow Fever Epidemic of 1853.* Louisiana State University Press, Baton Rouge, 1966.

Duperier, Alfred. *Biography.* Collection 55, Weeks Family, Edith Garland Dupre Library, Special Collections and Archives, University of Louisiana, Lafayette.

Energy Information Administration. *Energy in the United States: 1635–2000.* U.S. Department of Energy Report DOE/EIA-0384(2003), September 7, 2004. Available at: http://www.eia.doe.gov/emeu/aer/eh/frame.html.

Ellis, Capt. Thomas H. *Account of the Storm on Last Island.* Bethany Ewald Bultman Papers, Historic New Orleans Collection, New Orleans; also held in (Louise) Butler Writings, box 5, folder 2, no. 1069, S-19-21, South Reading Room, Special Collections, Louisiana State University Libraries, Baton Rouge.

Elson, Louis Charles, ed. *University Musical Encyclopedia: Musicians' Practical Instructor,* vol. 1. University Society Inc., New York, 1914.

Emanuel, Kerry. *Divine Wind: The History and Science of Hurricanes.* Oxford University Press, New York, 2005.

English, T. J. *Paddy Whacked: The Untold Story of the Irish American Gangster.* HarperCollins, 2005.

Espy, James P. *The Philosophy of Storms.* Charles C. Little & James Brown, Boston, 1841.

Etheridge, D. M., L. P. Steele, R. L. Langenfelds, and R. J. Francey. "Natural and Anthropogenic Changes in Atmospheric CO_2 over the Last One Thousand Years from Air in Arctic Ice and Firn." *Journal of Geophysical Research* 101 (1996): 4115–4128.

Fama, Anthony P. *Plaquemine: A Long, Long Time Ago.* Anthony P. Fama, Plaquemine, La., 2004.

Fenner, E. D. *History of the Epidemic Yellow Fever at New Orleans, La. in 1853.* Hall, Clayton & Co., New York, 1854.

Field, Martha R., M. R. S. Field, and J. McLaughlin. *Louisiana Voyages: The Travel Writings of Catharine Cole.* University Press of Mississippi, Jackson, 2006.

Fleming, James Rodger. *Meteorology in America, 1800–1870.* Johns Hopkins University Press, Baltimore, 1990.

Follett, Richard. *The Sugar Masters.* Louisiana State University Press, Baton Rouge, 2005.

Francey, R. J., C. E. Allison, D. M. Etheridge, C. M. Trudinger, I. G. Enting, M. Leuenberger, R. L. Langenfelds, E. Michel, and L. P. Steele. "A 1,000-Year High Precision Record of d 13C in Atmospheric CO_2." *Tellus* 51B (1999): 170–193.

Fraser, D. E. "Recent Deltaic Deposits of the Mississippi River: Their Development and Chronology." *Transactions of the Gulf Coast Association Geological Society* 27 (1967): 287–315.

French, B. F. *Historical Memoirs of Louisiana from the First Settlement of the Colony to the Departure of Governor O'Reilly in 1770 with Historical and Biographical Notes Forming the Fifth of the Series of Historical Collections of Louisiana.* Lamport, Blakeman and Law, 1853. Available online through the Library of Congress.

Gayarre, Charles. *History of Louisiana: The French Domination,* vol. 1. F. F. Hansell and Bro., New Orleans, 1903.

Gerdes, F. H. "General Reconnaissance of the Gulf Coast of Louisiana, from the South West Pass to the Bay of Atchafalaya: Survey of the United States Coast." Section 8, register no. 442, January and February 1853.

———. "Preliminary Chart of Ship Island Shoal, Louisiana." U.S. Coast Survey, 1853.

———. "Appendix 21: Extracts of the Report of F. H. Gerdes," in *Report to the Superintendent of the Coast Survey Showing the Progress of the Survey During the Year 1853* by A. D. Bache. Robert Armstrong, Washington, D.C., 1854.

———. "Western Part of Isle Derniere, LA, Triangulation and Topography." United States Coast Survey, A. D. Bache, Superintendent, register no. 410, February 1853.

Gill, James. *Lords of Misrule: Mardi Gras and the Politics of Race in New Orleans.* University Press of Mississippi, Jackson, 1997.

Gomez, Gay Maria. *A Wetland Biography: Seasons on Louisiana's Chenier Plain.* University of Texas Press, Austin, 1998.

Goodell, William. *The American Slave Code in Theory and Practice: Its Distinctive Features Shown by Its Statutes.* John A. Gray, Printer, New York, 1853.

Gordon, John Steele. *Empire of Wealth: The Epic History of American Economic Power.* HarperCollins, New York, 2005.

Gore, Laura Locoul. *Memories of the Old Plantation Home and a Creole Family Album,* with commentary by Norman and Sand Marmillion. Zoe Co., Vacherie, La., 2001.

Gray, William M. "Global View of the Origin of Tropical Disturbances and Storms." *Monthly Weather Review* 96, no. 10 (October 1968). Available at: http://docs.lib.noaa.gov/rescue/mwr/096/mwr-096-10-0669.pdf.

Griffin, C. S. "The University of Kansas and the Sack of Lawrence: A Problem of Intellectual Honesty." *Kansas Historical Quarterly* 34, no. 4 (1968): 409–426. Available at: http://www.kshs.org/publicat/khq/1968/68_4_griffin.htm.

Guza, R., and E. Thornton. "Wave Setup on a Natural Beach." *Journal of Geophysical Research* 86, no. C5 (1981): 4133–4137.

Hall, Basil. *Travels in North America, in the Years 1827 and 1828,* vol. 3. Robert Caddell, Edinburgh, 1830.

Harper, Lewis. *Preliminary Report on the Geology and Agriculture of the State of Mississippi.* R. Barksdale, State Printer, Jackson, 1857.

Harwick, Susan Wiley. *Mythic Galveston: Reinventing America's Third Coast.* Johns Hopkins University Press, Baltimore, 2002.

Haven, Kendall. *100 Greatest Science Inventions of All Time.* Libraries Unlimited, Westport, Conn., 2005.

Haydel, Leonce. *La Paroisse de St. Jacques: A History in Words and Photographs.* Pelican Management Corp., Baton Rouge, La., 1988.

Hearn, Lafcadio. *Chita: A Memory of Last Island.* Harper and Brothers, New York, 1889 (originally published as "Chita: A Memory of Last Island: A Novelette," *Atlantic Monthly* 76, no. 409 [1888]: 621–635).

Henry, Joseph. "Eulogy on Prof. Alexander Dallas Bache," in *Annual Report of the Board of Regents of the Smithsonian Institution, Showing the Operations, Expenditures, and Condition of the Institution for the Year 1870.* 42nd Cong., 1st sess., ex. doc. no. 20, pp. 91–108. U.S. Government Printing Office, Washington, D.C., 1872.

———. *Scientific Writings of Joseph Henry,* vol. 2. Smithsonian Institution, Washington, D.C., 1886.

Henshaw, Leslie. "Nicholas Roosevelt's 1811 Steamboat *New Orleans:* Early Steamboat Travel on the Ohio River." *Ohio Archaeological and Historical Quarterly* 20 no. 4 (October 1911): 378–402.

Hilliar, Henry. "A Brief Record of the Stewarts of Bright in the County of Down in the Province of Ulster." Unpublished 1964 family document available at: http://raymondjohnson.net/genealogy/histories/StewartsOf Bright.php.

Hoffman, Georgia Dell. "Account of Michael Schlatre Jr. and His Family." Unpublished document, private collection, May 1987.

Holman, R. A., and Abby Sallenger. "Setup and Swash on a Natural Beach." *Journal of Geophysical Research* 90, no. C1 (1985): 945–953.

Huler, Scott. *Defining the Wind: The Beaufort Scale and How a Nineteenth-Century Admiral Turned Science into Poetry.* Crown/Random House, New York, 2004.

Humphreys, Margaret. *Yellow Fever and the South.* Rutgers University Press, New Brunswick, N.J., 1992.

Humphreys, A., and H. Abbot. "Report upon the Physics and Hydraulics of the Mississippi River." U.S. Government Printing Office, Washington, D.C., 1867.

Hunter, James Davison. *Culture Wars: The Struggle to Define America.* Basic Books, New York, 1992.

Iberville, Pierre. *Iberville's Gulf Journals,* ed. and trans. Richebourg G. McWilliams. University of Alabama Press, Tuscaloosa, 1991.

Jeter, Marvin D. "From Prehistory Through Protohistory to Ethnohistory In and Near the Northern Lower Mississippi Valley," in *America in 1492: The World of the Indian Peoples Before the Arrival of Columbus,* ed. Alvin M. Josephy Jr., pp. 177–223. Alfred A. Knopf, New York, 1991.

Johnson, Walter. *Soul by Soul: Life Inside the Antebellum Slave Market.* Harvard University Press, Cambridge, Mass., 1999.

Kane, Harnett. *Bayous of Louisiana.* William Morrow, New York, 1943.

————. *Plantation Parade: The Grand Manner in Louisiana.* William Morrow, New York, 1945.

Kelton, Pagerul. "The Great Southeastern Smallpox Epidemic, 1696–1700: The Region's First Major Epidemic," in *The Transformation of the Southeastern Indians, 1540–1760,* ed. Robbie Etheridge and Charles Hudson, pp. 21–38. University Press of Mississippi, Jackson, 2002.

Kett, Joseph F. *The Pursuit of Knowledge Under Difficulties: From Self-Improvement to Adult Education in America, 1750–1990.* Stanford University Press, Stanford, Calif., 1996.

King, Grace Elizabeth. *New Orleans: The Place and the People.* Macmillan and Co., New York, 1896.

Kiple, Kenneth, and Virginia King. *Another Dimension to the Black Diaspora: Diet, Disease, and Racism.* Cambridge University Press, New York, 2003.

Landsea, Christopher, Craig Anderson, Noel Charles, Gilbert Clark, Jason Dunion, Jose Fernandez Partagas, Paul Hungerford, Charlie Neumann, and Mark Zimmer. *The Atlantic Hurricane Database Reanalysis Project Documentation for 1851–1910: Alterations and Additions to the HURDAT Database.* National Oceanic and Atmospheric Administration (NOAA), Hurricane Research Division. Available at: http://www.aoml.noaa.gov/hrd/hurdat/Documentation.html.

Larson, Erik. *Isaac's Storm: A Man, a Time, and the Deadliest Hurricane in History.* Random House, New York, 1999.

Latrobe, John H. B. *Southern Travels: Journal of John H. B. Latrobe, 1834,* ed. Samuel Wilson. Historic New Orleans Collection, New Orleans, 1986.

Lemmons, Alfred E., John T. Magill, and Jason R. Wiese. *Charting Louisiana: Five Hundred Years of Maps.* Historic New Orleans Collection, New Orleans, 2003.

Ludlum, David M. *Early American Hurricanes, 1492–1870.* Historical Monograph Series. American Meteorological Society, Boston, 1968.

Lyell, Charles. *Principles of Geology; or, The Modern Changes of the Earth and Its Inhabitants Considered as Illustrative of Geology,* 9th and entirely revised edition. John Murray, London, 1853 (originally published in three volumes: vol. 1 in 1830, vol. 2 in 1832, and vol. 3 in 1833).

————. *A Second Visit to the United States of North America,* vol. 2. John Murray, London, 1849.

Mahon, Charles. *Map of the Alluvial Region of the Mississippi Prepared to Accompany the Report by Humphreys and Abbott.* U.S. Mississippi

Delta Survey, plate II. War Department, Bureau of Topological Engineers, Washington, D.C., 1861.

McAllister, R. S. "Story Last Island Storm as Told by a Survivor." *Houma Courier* (centennial edition), May 3, 1934. McAllister's account originally appeared in *Southwestern Presbyterian,* April 9, 1891.

McBride, R. A., Shea Penland, W. Hiland, S. J. Williams, K. Westphal, B. Jaffe, and A. H. Sallenger. "Analysis of Barrier Shoreline Change in Louisiana from 1853 to 1989," in *Louisiana Barrier Island Erosion Study: Atlas of Shoreline Changes in Louisiana.* Miscellaneous Investigations Series I-2150-A. U.S. Geological Survey, Denver, Colo., 1992.

McBride, R. A., Shea Penland, Bruce Jaffe, S. J. Williams, A. H. Sallenger, and K. Westphal. *Shoreline Changes of the Isles Dernieres Barrier Island Arc, Louisiana, from 1853 to 1989.* Miscellaneous Investigations Series Map I-2186. U.S. Geological Survey, Denver, Colo., 1991.

McPhee, John. *The Control of Nature.* Farrar, Straus and Giroux, New York, 1990.

Miller, DeMond Shondell, and Jason David Rivera. *Hurricane Katrina and the Redefinition of Landscape.* Rowman & Littlefield, Lanham, Md., 2008.

Molinari, John, Paul Moore, and Vincent Idone. "Convective Structure of Hurricanes as Revealed by Lightning Locations." *Monthly Weather Review* 127, no. 4 (April 1999): 520–534.

Momaday, N. Scott. "The Becoming of the Native: Man in America Before Columbus," in *America in 1492: The World of the Indian Peoples Before the Arrival of Columbus,* ed. Alvin M. Josephy Jr., pp. 13–20. Alfred A. Knopf, New York, 1991.

Monmonier, Mark. *Air Apparent: How Meteorologists Learned to Map, Predict, and Dramatize Weather.* University of Chicago Press, Chicago, 2000.

Morgan, J. P. "Recent Geological History of the Timbalier Bay Area and Adjacent Continental Shelf." Museum of Geosciences, Louisiana State University, *Mélanges* 9 (1974): 17.

Murray, Charles Augustus. *Travels in North America During the Years 1834, 1835, and 1836,* vol. 2. Richard Bentley, London, 1839.

Murray, J. E. "Stature Among Members of a Nineteenth-Century American Shaker Commune." *Annals of Human Biology* 20, no. 2 (1993): 121–129.

National Academy of Sciences. "Surface Temperature Reconstructions for the Last Two Thousand Years." Report of the Committee on Surface Temperature Reconstructions for the Last Two Thousand Years, Gerald R. North, chair. National Academies Press, Washington, D.C., June 2006.

National Hurricane Center. "Worldwide Tropical Cyclone Names." Available at: http://www.nhc.noaa.gov/aboutnames.shtml (last modified September 23, 2008) and http://www.nhc.noaa.gov/aboutnames_history .shtml (last modified February 13, 2007).

National Oceanic and Atmospheric Administration (NOAA). "An Act to Provide for Surveying the Coasts of the United States" (initial legislation leading to the formation of the U.S. Coast Survey). 9th Cong., sess. 2, ch. 8, 2 Stat. 413–414 (1807). Available at: http://www .history.noaa.gov/legacy/act1.html.

———. "NOAA Revisits Historic Hurricanes." Hurricane Research Division. Available at: http://www.aoml.noaa.gov/hrd/hurdat/.

Neftel, A., E. Moor, H. Oeschger, and B. Stauffer. "Evidence from Polar Ice Cores for the Increase in Atmospheric CO_2 in the Past Two Centuries." *Nature* 315 (May 2, 1985).

Neuman, Robert W., and Nancy W. Hawkins. *Louisiana Prehistory, 2nd ed.* Department of Culture, Recreation, and Tourism, Louisiana Archaeological Survey and Antiquities Commission, Baton Rouge, May 1993. Available at: http://www.crt.state.la.us/archaeology/lapre his/lapre.htm.

Nevils, Rene Pol, and Deborah Gore. *Ignatius Rising: The Life of John Kennedy Toole.* Louisiana State University Press, Baton Rouge, 2005.

Norman, Benjamin Moore. *Norman's New Orleans and Environs: Containing a Brief Historical Sketch of the Territory and State of Louisiana and the City of New Orleans.* B. M. Norman, New Orleans, 1845.

O'Connor, Mallory McCane. *Lost Cities of the Ancient Southeast.* University of Florida Press, Gainesville, 1995.

Olmsted, Denison. "Address on the Scientific Life and Labors of William C. Redfield, A.M." Delivered before the American Association for the Advancement of Science, August 14, 1857. E. Hayes, Publisher, New Haven, Conn., 1857.

Olmsted, Frederick Law. *The Cotton Kingdom,* ed. Arthur M. Schlesinger. Alfred A. Knopf, New York, 1953.

Padover, Saul K. *Jefferson: A Great American's Life and Ideas.* New American Library, Penguin Group, New York, 1952.

Partagas, Jose Fernandez, and H. F. Diaz. "A Reconstruction of Historical Tropical Cyclone Frequency in the Atlantic from Documentary and Other Historical Sources: 1851–1880, part 1, 1851–1870." NOAA, Climate Diagnostics Center, Boulder, Colo., 1995.

Patterson, Benton Rain. *The Generals: Andrew Jackson, Sir Edward Packenham, and the Road to the Battle of New Orleans.* New York University Press, New York, 2005.

Penland, Shea. "Katrina: Behind the Tragedy: Taming the River to Let in the Sea." *Natural History* (February 2005).

Penland, Shea, John Suter, and Ron Boyd. "Barrier Island Arcs Along Abandoned Mississippi River Deltas." *Marine Geology* (Elsevier) 63 (1985): 197–233.

Persac, A. *Norman's Chart of the Lower Mississippi River.* J. H. Colton & Co., New York, 1858.

Persac, Marie Adrien. "Plantations on the Mississippi from Natchez to New Orleans, 1858." Pelican Publishing Co., Gretna, La., 1979 (map reprint, wall edition).

Peterson, Merrill D. *John Brown: The Legend Revisited.* University of Virginia Press, Charlottesville, 2004.

Philbrick, Nathaniel. *In the Heart of the Sea: The Tragedy of the Whaleship Essex.* Penguin, New York, 2000.

Piantadosi, Claude A. *The Biology of Human Survival: Life and Death in Extreme Environments.* Oxford University Press, New York, 2003.

Picard, Liza. *Victorian London: The Tale of a City, 1840–1870.* St. Martin's Press, New York, 2006.

Piddington, Henry. *The Sailor's Horn-Book for the Law of Storms,* 3rd ed. Williams and Norgate, London, 1860; 2nd ed., Smith, Elder and Co., London, 1851.

Postman, Neil. *Amusing Ourselves to Death: Public Discourse in the Age of Show Business.* Viking, New York, 1985.

Prichard, Walter, Fred Kniffen, and Clair Brown. "Southern Louisiana and Southern Alabama in 1819: The Journal of James Leander Cathcart." *Louisiana Historical Quarterly* 28, no. 3 (July 1945): 735–921.

Pugh, W. W. "A Historical Sketch of Assumption Parish for Forty Years: 1820–1860." *Assumption Pioneer (Terrebonne Life Lines* 14, nos. 2 and 3). Parts of this document are available at: http://www.arcementfamily .com/HistoryAssumptionParish.htm.

———. "Reminiscences of an Old Fogy," copied from *The Pioneer of Assumption,* beginning June 18, 1881. Held as a bound volume at the Assumption Parish Library, Napoleonville, La.

Quimby, George Irving. *The Medora Site, West Baton Rouge Parish, Louisiana.* Field Museum of Natural History, Louisiana State Archaeological Survey, 1951.

Rahmstorf, Stefan. "A Semi-Empirical Approach to Projecting Future Sea-Level Rise." *Science* 315 (January 2007).

Redfield, William C. "Reply to Dr. Hare's Further Objections Relating to Whirlwind Storms; with Some Evidence of the Whirling Action of the Providence Tornado of August, 1838." *American Journal of Science and Arts* 43, no. 2 (April 1842).

Reid, William. *An Attempt to Develop the Law of Storms by Means of Facts: Arranged According to Place and Time; and Hence to Point Out a Cause for the Variable Winds, with the View to Practical Use in Navigation.* J. Weale, London, 1838.

————. *The Progress of the Development of the Law of Storms, and of the Variable Winds with the Practical Applications of the Subject to Navigation.* John Weale, London, 1848.

Richardson, Francis DuBose. "The Teche Country Fifty Years Ago." *Southern Bivouac* (January 1886).

Riggs, S., and D. Ames. *Drowning the North Carolina Coast: Sea-Level Rise and Estuarine Dynamics.* North Carolina Sea Grant, Raleigh, 2003.

Rightor, Henry. *Standard History of New Orleans, Louisiana.* Lewis Publishing Co., Chicago, 1900.

Roth, David. "Louisiana Hurricanes." Unpublished report. National Weather Service, Lake Charles, La., 2003. Available at: http://www.srh.noaa.gov/lch/research/lahur.php.

Royal Commission. *Official Catalogue of the Great Exhibition of the Works of Industry of All Nations.* Spicer Brothers, London, 1851.

Royal Cornwall Polytechnic Society. *Twenty-sixth Annual Report.* Vibert, Falmouth, U.K., 1858.

Ruth, John A. *Decorum: A Practical Treatise on Etiquette and Dress of the Best American Society.* C. L. Snyder & Co., Chicago, 1881.

Sacher, John M. *A Perfect War of Politics, Parties, Politicians, and Democracy in Louisiana, 1824–1861.* Louisiana State University Press, Baton Rouge, 2003.

Sales, Grover. *Jazz PB: America's Classical Music.* Da Capo Press, New York, 1992.

Sallenger, A., and R. Holman. "Wave Energy Saturation on a Natural Beach of Variable Slope." *Journal of Geophysical Research* 90, no. C14 (1985): 11939–11944.

Sallenger, A., C. Wright, and K. Doran. "Barrier Island Failure Modes Triggered by Hurricane Katrina and Long-Term Sea-Level Rise." Paper submitted to journal.

Sallenger, A., C. Wright, K. Doran, K. Guy, and K. Morgan. "Hurricane Rita and the Destruction of Holly Beach, Louisiana: Why the Chenier Plain Is Vulnerable to Storms," in *Geologists Look at America's Most Vulnerable Beachfront Communities.* Geological Society of America special paper. In press.

Sallenger, A., C. Wright, Jeff Lillycrop, Peter Howd, Hilary Stockdon, Kristy Guy, and Karen Morgan. "Extreme Changes to Barrier Islands Along the Central Gulf of Mexico Coast During Hurricane Katrina." U.S. Geological Survey circular 1306 (2007), pp. 113–118. Available at: http://pubs.usgs.gov/circ/1306/pdf/c1306_ch5_c.pdf.

Schafer, Judith K. *Becoming Free, Remaining Free: Manumission and Enslavement in New Orleans, 1846–1862.* Louisiana State University Press, Baton Rouge, 2003.

Schlatre, Michael. "The Last Island Disaster of August 10, 1856: Personal Narrative of His Experiences by One of the Survivors," with an introduction by Walter Prichard. *Louisiana Historical Quarterly* 20 (July 1937): 690–737.

Secord, James A. Introduction to *Principles in Geology* by Charles Lyell. Penguin Classics, New York, 1997 (reprint).

Shalowitz, Aaron L. *Shore and Sea Boundaries*, vol. 2. Publication 10-1. U.S. Coast and Geodetic Survey, U.S. Government Printing Office, Washington, D.C., 1964.

Shay, L. K., G. J. Goni, and P. G. Black. "Effects of a Warm Oceanic Feature on Hurricane Opal." *Monthly Weather Review* 128, no. 5 (May 2000): 1366–1383.

Smith, Edgar F. *The Life of Robert Hare, an American Chemist (1781–1858)*. Arno Press, New York, 1980.

Smithsonian Institution. *Annual Report of the Board of Regents of the Smithsonian Institution, Showing the Operations, Expenditures, and Condition of the Institution for the Year 1858*. U.S. Government Printing Office, Washington, D.C., 1859 (reprinted by Adamant Media Corp., 2000).

————. *Annual Report of the Board of Regents of the Smithsonian Institution, Showing the Operations, Expenditures, and Condition of the Institution for the Year 1872*. U.S. Government Printing Office, Washington, D.C., 1872.

Sources Behind the Project: Documenting the Louisiana Sugar Economy, 1844–1917. Available at: http://www.sussex.ac.uk/louisianasugar/1-2.html.

Sothern, James M. *Last Island*. Cheri Publications, Houma, La., 1980.

Southern, Eileen. *The Music of Black Americans: A History*. W. W. Norton & Co., New York, 1997.

Sparks, William Henry. *The Memories of Fifty Years: Containing Brief Biographical Notices of Distinguished Americans, and Anecdotes of Remarkable Men*. Claxton, Remsen, & Haffelfinger, Philadelphia, 1872.

Stanton, Doug. *In Harm's Way: The Sinking of the USS Indianapolis and the Extraordinary Story of Its Survivors*. Henry Holt, New York, 2002.

Star, S. Frederick, ed. *Inventing New Orleans: Writings of Lafcadio Hearn*. University Press of Mississippi, Jackson, 2001.

Sternberg, Mary Ann. *Along the River Road: Past and Present on Louisiana's Historic Byway*. Louisiana State University Press, Baton Rouge, 1996.

Streatfeild, Dominic. *Cocaine: An Unauthorized Biography*. St. Martin's Press, New York, 2001.

Stuart, James. *Three Years in North America*, vol. 2. Robert Cadell, Edinburgh; Whitaker, London, 1833.

Stuiver, M., R. L. Burk, and P. D. Quay. "13C/12C Ratios and the Transfer of Biospheric Carbon to the Atmosphere." *Journal of Geophysical Research* 89 (1984): 1731–1748.

Sumner, Charles. *The Crime Against Kansas: The Apologies for the Crime, the True Remedy: Speech of Hon. Charles Sumner, in the Senate of the United States, 19th and 20th May, 1856.* Cornell University Library Digital Collections, Ithaca, N.Y., 2007.

Sunder, Marco. "The Height of Tennessee Convicts: Another Piece of the Antebellum Puzzle." *Economics and Human Biology* 2, no. 1 (2004): 75–86.

Tademy, Lalita. *Cane River.* Warner Books, New York, 2001.

Thornton, E., and R. Guza. "Energy Saturation and Phase Speeds Measured on a Natural Beach." *Journal of Geophysical Research* 87, no. C12 (1982): 9499–9508.

Tidwell, Mike. *Bayou Farewell: The Rich Life and Tragic Death of Louisiana's Cajun Country.* Pantheon Books/Random House, New York, 2003.

Times Picayune. "Mrs. Duperier, 98, Final Survivor of 1856 Disaster, Dies at New Iberia Home." *Times Picayune*, April 14, 1936.

Tompkins, F. H. *Riparian Lands of the Mississippi River.* A. L. Smith & Co., Chicago, 1901.

Toomey, David M. *Stormchasers: The Hurricane Hunters and Their Fateful Flight into Hurricane Janet.* W. W. Norton & Co., New York, 2002.

Tyndale, John. "Further Researches on the Absorption and Radiation of Heat by Gaseous Matter" (1862), in *Contributions to Molecular Physics in the Domain of Radiant Heat*, pp. 69–121. Appleton, New York, 1873.

Twain, Mark. *Life on the Mississippi.* New American Library/Penguin, New York, 2001 (originally published by American Publishing Co., Hartford, Conn., 1883).

Van Heerden, Ivor, and Mike Bryan. *The Storm: What Went Wrong and Why During Hurricane Katrina—The Inside Story from One Louisiana Scientist.* Viking, New York, 2006.

Volo, James M., and Dorothy Denneen Volo. *The Antebellum Period.* Greenwood Press, Westport, Conn., 2004.

Wakin, Edward. *Enter the Irish-American.* AuthorHouse, 2002 (originally published by Crowell in 1976).

Wang, D., D. Mitchell, W. Teague, E. Jarosz, and M. Hulbert. "Extreme Waves Under Hurricane Ivan." *Science* 309 (August 5, 2005): 896.

Warner, Charles Dudley. *The Complete Writings of Charles Dudley Warner: Studies in the South and West with Comments on Canada*, vol. 3. American Publishing Co., Hartford, Conn., 1904.

Weart, Spencer R. *The Discovery of Global Warming.* Harvard University Press, Cambridge, Mass., 2003.

White, Loring. *Ragging It: Getting Ragtime into History (and Some History into Ragtime).* iUniverse, 2005.

Williams, J., Shea Penland, and A. Sallenger. *Louisiana Barrier Island Erosion Study: Atlas of Shoreline Changes in Louisiana.* U.S. Geological Survey, Miscellaneous Investigations Series I-2150-A, 1992.

Wilson, James G., and John Fiske. *Appleton's Cyclopaedia of American Biography.* Gale Research Co., Detroit, 1968.

Wilson, Samuel, Patricia Brady, and Lynn D. Adams, eds. *Queen of the South: New Orleans, 1853–1862: The Journal of Thomas K. Wharton.* Historic New Orleans Collection and New York Public Library, New Orleans and New York, 1999.

Worcester, Nancy. "Nourishing Ourselves," in *Women's Health: Readings on Social, Economic, and Political Issues,* ed. Nancy Worcester and Mariamne H. Whatley, 4th ed. Kendall/Hunt Publishing Co., Dubuque, Iowa, 2004.

Youmans, William Jay. *Pioneers of Science in America: Sketches of Their Lives and Scientific Work.* D. Appleton and Co., New York, 1896.

Zietz, Karyl Lynn. *The National Trust Guide to Great Opera Houses in America.* John Wiley & Sons, New York, 1996.

{ INDEX }

ABBY (ASBURY) SALLENGER received his
BA in Geology and PhD in Marine Science from
the University of Virginia and is the former chief
scientist of the U.S. Geological Survey's Center
for Coastal Geology. He presently leads the
USGS Storm Impact research group, investigating how the coast changes during extreme storms,
such as Hurricanes Isabel, Ivan, Katrina, and Ike.
As an undergraduate at U.Va., Abby was a stu-
dent athlete, playing four years of intercollegiate
football. He and his wife live in Florida.